Penguin Handbooks
Vegetable Cookery

Nika Hazelton was educated in Italy, Switzerland
and England. She has worked on *Fortune*,
Harper's Bazaar and other magazines in the United
States, which is now her permanent home except
for trips. In the past she has also worked as an
advertising copywriter, but now she is a freelance
contributor to *House and Garden*, *Town and Country*,
the American *National Review* and several other
periodicals. Among her books are *Reminiscence and
Ravioli*, *The Art of Cheese Cookery*, *The Continental Flavour*,
The Art of Scandinavian Cooking, *The Best of Italian
Cooking*, *The Swiss Cookbook* and *The Belgian Cookbook*.
Her book, *Danish Cooking*, has been published in
Penguins. She loves to travel to different and exotic
places – such as Lapland at Christmas-time. She
adores both the Arctic North and the Mediterranean.

D1352451

Nika Hazelton

Vegetable Cookery

Illustrated by M. J. Mott

PENGUIN BOOKS

Penguin Books Ltd, Harmondsworth,
Middlesex, England
Penguin Books, 625 Madison Avenue,
New York, New York 10022, U.S.A.
Penguin Books Australia Ltd, Ringwood,
Victoria, Australia
Penguin Books Canada Ltd, 2801 John Street,
Markham, Ontario, Canada L3R 1B4
Penguin Books (N.Z.) Ltd, 182–190 Wairau Road,
Auckland 10, New Zealand

Published in Penguin Books 1979

Made and printed in Great Britain by
Richard Clay (The Chaucer Press) Ltd
Bungay, Suffolk
Set in Monotype Baskerville

For my son
JULIAN

Contents

Vegetable Cookery

Introduction

This book is about fresh vegetables, their history, ways of keeping and preparing them, their nutritional value. I have called a vegetable any part of a plant eaten as a vegetable rather than as a fruit.

Space forbade giving more botanical, historical and other information, as well as growing or preserving instructions.* I have omitted naming leading varieties and brand names of vegetables because these vary according to the parts of the country where they are grown and to the growers. Besides, new varieties are constantly being developed.

The recipes reflect my personal preferences. I have tried not to repeat the excellent basic recipes found in standard cookbooks. I have chosen dishes in which a specific vegetable is the main ingredient. This excludes many superb soups, stews and casseroles in which vegetables play a secondary part. My basic instructions reflect my own experiences as well as my personal tastes. I think that, above all, vegetables should be eaten as fresh as is possible, and I don't agree that they can be stored as long as suggested by some other books. I consider over-long cooking the death of almost all vegetables and I also think that, in general, vegetables should be cooked simply to let their own flavour dominate without confusing it with too many herbs, seasonings and other ingredients. Vegetable cookery is not difficult and rather a matter of timing. Most of it is more-or-less cookery that does not have to be measured out carefully: this will in many cases be clear from the equivalents given for metric and British measurements, which

* For further information see: M. Grieve, *A Modern Herbal* (Peregrine, 1976); Arthur J. Simons, *The New Vegetable Grower's Handbook* (1962); David Mabey, *The Vegetable Grower's Calendar* (1978); Helge Rubinstein and Sheila Bush, *The Penguin Freezer Cookbook* (1973); and David and Rose Mabey, *The Penguin Book of Jams, Pickles and Chutneys* (1976) (all Penguin Handbooks).

have in individual cases been chosen for convenience (in buying, for instance) rather than worked out on an exact scale.

The nutritional statements and the caloric figures are based upon the definitive source on the subject, *Composition of Foods, Hand Book no. 3* (Agricultural Research Service of the United States Department of Agriculture). The caloric values are based upon 100 g, close enough to 4 oz, an average vegetable helping. Generally speaking, there is very little difference in the amount of calories in cooked, unseasoned, fresh vegetables, unseasoned, tinned vegetables or cooked, unseasoned, frozen vegetables.

Finally, I may add that this book is based upon a lifetime preference for vegetables over other foods.

Note

There are occasionally discrepancies in the metric/imperial equivalents in the recipes; this is unavoidable in conversion and the reader should always follow one system or the other and not attempt a combination of the two.

Vegetables Then and Now

Wheat and barley, two of our oldest crops, came into cultivation in the Middle East between 8000 and 5000 B.C. and rice was a staple crop in China as early as 2800 B.C. Whether this early crop cultivation occurred by accident or on purpose we cannot know, but we do know that it was the essential step towards civilization. Agriculture has been the only way possible for man to accumulate the necessities of life and to live the settled, stable life without which civilization cannot develop.

The transition from a food-collecting way of life to a food-cultivating culture was of necessity a slow one, taking thousands of years, during which many plants evolved from their original wild state through seed selection, hybridization and environmental conditions. Food plants originated in many parts of the world and it is obviously impossible to say with total accuracy what took place when, where and how, nor is it possible to discover the ancestors of all food plants. In the case of the cucumber, onion, sweet corn, white and sweet potato, to mention a few, it is impossible to identify their wild ancestors with more than speculation.

The presence of food plants in different parts of the world is largely due to the activities of man. In very early times, food plants travelled to parts of the world that were easily reached by land. In later, but still early, times, the great seafaring and empire-building nations of antiquity, such as the Phoenicians, the Persians, the Romans and the Arabs, introduced their own food plants to places that were not familiar with them. Another great interchange of crops took place after 1492, when Columbus, returning from his first voyage, took back to Spain the first corn ever to reach Europe and, on his second voyage, brought back to America European seeds. But the exchange of food plants was not limited to America and Europe. Casually, the ships of the slave traders, along with their infamous cargoes, brought to America the food crops of West Africa which the Negroes were used to, such as yams and pigeon peas, and took to Africa American crops such as corn and cassava. These became widely cultivated in a short time, supplementing the limited crops native to the regions south of the Sahara. Other tradings between continents brought the banana and rice to Africa probably via Portuguese ships coming from Asia. In Australia, food crops date from the first European settlements at the end of the eighteenth century since the native aborigines did not cultivate plants. Coffee, which originated in Ethiopia, travelled first from Mocha and then from Java to South America where it became a primary cash crop, and pineapple, from Brazil, became equally important to Hawaii and some Caribbean islands.

In the eighteenth century seed selection was a fine art, and the emergence of the science of genetics in the nineteenth century enabled plant breeders to select suitable parent plants, or hybridize them, or produce new genetic variations by treating plants with chemicals or even X-rays. Experiments in radiation genetics have produced rust-resistant oats and peanuts with a 30 per cent higher yield. Science did not only more than double the yield of many crops during the last century but also increased the plants' tolerance to heat and frost, their suitability for various soils and climates and their resistance to diseases and pests. Some of the breeding objectives of commercial shippers and processors differ from those of the home gardener and roadside-stand owner. Commercial growers and shippers labour under the external pressures of mass-merchandising demands, such as the requirement for carrots and potatoes of a size and quality that can be uniformly graded and packaged. The supermarket green bean must have a high fibre content so that it can remain on the shelves for a week before wilting, whereas the home gardener's tender, low-fibre bean goes into the pot soon after it is picked. Another objective again is size, with the trend to smaller families today. A 3-kg (6-lb) head of cabbage for a family of three sits around in the refrigerator for two weeks and a 1-kg (2–2½-lb) size would be more practical.

The most spectacular results of scientific breeding are the plants that could make all the difference to malnutrition in some parts of the world if a host of social and physical obstacles could be overcome. There are new rice varieties that have increased yields from the world average of 600 kg (1,300 lb) of milled rice an acre to between 750 and 1,000 kg (1,700 and 2,100 lb), and that are more pest resistant, adapt better to new growing conditions and need far less fertilizer. A new type of corn has been developed which has nearly doubled the effective protein content of normal corn, surpassing that of milk.

Closely linked to the new breeding is the advent of the mechanical harvester which has already taken over much of the work of tens of thousands of agricultural workers. Lettuce, celery, spinach, cauliflower, tomatoes, corn, onions and peas are among the mechanized vegetable crops, and more and more mechanical harvesting is done for fruits. Yet harvesters are harder on plants than skilled human hands; with beans, for instance, a greater quantity of immature and broken beans and leaves are left which have to be removed from the fields. On the other hand, mechanical harvesters are clever and constantly improved upon.

Next comes the costly job of getting the vegetables to the packing plant in good condition, and the problems of cooling them before and after packing, of proper moisture, ventilation and so on, which are of a technical complexity quite unknown to the layman. A leaf of lettuce, besides being one of nature's wonders, is also a wonder of scientific ingenuity by the time it reaches our table, but already in 1969 its marketing cost amounted to 63 per cent of the price the consumer paid for it.

The recent boom in home vegetable-gardening, and the increased amount of travel which has introduced people to unfamiliar vegetables and interested them in experimenting in the garden, have intensified work on varieties and hybrids bred especially for the home gardener. Some of the research includes development of earlier maturing varieties, for gardeners living where the growing seasons are short, and of more compact growing habits, to suit small spaces. Ordinary vining plants, such as cucumbers, are encouraged to grow on little bushes rather than on rambling, space-consuming vines. To breed disease- and insect-resistance is another goal, partly because of the influence of the 'organic people' and of government regulations about some chemical sprays. As experimentation expands, home gardeners will be moving away from chemical gardening practices towards simpler, more natural ones, like companion planting and plant-based sprays, helped by the work that is being done on biological controls, such as combating insects with microbial insecticides which kill only what they are meant to kill.

With all of the plant breeder's relentless search for brave new vegetables, one might well ask what has happened to the flavour of those beauties bred for commerce. It is heartwarming to know that at last there is beginning to be a renewed emphasis on what are charmingly called 'quality factors'. The reason given for this is that technical questions such as the ones mentioned above have come such a long way that breeders can now take a second look at things like flavour. Added to that is the public demand for better-tasting vegetables, thanks to the boom in home gardening and the general awareness of natural foods.

Akee, Ackee

(*Blighia sapida*)

Akee is the fruit of a tropical evergreen tree of West African origin which is now grown in the West Indies; its edible part looks like a tiny creased brain. Because of its appearance and rather oily consistency, akee is known as 'the poor man's scrambled eggs' in Jamaica where, together with salt codfish, it has become the island's national dish. However, akee, which is rather bland, is also used with meats, cheese and in *au gratin* dishes, or boiled or fried.

The akee fruit is about 7 or 8 cm (3 inches) long and red when ripe. The ripe fruit opens naturally, usually displaying three black seeds in each fruit. These seeds are surrounded by a cream-coloured aril which is the edible part of the akee. Great care must be taken to avoid the pink tissue joining the aril to the seed since it is highly poisonous, as are the under-ripe or over-ripe fruit. Only ripe, naturally-opened fruit should be used. In spite of these inherent dangers, akee is widely used and tinned for export – it is perfectly safe in this form, as all the Jamaican expatriates sighing for akee the world over can testify.

The tree belongs to the Sapindaceae (soapberry) family. It is medium-sized, with glossy leaves, and is cultivated as a handsome ornament in many warm countries. It is named after Captain William Bligh, of *Mutiny on the Bounty* fame, who discovered it on one of his voyages and brought it to the West Indies.

Jamaican Salt Cod and Akee

4–6 servings
Serve with rice and beans.

500 g (1 lb) salt cod
500 g (1 lb) fresh akees or one
   500-g (16- to 19-oz) tin akees,
   drained
4 slices lean bacon, diced, or
   110 g (4 oz) blanched salt
   pork, diced
1 onion, cut into thin rings
2 medium onions, chopped

1 garlic clove, crushed
2 medium tomatoes, peeled and
   chopped
¼ tsp dried thyme
½ tsp finely chopped, seeded hot
   pepper (or to taste, or hot
   pepper sauce to taste)
30 g (1 oz) melted butter

Soak the cod in water to cover overnight. Drain. Cook in fresh water to cover until flaky and tender. Drain and remove any skin and bones. Flake the fish. While the fish is cooking, cook the fresh akees over low heat in water to cover for 15 minutes. Drain and add to the fish. In a large frying pan, cook the bacon or the salt pork until crisp. Remove the cooked bacon or pork bits with a slotted spoon and add to the fish and the akees. Pour off half of the fat. Cook the sliced onion in the remaining fat until crisp, put aside, then cook the chopped onion and garlic until the onion is tender and golden brown. Add the tomatoes, the thyme and the hot pepper. Cook, stirring constantly, for about 5 minutes. Add the flaked fish, the akees and the bacon or pork bits. Stir carefully with a fork. Cook over low heat, stirring frequently, for about 5 minutes. The dish must be thoroughly blended and heated through. Stir the melted butter into the dish. Turn into a heated serving dish and garnish with the onion slices.

Akees and Cheese

4 servings
Serve on hot boiled rice or toast.

30 g (1 oz) butter
1 small onion, finely chopped
1 500-g (16- to 19-oz) tin akees,
   drained

110 g (4 oz) grated Gruyère or
   Cheddar cheese
freshly ground pepper
2 tbsps finely chopped parsley

Heat the butter in a frying pan. Cook the onion until it is soft and golden. Add the akees. Cook, stirring with a fork as you would cook scrambled eggs, for 3 to 4 minutes or until thoroughly heated through. Stir in the cheese. Cook, stirring all the time, until the cheese is melted. Remove from heat and season with pepper. Sprinkle with the parsley before serving.

Artichoke

(Cynara scolymus)

For Jerusalem Artichoke, see page 184.

Globe artichokes are the fleshy, leafy buds of a plant that grows to 1–1½ metres (3–5 feet) and resembles a thistle in size and habit. The edible parts of the formidable-looking vegetable are the tender bases of the scale-like, at times spiky, leaves and the thickened receptacle of the bloom cluster, the part that would produce the plant's flowers. Though some varieties are eaten raw

in southern Europe because they are tender enough, globe artichokes are generally cooked. Since only a very small part of the vegetable is edible, artichokes, alone among vegetables, present an astonishing sight after being eaten, for there is then more of them, in volume, than before – whole platefuls of laboriously nibbled leaves and cast-off fuzz.

The artichoke is believed to be native to the western and central Mediterranean area, from where it was carried to the eastern part in ancient times. A close relation, which the ancients knew, was the cardoon, of which the tender stalks were eaten. In the second century A.D. it fetched the highest price on the vegetable markets of Rome, though Pliny the Elder considered it monstrous. The globe artichoke as we know it was first recorded in Naples around 1400. From Italy it went to France and England where Henry VIII fancied it greatly, possibly because of its alleged virtues as an aphrodisiac. But its greatest use was in Spain, Italy and other Mediterranean and Near Eastern countries. The name itself is of Arabic origin, *al-kharshuf*, which became *artichaut* in French, *carciofo* in Italian, *alcachofa* in Spanish and 'artichoke' in English, as early as the 1530s.

Globe artichokes have only recently become popular in the United Kingdom, and it is astonishing to see how many people still don't know what to do with them other than eating them boiled whole, tearing off leaf after leaf, dipping each one into a sauce and scraping off its bottom with the teeth until eventually a core of inedible, light, thin fuzz, the 'choke', is reached. This covers the bottom, the best part of the vegetable, and is easily scraped or cut off with a knife or fork. French cookery does wonders with these bottoms, and Italians quarter and slice the vegetable to be braised, singly or with other foods, or deep fried. Occasionally it is possible to find small artichokes, though none of them as small and tender as the violet-hued artichokes of Venice, which can be deep-fried and eaten *in toto*, or the really tiny *carciofini* which are pickled for an hors d'œuvre.

How to buy

Buy uniformly solid heads which are heavy in relation to size, with thick, fresh-looking, compact leaves without a blemish. Avoid soft artichokes, with loose, spreading leaves and discolorations.

Size has little if anything to do with flavour. Choose large artichokes for stuffing and for recipes using artichoke bottoms and hearts. Artichoke hearts and bottoms are also available tinned, ready for eating, or pickled. There is even an Italian aperitif made from artichokes, called Cynar.

How to keep

Refrigerated in a plastic bag or closed container, to prevent them from drying out, they will keep for several days.

Nutritive values

Artichokes contain small amounts of vitamins and mineral salts. Cooked: 50 to 60 calories per 100 g ($3\frac{1}{2}$ oz).

Vegetable Cookery

How to use

Important! Once they are cut, artichokes discolour rapidly on contact with air. To prevent this, before starting work on them have a bowl of water acidulated with lemon juice ready (about 3 tablespoons of lemon juice to 1 litre or quart of water). Work as fast as you can and drop the prepared artichoke pieces into the water as soon as you've finished with them. Keep them there until cooking time, but dry thoroughly on kitchen paper before using in the recipe. Finicky cooks are advised that contact with carbon knives, and with iron, steel or aluminium, also darkens artichokes and gives them a slightly harsh flavour. They are best cut up with stainless-steel knives and boiled in stainless-steel or enamelled cookware. If at all possible, artichokes should be sautéed in non-aluminium or non-iron frying pans, such as tinned copper or earthenware.

Some recipes advocate cooking artichokes *au blanc*, that is, after the artichokes have been rubbed with lemon, they are poached in acidulated water with a sprinkle of flour and a little oil. This does keep them white, but also removes quite a lot of their flavour. I do not think it necessary at all to do this, but John Evelyn in his *Acetaria* did, even then, and his were the days when English artichoke plants were exported to France and the Low Countries.

Whole artichokes: Since they are laborious eating, they are best served as a separate course.

Wash the artichoke and carefully break off the stem if you can, or cut it off with a knife either flush with the base or leaving a 1½ to 2½ cm (½ to 1 inch) stub. Pull off and throw away the small leaves at the base and any tough and discoloured leaves. Trim the base by paring from the base (and, if necessary, the stubs of the stem) spirally, cutting off all the dark green, uneven and tough parts. Dip the artichoke quickly in acidulated water. Then lay it on its side and cut off evenly about one third of the top, with a sharp knife. Or else with kitchen scissors cut off the spiny top of each leaf. Cook in boiling acidulated and salted water (add 1 tablespoon olive oil to each litre or quart of water) until tender, from 15 to 30 minutes, depending on size and variety. Drain and stand artichokes bottom-side up on a plate to drain off any excess liquid.

Alternatively, prepare the artichokes as above. Stand them upright in a deep saucepan large enough to hold them snugly. Add ¼ teaspoon salt for each artichoke and 5 to 7 cm (2 to 3 inches) of boiling water and 1 to 2 tablespoons olive oil. Cover and boil gently for 15 to 30 minutes or until tender or until the base can be pierced with a fork. Lift out the cooked artichokes and turn them upside down to drain. If the artichokes are to be stuffed, gently spread the leaves to make room for the stuffing and scrape out the centre fuzz, or choke, with a spoon.

Artichokes can be cooked in plain boiling salted water, but the lemon juice and olive oil give them a better taste and better-looking, glistening leaves.

Artichoke hearts and bottoms: There is a difference between artichoke hearts and bottoms, though the terms are often used interchangeably. Artichoke hearts have leaves or parts of leaves that are tender and chokes that are infantile enough to be ignored. Artichoke bottoms, the French *fonds d'artichaut*, are the fuzzless bottoms of more mature vegetables.

Have acidulated water ready before starting.

For artichoke hearts, prepare the stem and outer leaves as for whole artichokes. Proceed, removing leaves until only the very tender, greenish-white ones remain. Lay the artichoke on its side and cut off the top third of the remaining leaves. For artichoke bottoms, do the same but cut off two thirds to four fifths of the remaining leaves. In both cases, starting from the bottom, peel in a spiral motion until the whole base is smooth and rounded. Remove the fuzz if the artichoke is to be braised or sautéed; if it is to be blanched or boiled, remove the fuzz after boiling. Drop the finished hearts and bottoms into acidulated water. Drain, dry and cook according to recipe. Alternatively, cook covered (with three parts butter to one part olive oil and the juice of a lemon) or uncovered (in a little boiling salted water) until just tender; cooking time depends on size, but ranges, generally speaking, from 5 to 15 minutes. Do not overcook. You may add a little olive oil to the water and a sprinkling of herbs, such as sprigs of fresh rosemary or thyme or their equivalent in dried herbs.

Depending on the recipe, the hearts and bottoms may be blanched (to blanch, plunge into boiling water for 3 minutes, then drain) before using or they may be used directly after they are prepared.

Quartered and sliced artichokes: Prepare the artichokes as above, until only the tender, greenish-white leaves remain. Then lay each artichoke on its side. Cut off the green top part of the leaves in one stroke. Dip artichoke in acidulated water and shake dry. Cut the artichoke into four parts as you would an apple. Drop three parts into the acidulated water and work on one part at a time. Working quickly, core each part, removing the fuzz or choke, as you would core an apple. Drop immediately back into acidulated water.

Small tender artichokes may be quartered, older artichokes need to have the prepared quarters thinly sliced: the tougher the artichoke, the thinner the slice.

Fats to use in artichoke cookery: Artichokes are robust vegetables which, except for artichoke hearts and bottoms, seem to need the heartiness of olive oil. The hearts and bottoms are delicate enough to be cooked with butter. Using only olive oil in braising artichokes would make for too rich a dish; it is better to use even parts of olive oil and water or stock.

Stuffed Hors d'OEuvre Artichokes

6 servings

6 medium artichokes
acidulated water made with 1 l (qt) water and 3 tbsps lemon juice
150 g (5 oz) finely chopped parsley
3 anchovies, cut up small
1 tbsp capers, drained
2 tbsps finely chopped fresh basil or 2 tsps dried basil, crumbled

1 tsp salt
$\frac{1}{4}$ tsp freshly ground pepper
1 lemon, in six slices
3 tbsps olive oil
boiling water
6 dl (about 1 pt) French dressing made with lemon

Prepare as for whole artichokes (see page 22), then put upside down on a chopping board and press to open them. Drop the artichokes into the acidulated water to prevent discolouring. Taking out one artichoke at a time, dig out the fuzzy chokes with the point of a knife or a spoon. Drop back into water. Combine the parsley, the anchovies, the capers, the basil and the salt and pepper and mix well. Drain one artichoke at a time and stuff it with some of the parsley mixture. Tie each artichoke with a string to prevent it from opening during cooking. Place the artichokes side by side in a deep frying pan or saucepan just large enough to hold them tightly. Top each with a slice of lemon. Pour the olive oil into the frying pan and add about 2 cm (1 inch) boiling water. Cook without a cover for 3 minutes. Turn heat to low, cover and simmer for about 20 to 30 minutes or until the artichokes are tender. Check for moisture; if necessary, add a little more water and olive oil to keep the level. When cooked, transfer to serving dish. Cool. Pour the French dressing into six small, individual bowls. Place a bowl and one artichoke on each plate. Use the French dressing as a dip.

Fried Artichokes

4 servings

4 medium artichokes	2 eggs, beaten with 1 tbsp olive oil
acidulated water	olive or groundnut oil
flour	salt

Prepare the artichokes and cut them into thin slices. Drop the finished slices into the acidulated water. In a deep frying pan, heat about 5 cm (2 inches) of olive or groundnut oil to the smoking point. As the oil heats, drain the artichokes and dry them thoroughly between layers of kitchen paper. Dip a few slices at a time first into the flour and then into the beaten egg. Fry in the hot oil until crisp and golden. Remove with a slotted spoon and drain in a serving dish lined with a triple layer of kitchen paper. Keep the fried artichokes warm in a low oven as you fry the remaining slices. When all the slices are fried, blot the top layers in the dish with kitchen paper to drain them thoroughly. Pull the paper which lines the dish out from under the artichokes, sprinkle with salt and serve very hot.

Artichokes and Peas

4–6 servings
Serve with a cheese soufflé.

2–3 slices lean bacon
½ small onion
3 tbsps chopped parsley
1 small garlic clove
30 g (1 oz) butter
2 tbsps olive oil
6 medium artichokes, trimmed
and thinly sliced
2 tbsps minced fresh basil or 1
tsp dried basil, crumbled

salt
freshly ground pepper
about 1 dl (4–6 tbsps) hot
chicken stock
1 kg (2 lb) peas, shelled, or about
350 g (12 oz) frozen peas,
barely thawed

Combine the bacon, the onion, the parsley and the garlic clove on a board and chop very fine. Heat the butter and the olive oil in a heavy casserole. Add the bacon mixture. Cook, stirring constantly, for 3 to 4 minutes. Add the artichokes, the basil, salt and pepper and one third of the stock. Simmer, covered, over low heat for 10 minutes, stirring frequently. Add the peas and, if necessary to prevent scorching, more stock. Simmer covered for about 5 to 10 more minutes, or until the vegetables are tender.

Tuscan Artichoke Flan

4 servings
Serve as a main dish, with a tomato salad. Instead of the nutmeg flavouring, use any favourite herb in desired amounts.

6 medium artichokes
acidulated water
flour
2·5 dl (8 fl oz) olive oil
6 eggs

4 tbsps cream or milk
salt
freshly ground pepper
⅛ tsp ground nutmeg

Prepare the artichokes and cut them into thin slices. Drop the finished slices into the acidulated water. When ready to use, drain the artichokes and dry thoroughly between layers of kitchen paper. Coat the pieces with the flour and shake off excess. Heat the olive oil to smoking point. Fry the artichokes until crisp and golden. Drain on kitchen paper. Butter a shallow 1½-litre (or 1½-quart) baking dish. Put the artichokes into it. Beat together the eggs and the cream. Season with salt and pepper and the nutmeg or the herbs. Pour the mixture over the artichokes. Cook in a preheated moderate oven (Gas 4, 350° F, 180° C) for 15 to 20 minutes or until golden and puffy. Serve immediately.

Ragoût of Artichoke Hearts

4 servings

8 medium raw artichoke hearts or bottoms
30 g (1 oz) butter
1 tbsp olive oil
1 medium onion, chopped fine
1 garlic clove, crushed
4 small-to-medium ripe tomatoes, peeled, seeded and chopped fine

4 tbsps finely chopped parsley
salt
freshly ground pepper
2 tbsps drained capers or 110 g (4 oz) black olives, stoned and chopped

Cut the artichoke hearts into quarters. Heat the butter and the olive oil in a deep frying pan. Cook the onion and the garlic, stirring constantly, until the onion is soft. Add the artichoke quarters. Cook over low heat, stirring frequently and carefully, for about 7 to 10 minutes or until half tender. Add the tomatoes and the parsley. Season with salt and pepper. Simmer, covered, for 10 more minutes or until tender. Stir in the capers or the olives. Serve very hot.

Purée of Artichoke Hearts

4 servings
Serve with fillets of sole or lamb chops.

8 large braised artichoke hearts or bottoms
4 tbsps double cream
60 g (2 oz) butter

salt
freshly ground white papper
2 tbsps finely chopped parsley

Cut the artichoke hearts into pieces. Purée the artichokes with the cream in a blender (you will probably need to do this in two or three batches). Heat the butter and add the artichoke purée. Season with salt and pepper. Mix well and heat through thoroughly. If too thick, add a little more cream, 1 tablespoon at a time. Serve in a heated serving dish, sprinkled with parsley.

Asparagus

(Asparagus officinalis)

The edible shoots or spear rising from a rootstock of a vegetable believed to be a native of the eastern Mediterranean countries and Asia Minor; the most important species of a lily family of over 200 different kinds, some edible, some not. Its taste is delicate yet distinctive, its shape, whether svelte or plump, always elegant and its colour, ranging from bright-green to snow-white (depending on the variety and the way it is grown), decorative on whatever kind of china it is served. Furthermore, asparagus is often served with fancy sauces, which may be one of the reasons why it is considered a symbol of epicurean eating. It always has been a popular vegetable, whether wild or cultivated. The Greeks ate it wild, the Romans both wild and cultivated. As early as 200 B.C. Cato gave excellent growing instructions and Pliny deplored a species that grew near Ravenna, of which three heads would weigh one pound. Generally speaking, the ancients preferred wild asparagus, and wild asparagus can still be bought – or picked – in Italy and Spain. Anybody who has tasted its superlative flavour, a kind of essence of asparagus, will feel somewhat let down by the tamer flavour of cultivated asparagus.

In France, asparagus came into vogue under Louis XIV, and from the court of the *Roi Soleil* it made its triumphant way to the big and smaller courts of Europe who took their cue from France where good living was concerned. Not that asparagus was ever cheap; Brillat Savarin tells of an incident (*c.* 1825) when he balked at paying 40 francs for a bundle of asparagus and was told

29

by the seller that it would be snapped up in a trice, which it was, by two Englishmen who went off whistling 'God Save the King'. England had known asparagus in the sixteenth and seventeenth centuries mainly as a 'salad herb', but in the early nineteenth century London asparagus was famous and the acreage devoted to its cultivation in places like Mortlake truly enormous.

The name is the Latinized form of the Greek name and it is basically the same in most European languages: *asperges* in French, *Spargel* in German, *asparagi* in Italian. In seventeenth-century English the name was corrupted to 'sparrowgrass' and Pepys mentions it as such.

Just as there are different varieties of cultivated asparagus, there are different national tastes. The English like green asparagus, and the thinner it is, the better it tastes. The opposite of this is the continental European taste for colossal snow-white stalks, which are milder in flavour though somehow more voluptuous. Italy favours purple-tipped asparagus.

The difference is achieved by different cultivation methods; green asparagus is cut after the shoots have risen into the open air, while white asparagus is grown buried in mounds of soil, which, ridged high over the roots, keep from the shoots the light that would make them green. The shoots are cut as soon as they start showing their tips. These luscious white asparagus have brought fame to Argenteuil in France and Malines in Belgium and to some towns in southern Germany such as Heidelberg, where at asparagus time the local restaurants prepare the vegetable in dozens of ways, attracting visitors from far away.

Americans and Europeans eat asparagus differently. In America, people cut off the tip, ignoring what goodness there is in the stalk. In Europe, on the contrary, asparagus is eaten with the fingers down to its last tender moment. I personally always peel asparagus and eat it down, using my fingers, since I can't bear to waste half an inch of this vegetable delight.

Asparagus has also been valued for its medicinal properties as long as it has been known. It is a diuretic and a laxative and said to be good for people of sedentary habits who suffer from dropsy. Others have advocated its use to restore eyesight and ease tooth-ache.

How to buy

Buy fresh asparagus that is a rich green or creamy-white colour, with closed, compact tips, round spears and a fresh look. The stalks should be tender but firm. Avoid asparagus that has ridged spears, open and spread-out tips, or mouldy or rotting tips. Tired old asparagus is not worth cooking since it is tough, stringy and poor in flavour.

White asparagus in thick stalks is also imported in tins or glass jars. It is tender all the way through, beautiful to look at and disappointingly bland in flavour. It is entirely a luxury for show.

How to keep

Refrigerate in a plastic bag or in the vegetable drawer in the refrigerator. Do not wash before storing. If the stalks seem a little limp, cut a thin diagonal slice from the ends and stand them in cold water for about 5 to 10 minutes; but cook asparagus as soon as possible. Raw, on refrigerator shelf: 3 days. Cooked and covered, on refrigerator shelf: 2 days.

Nutritive values

A good source of vitamin A and a fair one for vitamins B and C and for iron. About 90 per cent of its weight is water. Raw: 26 calories; cooked: 20 calories (per 100 g/3½ oz).

How to use

When ready to cook, lay the asparagus on a cutting board. Cut off the white part at the bottom of the stalks which is tough. Or snap it off, though it is impossible to snap evenly. Cut all the stalks the same length for better cooking and prettier serving. If the asparagus is very thin, it need not be peeled. But since most is not, it is better peeled with a swivel vegetable parer up to the tip, beginning at the bottom and leaving only the tender scales at the head. You have to judge where it starts to be tender. Peeled asparagus is usually totally edible. Then place the asparagus, tips down, in a deep bowl. Quickly run cold water over it. Shake the stalks to loosen any sand in the tips. Lift out and, if sandy, repeat the quick washing under running cold water until the water is clean. *Never soak asparagus.* The stalks may be used whole, tips only, cut into 4-cm ($1\frac{1}{2}$-inch) pieces or cut diagonally. Asparagus can be steamed, boiled or cooked in a pan. The most important thing, and it *is* important, is not to overcook it. It should be crisp and almost tender. The best way to find out is to stick the point of a knife into the thickest stalk; it should meet some resistance. It's been my experience that most recipes give you far too long a cooking time. You can always cook asparagus longer, but you can't un-cook it from mush.

To steam: Using soft kitchen string, tie the asparagus into serving-size bundles or, if it is a small amount, in one bundle. Stand the bundles in the bottom of a double boiler. Add enough boiling water to cover about 5 cm (2 inches) of the stem, more if the stalks are very long. Add about $\frac{1}{2}$ teaspoon salt. Cover with the inverted top part of the double boiler. Cook for about 5 to 15 minutes, depending on size and age. Remove from pan with tongs or two forks. Drain, cut and remove string, arrange on serving plate and season. Serve at once with butter or sauce.

To boil: Place the stalks (tied or untied) in a deep frying or other wide-bottomed pan. Pour in from 2 to 3 cm ($\frac{1}{2}$ to 1 inch) boiling water. Add about $\frac{1}{2}$ teaspoon salt. Cover the pan. Bring quickly to boiling point, lower heat to medium and cook for 5 to 10 minutes. Lift from pan with tongs or two forks, drain, arrange on serving plate and season. Serve at once with butter or sauce. The tips and stalks of cut-up asparagus should be cooked separately in a minimum of water. Cook the stalk pieces, covered, for about 2 to 3 minutes, then add the tips and cook 5 to 7 minutes longer or until barely tender.

To cook in a pan: This is the oriental way of cooking the vegetable. Cut the stalks on the diagonal into about $\frac{1}{2}$-cm ($\frac{1}{4}$-inch) slices; leave the tips whole. Heat just enough butter or oil in a frying pan to cover the bottom. Do not brown the butter. Add the slices and the tips and season lightly with salt and pepper. Cover the pan and bring it to steaming point. Then turn the heat to low and cook for about 3 to 5 minutes or until barely tender, shaking the pan frequently to prevent sticking.

Seasoning asparagus: Hot or cold, asparagus is a natural for all sorts of plain and fancy sauces. Melted butter or French dressing are the most common ones, hollandaise the great favourite. Personally I prefer to eat asparagus lightly seasoned with salt and pepper, with no sauce at all beyond a sprinkle of fresh lemon juice.

Asparagus in Cream

2–4 servings
The simpler the recipe the finer the asparagus taste.

1 kg (2 lb) asparagus, trimmed and peeled
30 g (1 oz) butter
asparagus cooking water

4 tbsps double cream, heated
salt
freshly ground white pepper
⅛ tsp ground nutmeg

Cook the asparagus in boiling salted water for 5 minutes only; it should be only half tender. Drain it carefully, reserving the cooking water. Place it in a casserole that can go to the table. Add the butter and 2 tablespoons of the cooking water. Simmer, covered, over very low heat for about 10 minutes, or until the asparagus is tender. Shake the casserole frequently to prevent sticking and, if necessary, add a little more water, 1 tablespoon at a time. Stir a little salt and pepper and the nutmeg into the hot cream. Pour over the asparagus. Cook for 2 to 3 more minutes, or until thoroughly heated through. Serve very hot.

Asparagus Milanaise

4 servings
The eggs make this a main course.

1 kg (2 lb) asparagus
80 g (3 oz) grated Parmesan or Gruyère cheese

60 g (2 oz) butter, hot and browned
4 or 8 butter-fried eggs (optional)

Cook the asparagus until just tender. Drain it carefully. Butter a shallow baking dish generously and heat it in a low oven. Lay half of the asparagus in the dish. Sprinkle the tips with half of the grated cheese. Repeat with the remaining asparagus and the

33

remaining cheese. Drizzle the butter over the asparagus tips. Lay the fried eggs on top of the asparagus and serve very hot.

Flemish Asparagus

4 servings
This may be a light main dish, followed by salad, cheese and fruit. Allow 1 lb asparagus for each serving.

4 hard-boiled eggs, mashed
250 g (8 oz) butter, melted
salt
freshly ground pepper

2 tbsps fresh lemon juice
2 tbsps finely chopped parsley
2 kg (4 lb) asparagus, trimmed
  and peeled

Combine the mashed eggs, the butter, the salt and the pepper in a small saucepan. Cook over low heat long enough to heat through thoroughly. Remove from heat and stir in the lemon juice and the parsley. Keep hot while the asparagus is cooking, then turn into a sauce boat and serve as soon as the asparagus is ready. Cook and drain the asparagus and place the spears side by side on a clean kitchen towel. Line a serving platter with a large napkin in such a way that half of the napkin overlaps the dish. Place the asparagus on the napkin and cover with the overlapping part of the napkin. This will absorb any remaining moisture in the asparagus.

Piquant Green Sauce for Cold Asparagus

6 servings
This sauce takes the place of the usual vinaigrette and may be used for any cooked cold vegetables as well as for seafood.

good 1 dl ($\frac{1}{6}$ pt) olive oil
110 g (4 oz) parsley
1 hard-boiled egg, chopped
2 tbsps drained capers
1 tbsp finely chopped onion
1 garlic clove, finely chopped
2 anchovies, chopped, or 1 tbsp
  anchovy paste

1–2 tbsps chopped fresh basil or
  1 tsp dried basil
1 tsp salt
$\frac{1}{4}$ tsp freshly ground pepper
juice of 2 lemons
1$\frac{1}{2}$ kg (3 lb) cooked cold
  asparagus

Blend all the ingredients except the asparagus to a purée. Pour the sauce into six individual little bowls (such as little white soufflé bowls) and chill. At serving time, divide the asparagus into six servings and place each on a plate. Set the bowls with the sauce on the plate for dipping.

Aubergine, Eggplant

(*Solanum melongena*)

Aubergines belong to the nightshade family, which includes potatoes, tomatoes and pepper, tobacco, belladonna, petunias and jessamine. The fruit, which is botanically a berry, and which we eat as a vegetable, varies in length from 10 to 30 cm (4 to 12 inches) and comes in different round, oblong, pearl-like and long shapes. Aubergines grow on an annual bushy plant which needs a

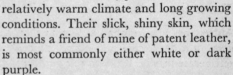

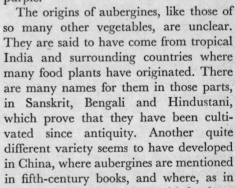

relatively warm climate and long growing conditions. Their slick, shiny skin, which reminds a friend of mine of patent leather, is most commonly either white or dark purple.

The origins of aubergines, like those of so many other vegetables, are unclear. They are said to have come from tropical India and surrounding countries where many food plants have originated. There are many names for them in those parts, in Sanskrit, Bengali and Hindustani, which prove that they have been cultivated since antiquity. Another quite different variety seems to have developed in China, where aubergines are mentioned in fifth-century books, and where, as in India, it is a popular vegetable to this day. In the Arabic lands we hear about aubergines in the ninth and tenth centuries, since when they have remained one of the major foods. The Arabs carried them into Spain and from there they reached northern Europe, first as a curiosity in the thirteenth century, but becoming better known by the mid sixteenth century. The Italians grew different kinds of aubergine even at that early time, of varying colours and sizes, and took them north. But in the rest of Europe aubergines never became as popular as in the Mediterranean and Near Eastern countries and in England not even the two names of the vegetable are recorded before the later eighteenth century. The Spaniards introduced them into the New World, specifically into Brazil, but in the United States 'eggplants' were grown for ornamental use only until some fifty or sixty years ago.

How to buy

Buy fruit that is firm, smooth, of a uniformly glossy colour and heavy for its size. Choose small rather than large fruit. Avoid oversize fruit, or fruit with large, rough, spongy places and with dark-brown spots for these are a sign of decay.

How to keep

Aubergines are perishable. Use as soon as possible. Until then, keep in a dark, cool and humid place, such as a basement. Or refrigerate briefly. Raw, on refrigerator shelf: 3 to 4 days. Cooked and covered, on refrigerator shelf: 3 to 4 days.

Nutritive values

There is little nutrition in aubergines, but they add interesting flavour and texture variety to menus. Cooked and drained: 19 calories per 100 g ($3\frac{1}{2}$ oz).

How to use

Aubergines can be prepared in many ways, depending on their size and the nationality of the cuisine. Whether they should be peeled or not depends on the size and the toughness of the skin. The commonly sold large aubergines have a tough skin, but the skin of the small, long, skinny ones or the tiny ones is tender and edible. Aubergines are a watery fruit and there are two schools of thought as to whether the water, which is a little bitter, should be drained before cooking. Again, it depends on size, variety and use.

If the water is to be drained, wash, trim off the stem, peel or not. Cut the aubergine into halves lengthwise and cut several gashes lengthways into the flesh. Or cut into thick slices. Sprinkle about 1 tablespoon of salt on the flesh of each aubergine half. Lay the halves cut-side down, or the slices side by side, on a kitchen towel or several thicknesses of kitchen paper. Let them stand at room temperature from 15 to 30 minutes. Squeeze the halves or slices gently with the back of a spoon to extract as much moisture as possible without damaging the fruit. Dry the halves or slices with another kitchen towel or more kitchen paper before using.

Otherwise, peel or not. Cut into slices, strips or cubes. Do this just before using because aubergines darken quickly when cut surfaces are exposed to the air.

To boil: Aubergines are seldom boiled by themselves; more usually, they are added to stews or dishes with liquid in which they will cook. In this case, it is best quickly to sauté the sliced or cubed aubergines first in a little hot butter or oil; this helps them keep their shape and adds to their flavour.

To pan fry: Slice, cube or cut the aubergine into strips. Sauté in a little hot butter or oil, turning over once, for 5 to 7 minutes or until golden brown. Or dip in flour and sauté as above. Season with salt and pepper.

To deep fry: Cut into strips. Roll in seasoned flour, dip into egg beaten with milk or water (1 egg and 2 tablespoons of milk or water) and roll in fine dry breadcrumbs. Fry in deep hot fat (375 to 385° F, 190 to 195° C, on frying thermometer) for a few minutes (time depends on the size of the strips) and drain on kitchen paper. Serve immediately, with lemon wedges.

To grill: Cut washed and trimmed aubergines into four or eight wedges, depending on size, or the same number of thick slices. With a pastry brush, brush all the cut surfaces with melted butter or with vegetable or olive oil. Sprinkle with salt and pepper, and any desired herbs. Place on grill pan or barbecue and grill about 7 to 10 cm (3 to 4 inches) away from heat, for about 10 minutes. Turn over once or twice to ensure even cooking, and brush repeatedly with melted butter or oil.

Aubergine with Beans

4–6 servings

1½ kg (3 lb) large aubergines
6 tbsps olive oil
1 medium onion, chopped
1 garlic clove, finely chopped
2 large ripe tomatoes, peeled,
  seeded and chopped
2 tbsps finely chopped parsley
2 tbsps chopped fresh basil or 2
  tsps dried basil

100–200 g (4–6 oz) cooked
  kidney beans (if tinned, rinse
  under running cold water and
  drain thoroughly)
2–3 tbsps fresh lemon juice
salt
freshly ground pepper
2 tbsps drained capers (optional)

Put the aubergines in a baking dish and prick three times with a fork. Bake in a preheated moderate oven (Gas 4, 350° F, 180° C) for about 30 to 45 minutes or until soft. Cool. Slit open the skin. Remove most of the seeds with a teaspoon. Mash the pulp with a fork. Heat 4 tablespoons of the oil in a frying pan. Cook the onion and garlic in it until soft and golden. Stir into the aubergine and mix well. Add the tomatoes, the parsley, the basil and the beans. Mix gently, taking care not to break the beans. Combine the remaining 2 tablespoons of oil and the lemon juice. Stir into the aubergine mixture. Season with salt and pepper and, if necessary, add a little more lemon juice. Sprinkle with the capers.

Aubergine Parmigiana

6 servings

1½ kg (3 lb) aubergines
salt
flour
2 eggs, beaten with 2 tsps olive
  oil
fine dry breadcrumbs
olive oil
2 tbsps chopped fresh basil or 2
  tsps dried basil

4½ dl (¾ pt) tinned tomatoes,
  forced through a sieve and
  heated
250 g (8 oz) mozzarella cheese,
  thinly sliced
60 g (2 oz) grated Parmesan
  cheese

Trim but do not peel the aubergines. Cut into ½-cm (¼-inch)

slices. Put the slices on a large platter and sprinkle each slice with salt. Let stand at room temperature for about 30 minutes to draw out excess moisture. Drain and dry the slices with kitchen paper. Dip each one into the flour and shake off excess. Dip into the beaten eggs, shake off excess egg and dip into breadcrumbs. Heat enough olive oil to cover well the bottom of a large frying pan. Fry the slices, a few at a time, until golden on both sides, turning over once. Drain on kitchen paper. Stir the basil into the tomatoes. Spoon a little of this tomato sauce into a buttered 2-litre or 2-quart baking dish. Arrange one third of the fried aubergine slices, overlapping, on the sauce. Top with layers of one third of the mozzarella, one third of the remaining tomato sauce and one third of the grated Parmesan. Repeat until all the ingredients are used. Bake in a preheated moderate oven (Gas 4, 350° F, 180° C) for about 20 to 30 minutes or until bubbly.

Tortino di Melanzane (Aubergine and Egg Puff)

4–6 servings
A good main dish, served with tomato salad.

4 small aubergines, each about 15 cm (6 inches) long	3 tbsps milk
	4 tbsps chopped parsley
salt	1 tbsp chopped fresh marjoram
flour	or $\frac{1}{2}$ tsp dried marjoram
olive oil	salt
10 eggs	freshly ground pepper

Trim and peel the aubergines. Cut into $\frac{1}{2}$-cm ($\frac{1}{4}$-inch) slices. Put the slices on a large platter and sprinkle each slice with salt. Let stand at room temperature for about 30 minutes to draw out excess moisture. Drain and dry the slices with kitchen paper. Coat them with flour, shaking off excess. Pour $\frac{1}{2}$ cm ($\frac{1}{4}$ inch) olive oil into a large frying pan. Heat the oil to smoking point. Fry a few aubergine slices at a time for about 2 minutes on each side in the hot oil, turning as each side gets golden brown. Add more oil, to keep the original level. Remove with a slotted spoon and drain on kitchen paper. Arrange the fried slices in overlapping rows in a $1\frac{1}{2}$-litre or $1\frac{1}{2}$-quart deep baking dish. Beat together the eggs, milk, parsley and marjoram. Season with very little salt and pepper, taking into account that the aubergines have been salted. Pour the mixture over the aubergines. Cook in a preheated hot oven (Gas 6, 400° F, 210° C) for about 20 minutes, or until puffed and golden brown.

Baked Aubergine, Mozzarella, Eggs and Tomatoes

3–4 servings

4 small aubergines, each about
   15 cm (6 inches) long
salt
4 anchovies, drained and cut up
2 large, ripe, firm tomatoes,
   peeled and cut into ½-cm
   (¼-inch) slices
3 hard-boiled eggs, sliced
1 mozzarella cheese weighing
   approximately 250–350 g
   (8–12 oz), cut into ½-cm
   (¼-inch) slices

freshly ground pepper
60 g (2 oz) parsley sprigs
3 tbsps fresh basil leaves or 2
   tbsps dried basil
2 garlic cloves
3 tbsps olive oil

Trim and peel the aubergines. Cut into ½-cm (¼-inch) slices. Put the slices on a large platter and sprinkle each slice with salt. Leave them at room temperature to draw out excess moisture. Drain and dry the slices with kitchen paper. Spread a little anchovy on each tomato slice. In a buttered, shallow, oven-proof dish which can go to the table or a pie plate, make well-over-lapping rows of aubergine, egg, tomato and mozzarella slices, in that order. Sprinkle with pepper, not salt (the aubergine slices and the anchovies are both salty). Chop the parsley, basil and garlic cloves together. Sprinkle the mixture over the vegetables and cheese, then sprinkle with the olive oil. Cover the dish with foil and bake in a preheated moderate oven (Gas 4, 350° F, 180° C) for 30 minutes. Remove the foil and bake for about 10 more minutes, to let any excessive moisture in the dish evaporate. Serve either hot, lukewarm or cold, but not chilled.

Aubergine Casserole

4–6 servings

The flavour trick is to sauté the vegetables separately in olive oil before cooking them with the tomatoes.

1½ kg (3 lb) aubergines, peeled and cut into cubes of 2–3 cm (1 inch)

1 dl (4 fl oz) olive oil

3 medium sweet green peppers, seeded and cut into strips

3 small onions, thinly sliced

2 whole garlic cloves

500 g (1 lb) peeled and chopped tomatoes or tinned plum tomatoes, drained and chopped

salt

freshly ground pepper

½ tsp dried thyme or oregano or basil

4 tbsps minced parsley

60 g (2 oz) currants, plumped in water, or 1 dozen black olives, stoned and halved

Put the aubergine into a strainer and sprinkle with about 2 to 3 tablespoons salt. Place the strainer over a bowl. Let it stand at room temperature for about 1 hour, stirring and squeezing the aubergine with the hands, in order to extract moisture. It will be mushed up, but this does not matter. Heat the olive oil in a frying pan. Over medium heat, cook the pepper strips in the oil, stirring frequently, until they are semi-soft. Using a slotted spoon, transfer the pepper strips to a casserole. In the same hot oil, cook the aubergine for about 3 to 4 minutes, then transfer it to the casserole. Now cook the onions and garlic in the remaining oil until they are semi-soft and barely golden. Add the onions to the vegetables in the casserole. Add the tomatoes, the salt and pepper, the thyme, the parsley and the currants or olives to the casserole. Mix well. Simmer over low heat for about 20 minutes, or until tender but not overcooked. Check occasionally for moisture; if necessary, add a little hot water, 1 tablespoon at a time, to prevent scorching. Serve hot or cold.

Caponata Siciliana (Pickled Aubergine)

8 servings
Whatever is not eaten at one sitting can be stored in a closed container in the refrigerator for 2 to 3 weeks.

2 kg (4 lb) aubergines
4½ dl (¾ pt) olive oil (it must be olive oil)
4 large onions, thinly sliced
250 g (½ lb) tinned tomatoes, forced through a sieve
4 celery stalks, white part only, thinly sliced
60 g (2 oz) drained capers

30 g (1 oz) parsley, finely chopped
12 black olives, stoned and halved
2 tbsps pine nuts
1 dl (4 fl oz) wine vinegar
3 tbsps sugar
salt
freshly ground pepper

Peel the aubergines and cut them into 2- or 3-cm (1-inch) cubes. Heat two thirds of the olive oil in a large, deep frying pan. Cook the aubergines in it until they are soft and brown, stirring constantly. Remove them with a slotted spoon to a dish and reserve. Add the remaining oil to the frying pan. Cook the onions, stirring constantly, until they are soft and golden. Add the tomatoes and the celery. Cook over medium heat, stirring frequently, until the celery is tender. To prevent scorching, add a tablespoon or two of water, if necessary. Add the capers, the parsley, the olives, the pine nuts and the fried aubergines. Mix well. Cook for about 1 minute and remove from heat. Heat the vinegar in a small saucepan and dissolve the sugar in it. Stir the vinegar into the aubergine mixture. Season with salt and pepper. Simmer, covered, over lowest possible heat for about 15 minutes. Stir frequently and add a tablespoon of water if there is danger of scorching, but go easy on the water because the finished dish must not be soupy. Cool before serving.

Avocado, Avocado Pear

(*Persea americana*)

The avocado is the pear-shaped fruit of a handsome glossy-leafed shade tree native to Central America. It is prized for its appetizing, rich, smooth and bland flesh which is yellowish-green in colour. This buttery flesh, which is easy to eat, surrounds a large, inedible stone from which a plant may be grown. Home gardeners do this with more enthusiasm than success, producing sad, tall, spindly stems with a few top leaves, which they cannot bear to throw away.

Botanically the avocado (which, strictly speaking, is a berry) is divided into three races – Mexican, Guatemalan and West Indian – which have been crossed into numerous varieties. The fruit can weigh as much as $1\frac{1}{2}$ to 2 kg (3 to 4 lb), be roundish rather than pear shaped, have a skin as thin as that of an apple or one that is coarse and pebbly, be greenish or russet in colour. Though a fruit, avocados are treated generally as a vegetable in appetizers, salads and soups. The cavity left by the removal of the stone makes the half shell a natural container for all sorts of fillings.

Avocados have been a staple food of Central and tropical South America since pre-Columbian days. Once an exotic rarity, they now are widely grown not only in the West Indies and Central America but also in the southern United States, South Africa, Australia, Israel and some Mediterranean countries.

The name is apparently an attempt to reproduce phonetically the Aztec name of *ahuacatl*. The great Indian civilizations of Mexico, Central America and northern South America widely cultivated avocados from seedling trees. The Spanish Conquest acquainted the Spaniards with the fruit; they liked it and took it back to Europe. But because of the difficulty of propagation, avocados did not become as well known as other New World fruits and vegetables. A report to Charles V of Spain in 1526 by the historian Ovido mentions avocados as similar to butter and 'very good eating'. The first reference in English is found in 1672, when W. Hughes, a physician to the English Crown, found the avocado in Jamaica and pronounced it a most rare and pleasant fruit, which also nourished the body and procured vigour.

The commercial growing of avocados became a viable proposition only after it was discovered, around 1900, that trees could be propagated by budding and grafting. The traditional way of growing them as seedling trees results in fruit that varies greatly in quality whereas grafting or budding produces fruit of uniform size and quality.

The three generally recognized races have flesh that varies from green to yellowish-white, but the flavour is invariably the same – bland, vaguely nutty, buttery and very soothing. In appearance, the Mexican avocado is a small, smooth-skinned fruit, usually purple or black in colour; the Guatemalan avocado is a medium-sized fruit, green, purple or black in colour with a more or less pebbly or rough skin; the West Indian avocado is a large, smooth-skinned fruit, green, red or purplish in colour. These races were the basis of about two dozen varieties now grown commercially.

How to buy

Buy fruit that is heavy, with a skin that is uniform in colour and without cracks or bruises. Avoid fruit with dark sunken spots and damaged skin surfaces. Generally the stone fits tightly in the cavity, but in some varieties the stones are often loose and rattling at maturity.

How to keep

To be good eating, avocados must be properly ripened, that is, they must be slightly soft. For immediate use, choose fruit that yields to gentle pressure. Whole avocados may be stored in the warmest part of the refrigerator for about 8 to 10 days, depending on ripeness. For later use, choose firm avocados. Keep them at room temperature and they will ripen, taking from about 3 days to a week and sometimes even longer. Never store unripe avocados in the refrigerator.

If half an avocado is to be stored, rub the cut surface with half a lemon to prevent discoloration. Keep the stone in its cavity since it also prevents discoloration. Wrap the fruit tightly in plastic wrap and refrigerate.

Nutritive values

Depending on their variety and size, avocados offer a fair amount of vitamins A and B_1, thiamine, riboflavin and ascorbic acid as well as iron, calcium and phosphorus. The oil content ranges from 5 to 25 per cent and is largely unsaturated. The low carbohydrate content makes the avocado useful in diabetic diets. It is easily digestible. It has 167 calories per 100 g ($3\frac{1}{2}$ oz).

How to use

Important: cut avocados discolour rapidly in contact with the air. When preparing the fruit, immediately rub the cut parts with half a lemon or dip in lemon juice.

To cut or to peel an avocado, use a stainless steel knife which retards darkening. Cut the fruit into halves lengthwise, twist halves a little to separate them and remove the stone. Scrape off any peel from the stone which may have clung to the cavity. To peel, lay the avocado, cut side down, on a board and pry off the skin with a paring knife or with the back of a teaspoon. Peeled avocados can be sliced, diced, mashed or puréed, and used raw or baked. Avocados are best combined raw with cooked foods; this should be done at the last moment, away from the heat. Apart from their use in salads, the best known avocado dish is the Mexican salad, guacamole, also used as a dip.

Cold Avocado Soup

4–6 servings
The soup should be well seasoned.

2 medium avocados
2 tbsps lime or lemon juice
9 dl (1½ pts) cold chicken stock,
  fat free
salt
freshly ground pepper

dash of Tabasco sauce
3 dl (½ pt) single cream or 1½ dl
  (¼ pt) sour cream and 1½ dl
  (¼ pt) single cream
paprika

Cut the avocados, remove the stone and scoop out the flesh. Place
in a blender with all the other ingredients, except the paprika.
Blend until smooth. Chill, covered, for 1 hour or longer. Serve
with a sprinkling of paprika.

Guacamole

about 4 cups
This is the true Mexican version of this popular avocado sauce, from The
Complete Book of Mexican Cooking *by Elisabeth Lambert Ortiz.* If
possible, make guacamole just before serving since avocado darkens. Or
cover tightly with plastic wrap or aluminium foil and use soon.*

2 large, very ripe avocados
1 medium tomato, peeled, seeded
  and chopped
½ small white onion, chopped
  fine
2 or more hot chilis, chopped

several sprigs of fresh coriander,
  finely chopped
salt
freshly ground pepper
pinch of sugar

Peel and mash the avocados with a fork. Mix well with the other
ingredients. Pile into a serving dish.

Note: I stir 1 to 2 tablespoons fresh lemon juice into my
guacamole because I think this freshens the dish. I also use whatever tinned chili peppers I have at hand; they should be drained,
seeded and rinsed before being chopped. Lastly, I frequently
serve guacamole in hollowed-out tomatoes, with a sprig of
coriander or parsley on top.

  *Bantam Books.

Cold Shrimp-Stuffed Avocados

6 servings
Serve with a salad of new potatoes dressed only with sour cream, a little mustard and salt and pepper.

3 large avocados
juice of 1 lemon
250 g (½ lb) cooked, shelled
   shrimps (reserve 6 whole
   shrimps), coarsely chopped
1 hot chili pepper, peeled if fresh,
   seeded, washed and chopped
   fine

1 hard-boiled egg, chopped
1 dozen green or black olives,
   stoned and chopped
mayonnaise
salt
freshly ground pepper
3 tbsps finely chopped coriander
   leaves or parsley

Cut the avocados into halves lengthwise. Remove the stone. Carefully scoop out the flesh without damaging the shells. Put the flesh into a bowl. Sprinkle each shell with a little lemon juice to prevent darkening. Mash the avocado flesh with a fork. Add the shrimps, the hot pepper, the egg and the olives. Mix well. Add enough mayonnaise, beginning with 4 tablespoons, to bind the ingredients together. Taste and season with salt and pepper. Stuff the avocado shells with this mixture. Top each shell with one of the reserved shrimps and sprinkle with a little coriander.

Avocado Soufflé

6 servings

60 g (2 oz) butter
60 g (2 oz) flour
½ l (⅘ pt) hot milk
1 tsp salt
freshly ground pepper

⅛ tsp ground nutmeg or cayenne
   pepper
2 medium ripe avocados
5 egg yolks, beaten
6 egg whites

Heat the butter in a saucepan large enough to hold all the ingredients and stir in the flour. Cook, stirring constantly, for 2 to 3 minutes; do not brown. Stir in the milk. Cook, stirring constantly, until smooth and thickened. Remove from heat and stir in the salt, the pepper and the nutmeg or cayenne. Cut the avocados into halves lengthwise and remove the stones. Scoop out the flesh. Press it through a fine sieve or purée it in the blender. Stir the egg yolks into the avocado purée and mix well. Stir the avocado mixture into the white sauce and blend thoroughly. Return the saucepan to very low heat. Cook, again stirring constantly, for 3 to 4 minutes or until just warm, and remove immediately from the heat. Do not heat too much. Beat the egg whites until stiff and fold carefully into the avocado mixture. Turn the mixture into a buttered 2-litre or 2-quart soufflé dish. Bake in a preheated moderate oven (Gas 5, 380° F, 195° C) for about 30 to 35 minutes.

Bamboo Shoots

(*Bambusa vulgaris*, *Phyllostachys pubescens* and other species)

The ivory-coloured young sprouts we eat come from the thick pointed shoots that emerge from the ground under a bamboo, a tropical plant. Left to grow, they would form new stems and end up as adult bamboos, often enormously tall plants, used for construction and in many other ways in tropical and sub-tropical Asia. Bamboo shoots are a staple of Chinese, Japanese, Korean and other Asian cooking. Non-oriental aficionados say that their taste is reminiscent of artichokes, but more realistically, it is bland and pleasantly crunchy; in cooking, bamboo shoots are basically fillers, added for texture contrast.

The two varieties mentioned above are the most widely cultivated as food plants, but the shoots from any number of wild bamboo species are also used. They are usually cut when 15 to 30 cm (6 inches to a foot) long and about 5 cm (2 inches) in diameter. Though some shoots are tender enough to be boiled as they are, usually the tight, tough, overlapping outer sheaths of the plant are stripped off. The shoots are then sliced or cubed and they are ready for cooking. They are usually eaten freshly boiled; oriental cooks take great care to add them to a dish for the least possible cooking time, so as not to rob them of their crispness. They can be pickled or deep fried; or they can be used much as mushrooms are used or for texture contrast in seafood, meat or vegetable dishes.

How to buy

Bamboo shoots reach us tinned, imported from the Far East in a lightly salted liquid.

How to keep

If not all the bamboo shoots in a tin are used in a recipe, they should be put into a clean glass jar filled with cold water and sealed with a tight lid. The jar should be placed in the warmest part of the refrigerator and the water changed daily. However, bamboo shoots should be used up as soon as possible or they lose what flavour they have and, more important, their crunchiness which, after all, is their *raison d'être*.

Nutritive values

Raw: 27 calories per 100 g (3½ oz).

Bamboo Shoots and Pork Soup

4–6 servings
Far Eastern cookery frequently combines pork and bamboo shoots.

30 g (1 oz) butter	1 tsp sugar
1 garlic clove, crushed	1½ l (2½ pts) chicken stock
½ tsp ground coriander	salt
¼ tsp cayenne pepper	250 g (8 oz) bamboo shoots,
2 tbsps soy sauce	drained and thinly sliced
110 g (4 oz) lean boneless pork,	110 g (4 oz) chopped watercress
thinly sliced	or spring-onion tops

Heat the butter in a large saucepan. Stir in the garlic, the coriander, the cayenne and the soy sauce. Cook, stirring constantly, for 2 minutes. Add the pork. Cook, stirring all the time, until the pork is browned on all sides. Add the sugar and the stock. Taste and, if necessary, add a little salt. Simmer, covered, for 10 to 15 minutes or until the pork is thoroughly cooked. Add the bamboo shoots and cook 3 minutes longer. Remove from heat and stir in the watercress. Serve very hot.

Bamboo Shoots and Spinach

3 servings

4 tbsps groundnut oil or vegetable
oil
125 g (4–5 oz) finely shredded
bamboo shoots
500 g (1 lb) spinach, trimmed,
washed and torn into bite-sized
pieces

2 tsps soy sauce
salt

Heat the oil in a frying pan or in a wok. Add the bamboo shoots.
Cook, stirring constantly, for 2 minutes. Add the spinach and
cook for 1 more minute. Stir in the soy sauce and a little salt.
Transfer to a hot serving dish and keep hot. Over high heat,
reduce the pan juices to 2 or 3 tablespoons. Pour over the vegetables and serve.

Banana

(genus *Musa*)

Bananas are the seedless fruit of a tropical plant of which there are more than 100 cultivated varieties, sterile hybrids which cannot be given exact species names. This most familiar of all tropical fruit is best known as a dessert fruit, with a yellowish-white soft pulp and a zip-off skin, but since it can also be used as a vegetable it is included in this book. Furthermore, there are a number of bananas which are strictly for cooking, less sweet and with a higher starch content, of which the large plantain (*Musa paradisiaca*) is the best known.

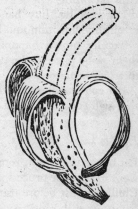

Bananas grow on trees which look vaguely like palms but which are really gigantic herbs that can grow up to 10 metres (30 feet), with enormous, oblong, droopy leaves. The wild varieties have seeds, but in the cultivated ones, grown for commerce, seedless fruit grows from the female flower in a bunch which may have 200 single bananas and weigh up to 35 kg (80 lb). Each plant bears a single crop, then it is cut down to resurrect from its own suckers.

Originally the banana was native to the humid tropics of east Asia. From there it spread to all the tropical world; today there is practically no hot region where it is not grown and does not form part of the local diet. Bananas are an ancient crop, mentioned in Greek, Latin and Arab writings; Alexander the Great noticed them when on his way to India. Portuguese navigators brought the fruit to the Canary Islands shortly after 1400 and from there it went to Hispaniola around 1516. Soon it became a great West Indian crop.

53

Vegetable Cookery

In some parts of the world, such as Hawaii and other Pacific Islands, and in the Far East, people eat the terminal buds of the banana plant much as palm cabbage. The leaves are used for wrapping up food for cooking, as we use aluminium foil. Bananas are also made into beer, liqueurs and a kind of powerful wine which I once drank in the north of Brazil and which laid me out flat.

How to buy

Buy firm, unblemished fruit, regardless of size, without bruises. Fully ripe bananas are yellow with brown flecks; use these first. Buy bananas by the bunch for single bananas deteriorate quicker. Avoid bruised, discoloured, over-soft fruit. Mould on the darkened skins means decay.

For keeping, buy bananas with green tips and an all-over greenish-yellow skin and let them ripen at room temperature.

Totally brown bananas need not always be rotten. Touch them *gently* to see if the flesh is still firm and not mushy and use them immediately.

For cooking, bananas should be still slightly green and firm, or they will cook into mush.

How to keep

Let bananas ripen at room temperature, in a cooler room if you want to slow the process. But never keep them in the refrigerator. Chill only just before using.

Nutritive values

Bananas provide good quantities of vitamin C and some vitamins A and B_1. They are low in protein and fat, high in carbohydrates and, when truly ripe, very easily digested. One medium banana: 85 to 100 calories.

How to use

Cut bananas darken rapidly when exposed to the air. To prevent this, rub or dip immediately in lemon juice. Use a stainless-steel rather than a carbon knife to slice them since this will help keep them light. When tearing a single banana from a bunch, be careful not to tear off any part of the skin of the adjoining fruit or it will darken where exposed to the air.

Curried Bananas

4 servings
Choose unripe, firm bananas or make the dish with plantains. Serve with a meat curry.

60 g (2 oz) butter
½ tsp turmeric
1 tsp curry powder or to taste
4 large bananas, peeled and cut
   into halves lengthwise

1 tsp salt
4–6 tbsps plain yoghurt

Heat the butter in a frying pan large enough to hold the banana halves side by side. Stir in the turmeric and the curry powder. Cook over medium heat, stirring constantly, for about 3 minutes. Add the bananas, lower the heat and sprinkle with salt. Cook for about 5 to 7 minutes or until heated through. Shake the pan frequently to prevent sticking, or stir gently with a wooden spoon. Turn over once, using two wooden spoons in order not to break the bananas. Spoon the yoghurt over the bananas. Turn the heat to medium. Cook for 3 to 5 more minutes, or until the yoghurt is heated through, shaking the pan frequently.

Banana and Mango Chutney

It is important to cook the mixture slowly, for a long time.

3 mangoes, each weighing about
   500 g (1 lb), or the equivalent
   in tinned mangoes
1 medium onion, finely chopped
1 large garlic clove, finely
   chopped
125 g (4–5 oz) golden raisins
5 large ripe bananas, sliced

2–3 tbsps finely chopped fresh
   ginger or 1 tbsp ground
   ginger
250 g (8 oz) sugar
1 tbsp salt
2½ dl (8 fl oz) cider vinegar
1 tsp Tabasco or hot pepper
   sauce, or to taste

Peel the mangoes. Cut the flesh from the stone and chop into pieces. Put the mangoes into a large saucepan and add the onion, garlic, raisins, bananas and ginger. Stir the sugar and salt into the vinegar until dissolved. Stir in the Tabasco sauce, beginning with 1 teaspoon. Pour the mixture over the fruit and mix well. Bring to boiling point and lower the heat to very low. Simmer, uncovered and stirring frequently, for about 2 hours, or until thick and cooked down. Cool and spoon into sterilized jars, or refrigerate. The chutney will keep at least two months in the refrigerator.

Barley

(genus *Hordeum*)

The edible grain of a grass, barley has a nut-like flavour and high amounts of carbohydrates. It is one of the oldest food plants, so old that it is impossible to be precise about its origins. Carbonized remains of one of the varieties, *Hordeum vulgare*, date back to the Neolithic and Bronze Ages in Europe. It was known in Egypt in 5000 B.C., in Europe 3,000 years ago and in China in 2000 B.C.

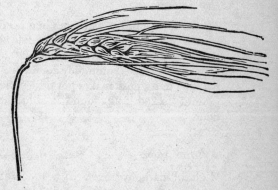

The Bible tells us barley was one of the foods destroyed by the plagues of Egypt (Exodus 9:31). Barley was the chief bread plant of the Hebrews, Greeks and Romans and of most of Europe until the end of the sixteenth century.

Today, barley is no longer an important food, in spite of its high nutritional value and palatable taste. About half of the world's crop is used as livestock fodder. The rest is used mostly for beer-making in which it is an essential ingredient. Malting barley (*Hordeum distichon*) is used in a process called 'malting' which germinates the grains and dries the very young seedlings to produce malt for brewing. The most illustrious use of the grain, however, is in the distillation of Scotch whisky.

The reason that barley has been so widely distributed is that it will grow in a great many different climates; there are varieties suitable for subarctic to subtropical areas. It has a short growing season (which can be less than ninety days), shorter than that of any other cereal, so that it is particularly useful at high altitudes

57

such as the slopes of the Himalayas and in the far north; I've seen
it grown in north Norway on the shores of an Arctic sea.

Barley was supplanted as the main bread cereal in Europe in
the seventeenth century by the more palatable wheat. Wheat,
with its high gluten content, lends itself to baking whereas barley
is deficient in gluten, an elastic protein substance which makes
a flour that will bake a porous loaf. Barley flour makes a very
heavy bread and is used for the unleavened flat breads of Scandi-
navia, making a virtue out of necessity.

Barley oddities are barley water, a soothing, refreshing drink,
once standard in English Victorian and Edwardian households,
and barley sugar, which, incidentally, no longer is made of barley
water and sugar, but of flavoured cane sugar.

How to buy

The barley we buy in packages in groceries is pearl barley, whole
kernels from which the outer husk has been removed and part of
the bran polished away. It comes in coarse, medium and small
sizes, but the one commonly found is medium. The removal of
only the outer husk makes pot barley. Scotch barley is a roughly-
ground husked grain found in some health stores, as is barley
flour.

Nutritive values

High in carbohydrates, with moderate amounts of calcium,
phosphorus and protein. Low in vitamins. Pearl barley, raw: 349
calories; Scotch barley, raw: 113 calories (per 100 g/3½ oz).

How to use

Like rice, barley is boiled or braised until tender, by itself or with
other foods, especially soups.

One measure raw pearl barley makes 2¼ to 2¾ measures cooked
barley.

Cream of Barley Soup

4–6 servings

30 g (1 oz) butter
75 g (scant 3 oz) medium
  barley
1 celery stalk, chopped
1 medium onion, chopped

1½ l (2½ pts) hot chicken stock
salt
freshly ground pepper
2½ dl (8 fl oz) single cream
paprika

Heat the butter in a large saucepan. Stir in the barley, the celery, and the onion. Cook, stirring constantly, for about 4 minutes. Do not brown. Add the stock. Taste and add salt and pepper. Bring to boiling point. Turn heat down immediately to very low. Simmer, covered, for about 30 minutes. Purée in a blender and return to saucepan. Add the cream and heat through but do not boil. Serve sprinkled with paprika.

Barley and Mushroom Casserole

4–6 servings
Serve in place of potatoes or rice.

30 g (1 oz) butter
1 small onion, chopped fine
250 g (8 oz) mushrooms, thinly
  sliced
250 g (8 oz) medium barley
½ tsp dried thyme or marjoram

4½ dl (¾ pt) hot chicken or beef
  stock
salt
freshly ground pepper
2 tbsps finely chopped parsley

Heat the butter in a heavy casserole. Stir in the onion. Cook for 3 to 4 minutes or until golden. Stir in the mushrooms. Cook, stirring constantly, for about 3 minutes. Stir in the barley. Cook, stirring all the time, for about 3 to 4 minutes or until the barley is golden. Stir in the thyme and the stock. Taste and add salt and pepper. Cover tightly and cook over low heat for about 20 minutes, or until the barley is tender and has absorbed all the liquid. Check occasionally for moisture; if necessary, cook without a lid to allow for evaporation or, if too dry, add a little more stock or water, 2 tablespoons at a time. Sprinkle with parsley before serving.

Beans

(Leguminosae)

The general name of some species of the large and varied Leguminosae family whose fruit is a pod which opens along two sutures when the seeds are ripe. Depending on the varieties, either the pod and seeds (as in green beans) or the seeds alone (as in kidney beans) are eaten.

Next to cereals, beans are the most important human food. The protein content of some varieties is higher than that of any other vegetable and can be a substitute for animal protein in human nutrition. Beans, which also have the advantage that they are easily grown, dried and stored (this last of great importance), are the basic food in many parts of the world where animal protein is scarce. Beans are also rich in vitamin B, minerals and carbohydrates. Best of all, beans are an easy-to-cook, palatable food which can be used in an enormous variety of dishes and as stretchers of other foods. Their importance in human nutrition cannot be exaggerated.

Different kinds of beans originated in the Far East, Africa, Europe and the Americas. Broad beans were cultivated in the Old World for over 4,000 years while in the New World kidney beans go back for more than 2,000 years. Beans played an important part not only in the diet of the Egyptians, the Greeks and the Romans, but also in their ritual offerings of food to the dead and to the powers of the underworld, in divinations and other cult activities. Chinese documents tell us how, in the first century A.D., merchants made their fortunes with a popular bean relish. Beans were a major food for the Indians of all the Americas; the Hopi made their Bean Festival a major part of their religion. Beans are part of folklore wherever they are used; magic beans, jumping beans, ghostly beans, laughing beans still enchant us.

For the cook, beans are divided into two main categories (though there is no botanical basis for this): those which are eaten fresh and whole, like French beans, and those which are shelled and eaten fresh or dried, like butter or kidney beans. In bean cookery, it should be remembered that different kinds of fresh beans may be substituted for each other, as may dried beans. Naturally, the flavour, texture and appearance of the finished dish will vary according to the beans used. Various kinds and groups of beans (and similar legumes) will be found under their own headings: Black-eye Pea, Broad Bean, Butter Bean, Chick Pea, French Bean, Grams, Lentil, Mange-tout, Pea, Peanut, Pigeon Pea, Soy Bean. General notes on the extensive haricot family are under Dried Beans.

Bean Sprouts

Bean sprouts are the seeds of grains or legumes that have germinated and, in doing so, converted their fats and starches into easily digestible vitamins, sugars and proteins. The taste of the pale, tender shoots, depending on the variety of bean sprouted, is crisp and usually pleasant and somewhat nut-like, and bland enough to be added to salads and main dishes. The ease with which sprouts can be produced at home or bought for little money in oriental stores could make them into a valuable addition to our nutrition, as they have been for thousands of years in China.

The most commonly sprouted bean is the small, round, green mung bean or green gram (*Phaseolus aureus*), native of tropical Asia, and cultivated in China for thousands of years. Bean sprouts are produced from other beans as well, notably soy beans, but the kind sold fresh or tinned in oriental stores and supermarkets are sprouted mung beans.

How to buy

Buy fresh-looking, crisp beans with moist tips. Short sprouts mean young, tender ones.

How to keep

Refrigerate in a plastic bag and use as soon as possible.

Nutritive values

Bean sprouts are a good source of proteins, vitamins A and C and minerals. Raw: 35 calories; cooked and drained: 28 calories (per 100 g/3½ oz).

How to use

Wash thoroughly and drain well. Chill in ice water for about 30 minutes if they are to be served raw in a salad. Do not remove the loose hulls or little roots from sprouted beans since they contain most of the vitamins and the flavour. If they are to be cooked, put in boiling salted water to cover for 2 to 3 minutes. Do not overcook: bean sprouts must be crisp.

Egg Fu Yung

4 servings

250 g (½ lb) bean sprouts
boiling water
6 eggs, beaten
2 tbsps grated onion
2 spring onions, white and green
   parts, thinly sliced
salt

freshly ground pepper
110 g (4 oz) cooked, peeled,
   chopped prawns, or cooked,
   shredded pork
vegetable oil
soy sauce

Cook the bean sprouts in boiling water to cover for 3 minutes. Drain. Combine the bean sprouts, eggs, grated onion, spring onions, salt and pepper and the prawns or pork. Heat about 1 teaspoon oil in a small frying pan. Add about 4 tablespoons of the egg mixture and cook until set, as you would a pancake. Sprinkle with soy sauce. Turn over with a spatula and cook on the other side. Transfer to a serving dish and keep warm in a low oven. Repeat until all the egg mixture is used.

Sautéed Sprouts and Radishes

4 servings

2 tbsps vegetable oil
3 bunches red radishes, thinly
   sliced
250 g (½ lb) bean sprouts, cooked
4 spring onions, white and green
   part, thinly sliced

1–2 tbsps sherry and/or soy sauce
salt
freshly ground pepper

Vegetable Cookery

Heat the oil in a large frying pan. Add the radishes. Cook over medium heat, stirring constantly, for 1 minute. Add the bean sprouts and the spring onions and cook for 1 more minute. Sprinkle with the sherry and season with salt and pepper. Cook, stirring constantly, for 2 to 3 more minutes. Serve very hot.

Beetroot, Red Beet

(*Beta vulgaris*)

Beets are a vegetable that provides both edible bulbous red roots and leafy green stalks. Of the two, the roots are far more universally used because they stay fresh longer and are easily stored.

There are four different varieties of beets that are commonly cultivated:

1. The garden beet, the vegetable that we mean when talking of beetroot.

2. The leaf beet, or chard, of which only the leaves and stalks are eaten: see pages 113–15.

3. The sugar beet, one of the world's major sources of sugar.

4. The mangold, or mangel-wurzel, a major livestock feed.

All of these are derivates of the wild *Beta maritima*, a sprawling plant from the seashores of Europe, which spread from the Mediterranean to the Caspian Sea. Originally, only the leaves of this plant were eaten, and the edible roots were unknown as food in pre-Christian times. The large fleshy roots are typical of cultivated varieties, not wild ones. There are some allusions in the second and third centuries in Roman literature to cooking the roots of the plant, then still in rudimentary form, but the next mention of beetroots is found in fifteenth-century English recipes. A few improved versions became known in the sixteenth century in Italy, France and Germany, though beetroots were not a major food. Today, they are easily grown, both in home gardens and commercially. In Europe, beets are particularly popular in the northern parts since they thrive in cool climates. It is impossible to think of German or Scandinavian cooking without beetroots in their pickled form.

How to buy

Beetroot is the one vegetable which is more often sold cooked than raw. Buy fresh beetroots with a good round shape, a smooth firm flesh and a rich, deep-red colour. If the green tops are on, they should be fresh-looking, but somewhat wilted tops do not affect the quality of the root. Cooked beetroots should have a loose but undamaged skin. Choose small or medium beets which are tender whereas large ones may be tough. Avoid spotted, pitted beetroots or ones with scales. Avoid also very large beets, or beets that are flabby and wilted.

For two or three servings you will need 500 g (1 lb) of medium-sized roots.

Beet tops: Frequently beet tops are taken from young plants and sold in bunches as salad greens or potherbs. Buy beet tops which are thin-ribbed, fresh and clean. Avoid wilted tops or tops with even a touch of slime.

How to keep

If the beetroots have tops, cut them off about 3 to 5 cm (1 to 2 inches) above the crown; leave root ends intact. If the beet tops are fresh, save them and store in refrigerator, using as soon as possible. Refrigerate the beetroots in a plastic bag or the vegetable drawer of the refrigerator. Uncooked, on refrigerator shelf or in vegetable drawer: 3 weeks. Cooked, covered, on refrigerator shelf: 1 week.

Nutritive values

Beetroots are a good source of vitamins A and C and they contain small amounts of minerals. They have a high sugar content. Cooked and drained: 32 calories per 100 g (3½ oz). Beet tops are an excellent source of vitamins A and C as well as calcium. Cooked and drained: 18 calories per 100 g (3½ oz).

How to use

To preserve their colour, beetroots are almost always cooked or baked whole until tender and then peeled. The exception are very small young beetroots which are scrubbed and cooked with their green tops. Since beetroots bleed easily, cut off any tops well above the crown; this keeps the colour loss during cooking to a minimum. Wash the beetroots and, if large, scrub with a vegetable brush. Cook whole and unpeeled in boiling unsalted water to cover until tender. Cooking time varies from about 15 minutes to an hour depending on the age and size of the beetroots. Drain and cool quickly under running cold water. Trim crown and root ends and rub off the skin. Use as directed in recipe. If the beetroots are not used at the time of cooking, do not trim or peel them, and store, covered, in the refrigerator. Alternatively, bake the beetroots until tender: they will be more flavourful than boiled ones. To bake, place the trimmed beetroots on a shallow baking sheet. Brush with a little oil and bake in a preheated moderate oven (Gas 4, 350° F, 180° C) until tender. Cool before peeling.

To cook beet tops: Wash and trim the leaves, discarding any that are damaged. If the tops are big, cut them and any very big leaves into pieces. Cook, covered, in just enough boiling salted water to prevent scorching. Do not overcook. Drain and use as in recipe, or serve with butter and lemon juice.

Beetroot Parmesan

4–6 servings

16 or 18 tiny cooked, peeled beetroots	freshly ground pepper
salt	1½ dl (¼ pt) double cream
	3 tbsps grated Parmesan cheese

Put the beetroots into a saucepan. Season with salt and pepper. Add the cream. Cook over low heat, stirring carefully, until the beetroots and the cream are heated through. Stir in the Parmesan cheese and cook until the cheese is melted and the cream thickened. Serve very hot.

Pickled Beetroot

4 servings
The universal Scandinavian relish. The cooked dressing improves the flavour greatly.

1½ dl (¼ pt) cider or white
   vinegar
1½ dl (¼ pt) water
60 g (2 oz) sugar
1 tsp salt

¼ tsp freshly ground pepper
500 g (1 lb) cooked, peeled and
   thinly-sliced beetroots
1 tbsp caraway seeds

Combine the vinegar, water, sugar, salt and pepper in a saucepan. Bring to boiling point. Cook for 3 to 5 minutes. Cool. Put the beetroots into a deep bowl and pour the dressing over them. Sprinkle with the caraway seeds. Cover the bowl. Let it stand at room temperature for about 4 hours or refrigerate overnight. Drain before serving.

Steamed Beetroots and Tops

4 servings
Delicious when the beetroots are small and very fresh.

2 bunches small beetroots, with
   fresh green tops
60 g (2 oz) butter or more to
   taste

salt
freshly ground pepper

Cut the beetroots from the tops. Trim and wash the beetroots. Peel with a vegetable peeler and cut into slices. Cut the stems from the leaves and wash the leaves in several changes of water. Shake dry. Put the cut beetroots into a saucepan. Add about half the butter and a little salt and pepper. Top with the leaves. Add the remaining butter and a little salt and pepper. Cook, covered, over medium heat for about 5 to 10 minutes, tossing occasionally. The dish is ready when the beetroots are tender and the pan juices have cooked down to a few tablespoonfuls.

Beetroot Salad à la Crème

4 servings

4 large beetroots, cooked, peeled
   and cut into thin slices
1 tbsp Dijon mustard
1½ dl (¼ pt) double cream,
   lightly whipped

juice of ½ lemon
salt
freshly ground pepper
1 hard-boiled egg, chopped fine

Arrange the beetroots in overlapping slices on a shallow serving
dish. Chill well. Stir the mustard into the cream and then stir in
the lemon juice and salt and pepper. Pour the dressing over the
beetroots. Sprinkle with the chopped egg.

Black-eye Pea, Cow Pea

(*Vigna unguiculata* or *Vigna sinensis*)

In spite of their appearance and name, black-eye peas are botanically closer to the bean than to the pea. They are the edible seeds, marked with a black eye, of an annual leguminous vine. Black-eye peas are thought to be natives of Africa, but also grow throughout tropical Asia, where they are an important staple. They reached America, specifically Jamaica, in 1675 via African slave traders and from there spread to the other islands as well as to the Atlantic coast of the mainland; there they became widely grown in the Deep South, of which one may call them a speciality.

In Africa and America it is the seed of a small, erect plant which is used, most often dried. China grows a tall, climbing variety for the edible pods, as well as a variety with very long pods, known as yard-long beans, which is perhaps a different species (*Vigna sesquipedalis*).

Black-eye peas are harvested when the pods begin to fade. They are then shelled and usually cooked with a piece of pork. Dried black-eye peas are treated and cooked like dried beans.

Nutritive values

Fresh, raw: 127 calories; cooked and drained: 108 calories; dried, cooked: 76 calories (per 100 g/3½ oz).

Southern Black-eye Peas

6 servings
The dish should have a little sauce, but not be soupy.

1 l (1 qt) water
250 g (½ lb) blanched salt pork or bacon,* cut into small pieces
500 g (1 lb) dried black-eye peas, soaked and ready to cook

2 onions, chopped
¼ tsp hot pepper flakes or Tabasco sauce, or to taste
salt
freshly ground pepper
60 g (2 oz) butter

*To blanch the bacon, cover with boiling water and let stand for 5 minutes. Drain.

Pour the water into a large, heavy saucepan. Add the pork and bring to boiling point. Lower the heat and simmer, covered, for 30 to 45 minutes. Add the peas, the onions and the hot pepper flakes. Simmer, covered, over low heat for about 1 hour or until the peas are tender. Check for moisture. It may be necessary either to add a little more hot water, 2 tablespoons at a time, or to cook without a cover to reduce the pan liquid. Add salt and pepper. Stir in the butter and cook for 5 more minutes.

Broad Bean, Fava Bean, Ful

(Vicia faba)

Broad beans are one of the most ancient vegetables cultivated in the Western world, and for centuries they were the only readily available beans in Europe. Grown since prehistoric times, the ancient beans were small-seeded varieties rather than the large-seeded broad beans we eat today. All sorts of curious beliefs grew around them among the Mediterranean people of old. Egyptian priests thought them unclean, Pythagoras the Greek loathed them and a Roman pontifex was not allowed even to mention them since they were a funeral plant – bean feasts traditionally ended funerals. But the common Romans ate them, so much so that candidates for public office distributed broad beans at election time, when they were also used as counters in voting.

Broad beans have always been a staple of European and Mediterranean countries. In England they were cultivated as early as the Iron Age. Germany, where they are called *Saubohnen* (beg beans), France (*fèves*), Italy (*fave*) and the Arab countries (*ful* – specifically, *ful nabed*, as opposed to *ful medames*, the Egyptian brown bread) have made them part of their diets for centuries. They are grown world-wide now, throughout the temperate zone.

Broad beans have large, rich-green pods which can grow to well over 30 cm (12 inches) in length. They are heavy and their seeds are big and flat, resembling butter beans. The pods are not eaten unless they are very young. Usually the beans are shelled, to be eaten fresh or dried. When mature, broad beans have a tough skin which is better peeled off. If young and tender, or when peeled, fresh broad beans have a much more delicate flavour than most other beans.

Nutritive values

Broad beans are high in proteins and carbohydrates, and a good source of minerals and (when fresh) vitamins. Raw, immature beans, fresh: 105 calories; raw, mature beans, dried: 338 calories (per 100 g/3½ oz).

How to use

Cook fresh beans, covered, in a minimum of boiling salted water until just tender; cooking time depends on age and size of the beans, varying from 4 or 5 to 12 or even 15 minutes. Peeling off the skin of older beans reduces their cooking time considerably. Dried broad beans are cooked like other dried beans.

Roman Broad Beans

4 servings

The Romans, who claim to have the best fave *beans, make this dish with guanciale, pork jowl, which is hard to find in this country. In its stead, pancetta may be used, a tightly rolled cut of pork (it is the same cut as bacon) which is not smoked, but cured in salt and spices. Pancetta, found in Italian food stores, is used as a flavouring in the way we use bacon. It has a definite, pleasing flavour. When none is available, use prosciutto, or, at a pinch, bacon, though the flavour of the dish will be different. Serve with roast pork or lamb.*

2 kg (4 lb) broad beans, in the pod
1 tbsp lard or olive oil
1 small onion, chopped fine
110 g (4 oz) *pancetta* or bacon, cut into narrow strips

3 tbsps water or beef stock
salt
freshly ground pepper

Shell the broad beans. If they are very large, remove the tough skin with the tip of a sharp knife. Heat the lard in a heavy saucepan. Cook the onion in it until golden. Add the *pancetta* and cook 1 minute longer. Add the beans, the water and salt and pepper. Mix well. Simmer, covered, over low heat for 5 to 15 minutes, depending on the size and toughness of the beans. Stir frequently and check the moisture and seasoning.

Broad Bean Purée

4 servings
Serve with thick tomato slices sautéed in butter as an accompaniment to any lamb or veal dish or with roast chicken. Sprinkle the de-fatted meat juices over the purée.

2½ kg (5 lb) broad beans, in the pod	salt
boiling water	freshly ground pepper
80 g (3 oz) butter	⅛ tsp ground nutmeg

Shell the beans. If they are very large, remove the tough skin with the tip of a sharp knife. Cook, covered, in enough boiling water to cover the beans generously for about 10 minutes or until the beans are very tender. Drain and reserve the cooking water. Purée in a blender with 1 to 2 tablespoons of the cooking water or strain through a sieve. Return the bean purée to the heat and add the butter. Cook over very low heat, stirring constantly, for 5 minutes or until the beans are very hot. Season with salt and pepper and the nutmeg.

Broad Beans in Cream

4 servings

2 kg (4 lb) broad beans in the pod	salt
boiling water	freshly ground pepper
30 g (1 oz) butter, cut into pieces	⅛ tsp ground nutmeg
2 dl (6 fl oz) double cream	2 tbsps finely chopped parsley and chives, mixed

Shell the beans. Cook them in boiling water to cover for about 5 to 7 minutes or until almost tender. Drain. Stir in the butter and cook for 1 minute, stirring to coat the beans. Stir in the cream and season with salt and pepper and the nutmeg. Cook over low heat for about 3 minutes or until the cream is hot and slightly thickened. Do not boil. Sprinkle with the herbs and serve very hot.

Broccoli

(Brassica oleracea, italica group)*

When we speak of broccoli, we usually mean sprouting broccoli, a cluster of green flowerbuds branching from a thick green stem, with additional, smaller clusters sprouting from the stem at the attachment of the leaves. There is another variety, with a dense purple, green or white head which closely resembles the cauliflower. Broccoli is a close relative of cauliflower, which is *Brassica oleracea* (botrytis group), and less closely related to other oleracea such as cabbage, Brussels sprouts and kale.

Like other cabbages, broccoli is a native of the Mediterranean countries and Asia Minor. The Romans, according to Pliny, grew and ate it in the first century A.D. The vegetable has remained popular in Italy, especially in Rome, in a different variety that tends to be green in colour. It is especially flavourful, and is known as Italian broccoli or calabrese. In England, broccoli was introduced in the first part of the eighteenth century as 'Italian asparagus', a touching conceit, and more graphically as 'sprout cauliflower'. The French to this day treat it gingerly in their few recipes. The name is a diminutive of the Italian *brocco*, meaning 'arm' or 'branch'.

How to buy

Buy broccoli which has heads with tightly closed and compact bud clusters. The colour, depending on the variety, can be dark green, deep purple or a purplish green. Stalks and stem branches should be tender and firm, with fresh leaves.

Avoid bruised, wilted and flabby broccoli, or broccoli with open bud clusters, showing the yellow flower, and wooden-looking stalks.

How to keep

Place unwashed broccoli in a plastic bag and refrigerate. Broccoli is very perishable, so use as soon as possible. Uncooked, on refrigerator shelf or in vegetable drawer: 3 days. Cooked and covered, on refrigerator shelf: 1 to 3 days.

Nutritive values

An excellent source of vitamins A and C if the vegetable is cooked quickly in a minimum of water. A good source of riboflavin, iron and calcium. Cooked spears, boiled and drained: 28 calories per 100 g ($3\frac{1}{2}$ oz).

How to use

Wash broccoli thoroughly when ready to use, but do not soak for a prolonged time. Trim off only the toughest part of the stem. If the stalks are tough and more than 2 to 3 cm (1 inch) in diameter, peel them; this makes the whole stem edible and ensures quicker cooking. If even the peeled stems are larger than 3 cm (1 inch) in diameter, make four to six slashes through them up to the flowerets. This allows them to cook in the same time as the flowerets. Place in a saucepan with 3 cm (about 1 inch) boiling water or stand up in the bottom part of a double boiler. Cover the saucepan or use the inverted top part of the double boiler and cook for about 7 to 10 minutes or until barely tender. During cooking remove the cover several times to let the steam escape;

this keeps the broccoli green (purple broccoli cooks green whatever you do).

An alternative method is to divide the head into individual flowerets by slicing lengthwise from flowerets to the bottom of the stem. If the flowerets are large, slice them into halves or quarters. Cook in the smallest possible amount of boiling salted water to prevent scorching for about 4 to 5 minutes or until just tender and crisp, or braise with a little butter in a covered pan.

Broccoli may also be cut into thin diagonal slices (after the stem has been peeled) and sautéed quickly in hot fat until just crisp.

Broccoli cooks quickly and easily becomes overcooked and mushy. Cook until just tender and very crisp.

Broccoli Roman Style

3–4 servings

500 g (1 lb) broccoli
3 tbsps olive oil
1 garlic clove, sliced
salt
freshly ground pepper

2–3 anchovies, mashed, or 1 or
  2 tbsps anchovy paste
half a bottle dry red or white
  wine

Trim the broccoli and cut into flowerets. Peel the stalks and cut them into 5-cm (2-inch) pieces. Wash and drain. Heat the oil in a deep frying pan. Cook the garlic in it until it turns brown. Remove and throw away. Add the broccoli and season with salt and pepper. Cook, stirring constantly, for 2 to 3 minutes. Add the anchovies and the wine. Cook over low heat for about 5 to 10 minutes or until the broccoli is tender but still firm. Stir occasionally with a fork, being careful not to break the flowerets.

Hot or Cold Broccoli Salad with Caper Sauce

4 servings

500 g (1 lb) broccoli
1½ dl (¼ pt) olive oil
juice of 1 large lemon

4 tbsps drained small capers
freshly ground pepper

Trim the broccoli and cut into flowerets. Peel the stalks and cut them into 5-cm (2-inch) pieces. Wash and drain. Cook in boiling salted water to cover for 4 to 5 minutes or until barely tender. Drain and turn into a serving dish. Combine the remaining ingredients and mix well. Pour over the flowerets while they are still hot. Check the seasoning and toss gently with a fork.

Puréed Broccoli

4 servings

Puréed vegetables don't wilt while waiting; this is the reason so many restaurants serve vegetables this way. Keep warm in the top of a double boiler, over hot water.

500 g (1 lb) broccoli, washed and ready for cooking	salt
	freshly ground pepper
60 g (2 oz) butter, cut into pieces	2–4 tbsps double cream
	$\frac{1}{8}$ tsp ground nutmeg

Cook the broccoli until very tender and mushy. Drain and reserve the cooking liquid. Cut into pieces or mash with a fork. Strain through a sieve, or purée in a blender, adding a little of the cooking liquid for easier blending. Return the broccoli purée to the saucepan and stir in the butter. Season with salt and pepper. Cook over medium heat, stirring constantly, until the broccoli purée is on the dry side. Stir in 2 tablespoons of the cream. The purée should be creamy but not soupy; if necessary for the proper consistency, add a little more cream. Stir in the nutmeg and serve very hot.

Brussels Sprout

(Brassica oleracea gemmifera)

The plant, a member of the cabbage family, is a tall stemmed cabbage which, rather than producing one tall head, forms many tiny heads called sprouts at the bases of the leaves. By pulling away the lower leaves the sprouts are allowed to develop into an average size of 2 to 4 cm (1 to 1½ inches) in diameter. Brussels sprouts are a full-flavoured winter vegetable.

Their history is somewhat obscure. They are said to have been cultivated around Brussels in Belgium in the 1500s but they don't appear to have been well known until their cultivation spread into France between 1800 and 1850. By the latter date they had begun to be known in England but for a long time sprouts were a luxury vegetable, especially so when only tiny, fingernail-sized ones were prized for the delicacy of their taste. Now, sprouts are one of the perennial English winter vegetables, but all too often they are allowed to grow far too large, which coarsens their flavour and texture.

How to buy

Buy the smallest available sprouts, with compact heads, bright green in colour and free from all blemishes. Avoid soft, wilted, puffy heads or heads with loose or yellow leaves. Torn and smudgy leaves may hide insects.

How to keep

Discard loose or yellowed leaves before storing. Place unwashed sprouts in a plastic bag and refrigerate. Use as soon as possible: old sprouts acquire a strong flavour. Raw, on refrigerator shelf or in vegetable drawer: 1 to 2 days at peak, but will keep longer. Cooked and covered, on refrigerator shelf: 1 to 2 days.

Nutritive values

Brussels sprouts are a good source of vitamins A and C and a fair source of iron. Cooked and drained: 36 calories per 100 g (3½ oz).

How to use

Wash thoroughly and trim off stem ends and loose leaves. If there are signs of insects, soak 10 minutes in cold salted water and rinse several times in changes of water. Cook in 3 cm (about 1 inch) of boiling salted water without a cover for 4 minutes, then cover and cook for about 2 to 3 minutes longer, or until just tender. Drain. Do not overcook, for sprouts get mushy easily, acquire a strong flavour and lose vitamins.

Brussels Sprouts and Chestnuts

4–6 servings

500-g (16–19-oz) tin whole chestnuts	salt
750 g (1½ lb) Brussels sprouts, trimmed and washed	freshly ground pepper
	¼ tsp ground nutmeg
boiling salted water	3 tbsps double cream
60 g (2 oz) butter	3 tbsps parsley, finely chopped

Drain the chestnuts and wash them quickly under running cold water, taking care not to break them. Drain and dry with kitchen paper. Cook the Brussels sprouts in 3 cm (about 1 inch) boiling salted water until they are almost tender. Drain. Heat the butter and add the Brussels sprouts and the chestnuts. Season with salt and pepper and the nutmeg. Cover and cook over low heat, shaking the pan frequently, until the sprouts are tender. Add the cream, stir carefully with a fork and cook 1 minute longer. Turn into a heated serving dish and sprinkle with the parsley.

Italian Brussels Sprouts

4 servings

500 g (1 lb) Brussels sprouts,
   trimmed and washed
boiling salted water
4 tbsps olive oil
2 garlic cloves, sliced

salt
freshly ground pepper
2 tbsps fresh lemon juice
30 g (1 oz) freshly grated
   Parmesan cheese (optional)

Cook the sprouts in 3 cm (about 1 inch) boiling salted water until almost, but not quite, tender. Drain. While the sprouts are cooking, heat the oil in a large frying pan. Add the garlic. Cook over medium heat until the garlic is browned; remove the garlic and throw it away. Add the drained sprouts. Season with salt and pepper. Cook, stirring carefully with a fork so as not to break the sprouts, for about 2 to 3 minutes. Add the lemon juice and cook for 1 minute longer. Turn into a heated serving dish and sprinkle with the Parmesan. Serve immediately.

Brussels Sprouts with Lemon Sauce

3–4 servings

500 g (1 lb) Brussels sprouts,
   trimmed and washed
boiling salted water
1 large or 2 small egg yolks

salt
freshly ground pepper
2 tbsps fresh lemon juice or to
   taste

Cook the sprouts in 3 cm (about 1 inch) boiling salted water until tender but still firm. Drain the cooking liquid from the saucepan into a small bowl and reserve. Keep the sprouts warm in the saucepan in which they were cooked. Put the egg yolks into a heated serving dish and beat them well with a fork. Beat in about 1 to 2 tablespoons of the reserved cooking liquid. Season with salt and pepper and beat in the lemon juice. Mix well. Turn the sprouts into the sauce and toss to coat them with the sauce. Serve immediately.

Note: This simple sauce is equally good with other vegetables, such as green beans, cauliflower, broccoli and chick peas.

Buckwheat

(Fagopyrum saittatum or *esculentum)*

Buckwheat is an annual grain plant (though not a cereal grass like wheat), originating most probably in central China, of which the seed kernels are used as a cereal. Compared to other cereals, buckwheat is of recent use, the earliest mention being in tenth- and eleventh-century Chinese writings. Buckwheat came to Europe during the Middle Ages and was cultivated there first in the early part of the fifteenth century. Since it likes a cool climate and will grow on any kind of soil, buckwheat became widely cultivated in Russia and Poland, where it is now a staple grain. In the Slav countries, hulled buckwheat groats, called *kasha*, are part of the daily diet. Jewish cookery uses the same term. Buckwheat is also important in France and Germany. The name means 'beech wheat' from the German *Buche*, the word for 'beech', since its triangular fruit resembles a beech nut. Until the early nineteenth century buckwheat was a staple crop in Wales and Shropshire, but there, as in most of western Europe, it was used principally as an animal feed.

Ground into flour, the French and Americans use buckwheat in pancakes whereas in the orient it is made into soba noodles available in oriental foodstores. For pancakes it is usually mixed with wheat flour for a good colour and texture.

Nutritive values

High in carbohydrates with a fair supply of protein, some fat and small amounts of vitamins. Whole grain, raw: 335 calories per 100 g ($3\frac{1}{2}$ oz).

How to use

Cook buckwheat as you would cook rice or follow package directions.

Buckwheat (Kasha) Casserole

4 servings

1 egg
200 g (6 oz) medium buckwheat
   (*kasha*)
50 g (2 oz) butter
1 small onion, finely chopped

110 g (4 oz) mushrooms, thinly
   sliced
6 dl (1 pt) hot chicken stock or
   water

In a bowl, beat the egg and stir in the buckwheat. Mix well to coat all the grains. Heat the butter in a saucepan. Add the onion and cook for 2 minutes. Add the mushrooms. Cook, stirring constantly, for 2 minutes. Stir in the buckwheat mixture. Cook, stirring with a fork, for 3 to 4 minutes or until golden brown. Add three quarters of the chicken stock. Cook, tightly covered, for 15 minutes. After 10 minutes' cooking time, check for moisture. If the dish looks too dry, add the remaining stock.

Butter Bean, Lima Bean

(Phaseolus lunatus)

Butter beans are New World beans, natives of South America where different varieties have been cultivated for centuries. Largest of all the pulses, they grow as tall vines or as bushes, with large, dark-green pods which contain a few flat, smooth seeds, varying in colour from the palest green to buff and mottled buff colour. The pods are shelled and the beans eaten fresh or dried. Their taste is delicate and mealy.

Butter beans were introduced early into northern America via the Indian trade routes, which took them through Mexico into the south-west, then east to Florida and Virginia. The early explorers of the Americas used them for ships' stores, getting their supplies from local Indians and transporting the beans to many parts of the world. Records in the late 1700s often speak of these beans, which are now also grown in the West Indies, tropical Africa, New Guinea and northern Australia.

Butter beans are among the most popular American beans and considered finer than other beans; in Europe, tinned or frozen butter beans are only available in the whitish-green variety the Americans call 'baby limas'.

Nutritive values

A fair source of proteins and carbohydrates, with a fair amount of vitamins A and C. Young beans, cooked and drained: 99 calories per 100 g ($3\frac{1}{2}$ oz).

How to use

Cook frozen butter beans according to package directions, but remember that frequently the cooking time given is too long and overcooks the beans. Reheat tinned butter beans quickly in a little of their own liquid, just enough to prevent scorching. Dried butter beans are cooked like other dried beans.

Cabbage

(Brassica oleracea)

Cabbages are members of the large Brassica family, cousins to kale and collards, broccoli, cauliflower, Brussels sprouts and kohlrabi. When we speak of cabbage we mean the variety that has compact heads, the variety called *capitata*. There are cabbages with firm or loose heads, with flat or conical ones, plain or curly leaves, in shades of white, green or red. There are also

exotic ones which don't look much like cabbages, but still are true brassicas. In some form or another, cabbage is grown and eaten in most parts of the world. Almost any soil or climate will do, and in as little as three months' growing time, from seed to head, an acre of cabbage plants will yield a greater amount of green vegetables than any other plant.

The origin of cabbage is ancient and obscure, though there is some evidence that the eastern Mediterranean countries and Asia Minor may have been the place of origin of the species. A leafy wild variety was found on the coasts of Europe and, though there is no record of a hard-headed cabbage in ancient Roman writings, there are references to cultivated cabbage plants which must have been very different from the wild species. Types of kale and broccoli, with smooth or curly leaves, were probably known too. The Romans thought highly of the vegetable, as did the Greeks; Cato recommended it, raw or cooked, as surpassing all other vegetables. He also suggested eating as much as possible with vinegar before a feast and still more after (raw cabbage with vinegar is still recommended by some as a hangover cure).

The Celts are thought to have introduced cabbage into northern Europe, but that again is speculation. In any case, cabbage came and conquered and became so to speak the national vegetable of central and northern Europe. But hard-heading cabbage as we know it was unknown until the time of Charlemagne, who died in 814. In the thirteenth century Albert of Cologne refers to it and other writers of the time also make a distinction between hard-heading and non-heading cabbages (that is, coleworts). The 1440 *Feate of Gardening* devotes twenty-five poetic lines to their cultivation. The word 'cabbage' in English, and in other languages such as French, German, Norwegian and Swedish, can be traced to Celtic root words as easily as to the Latin *caput*. In due course, cabbage became the food of the masses and the poor, with national preferences for different kinds. Red varieties became popular in northern Europe and the savoyed varieties in the southern parts. But the most common of all is the smooth-leaved green or white kind. On the English market all these varieties are represented:

Spring cabbage is a term used for any green or white cabbage cut young, when only semi-hearted, regardless of the actual season.

Savoy is the general name for the wrinkled-leaf varieties. The word probably derives from the French province Savoie, and has been in English use since the middle of the sixteenth century. The flavour of Savoys is usually mild, and they are much used raw and shredded.

Green or white cabbages are usually smooth-leaved and include the varieties with the hardest heads and therefore better keeping-potential. Rounds and drumheads are of this group, as are the famous 'January King' (with slightly wrinkled leaves) and 'Winter Whites'.

Red cabbage is a variety which has been cultivated from those cabbages which have reddish outer leaves. They are usually smooth and hard, and a large proportion is used for pickling.

Sauerkraut, a fermented form of pickled cabbage, has been made for centuries in Germany and other countries: the very word was used in English from the early seventeenth century onwards. Nor is pickled cabbage limited to sauerkraut: the Koreans have kimchi (page 131) which transcends in power anything found in the Western world.

Chinese Cabbage, see p. 129.

How to buy

Buy firm heads that are heavy for their size. Outer leaves should be crisp and fresh looking, free of blemishes and with a fresh colour. Early cabbage and Savoy cabbage have softer, looser heads, but should have firm, crisp leaves. Avoid heads that are too white, indicating over-maturity, blemished leaves with coarse discoloured veins, or puffy heads. If leaf bases are separated from the stem, the cabbage may be strong in flavour and coarse in texture.

How to keep

Firm, hard cabbages will keep a week or more, soft-headed ones a few days. Storing them in the refrigerator in a plastic bag will prolong their useful life by several days. Cooked and covered, in the refrigerator, cabbage will keep up to four days.

Nutritive values

Raw cabbage is an excellent source of vitamin C, and of some vitamin A, as well as a fair source of minerals. Provided it is cooked quickly and used soon after it does not lose too much. Cabbage is ideal roughage to aid the digestion. Raw: 24 calories; cooked and drained: 20 calories (per 100 g/3½ oz).

How to use

Wash head thoroughly and trim any wilted leaves or tough stem end. Cut into wedges and remove the centre if the cabbage is old. Or shred cabbage on vegetable shredder or with a large wide knife, slicing across the head or, if the head is very large, after cutting into halves or quarters. Savoy cabbage is either cooked whole or cut into serving-size wedges. Cook all green cabbage quickly to avoid odours. Cook wedges without a cover in 3 cm (about 1 inch) of boiling salted water rapidly for about 2 to 3 minutes. Cover and cook a few more minutes, or until the cabbage is tender but still crisp. Drain and season.

Cook shredded cabbage without a cover in very little (about 1 cm or ½ inch) boiling salted water for 1 to 2 minutes; cover and cook for 1 to 2 minutes longer, depending on the size of the shreds. Do not overcook.

To braise cabbage, melt just enough butter or fat to cover the bottom of a large saucepan or frying pan. Add cabbage wedges or shreds. Cook over low to medium heat for 2 to 3 minutes, turning the vegetable with a fork until it is coated with fat. Add a little water or stock, cover the pan and steam for about 5 to 10 minutes, depending on the size of the cabbage. Season when cooked and do not overcook.

Red cabbage may be cooked by any of these methods, but add a little vinegar, lemon juice or a few pieces of a tart apple: these acids will hold the colour. When combining red cabbage with another dish, cook it separately and add it later because otherwise it will discolour the dish.

Raw cabbage for salads may be either grated, shredded or cut into fine shreds.

Creamed Cabbage

4–6 servings

This is a lighter dish than the usual creamed cabbage. You may add a handful or more cooked peas to the cabbage.

1 medium cabbage weighing approximately 1 kg (2 lb), trimmed and thinly shredded	3 dl (½ pt) milk or single cream salt freshly ground pepper
boiling salted water	ground nutmeg to taste
30–60 g (1–2 oz) butter	

Plunge the cabbage into a saucepan full of boiling salted water. Cook for 2 to 3 minutes. Drain and press out excess moisture. Put the cabbage into a saucepan. Add the butter, depending on taste, the milk, salt, pepper and nutmeg. Simmer, covered, over low heat, stirring frequently, for about 5 minutes or until the cabbage is heated through.

Cabbage Leaves Stuffed with Mushrooms

6 servings
Serve with roast pork or veal.

6 large cabbage leaves	75 g (2–3 oz) soft breadcrumbs
boiling water to cover	3 stalks celery, finely chopped
½ tsp salt	2 tbsps grated onion
60 g (2 oz) butter or margarine, melted	1 tsp salt
	½ tsp ground thyme
250 g (½ lb) fresh mushrooms, chopped	ground black pepper

Cut out the coarse, heavy stems at the base of the cabbage leaves. Put the leaves in a deep frying pan. Add boiling water to cover and the salt. Cook over high heat for about 3 minutes or until the leaves are soft but not mushy; cooking time depends on their tenderness. Lift the leaves out of the water, drain and reserve the cooking liquid. Dry the leaves thoroughly between layers of kitchen paper. Heat a little of the butter. Add the mushrooms. Cook over high heat, stirring constantly, for 2 to 3 minutes. Remove from heat and stir in the breadcrumbs, celery, onion, salt, thyme and pepper. Stir in the remaining butter and mix well. Cook over low heat, stirring constantly, until the mixture is well coated with the butter. Spread the cabbage leaves side by side on the kitchen table. Divide the stuffing up and place some on each leaf. Roll tightly and fasten with toothpicks. Place the cabbage leaves fastened-side down and side by side in a buttered shallow baking dish. Pour 1½ dl (¼ pint) of the reserved cabbage liquid around them. Bake in a preheated moderate oven (Gas 4, 350° F, 180° C) for about 20 minutes. Add more cabbage liquid if needed to prevent sticking.

Sweet-Sour Red Cabbage

4–6 servings
Serve with roast pork, goose or duck, or braised beef.

1 medium red cabbage, weighing approximately 1½ kg (3 lb)	salt
60 g (2 oz) butter	freshly ground pepper
1 tbsp sugar or more, according to taste	2 medium tart apples, peeled, cored and chopped
3 tbsps cider vinegar	1 dl (about 4 fl oz) red-currant jelly
3 tbsps water	

Remove the tough outer leaves and cut into quarters. Cut out the core and shred the cabbage fine. Wash and drain. In a heavy saucepan, melt the butter. Stir in the sugar; do not let the sugar brown. Add the cabbage. Cook over medium heat, stirring constantly, for about 3 to 4 minutes. Stir in the vinegar and the water, and season with salt and pepper. Simmer, covered, over lowest possible heat or on an asbestos mat, for about 1 hour, or until the cabbage is very tender. If necessary, add a little more water, 1 or 2 tablespoons at a time, to prevent scorching. Add the apples and the red-currant jelly and mix well. Taste the cabbage. It should be sweet-sour; if necessary, adjust the taste with more sugar and vinegar, ½ tablespoon of each at a time. Simmer, covered, for 30 more minutes. Stir occasionally and check for moisture, adding more water if necessary.

Sauerkraut Cooked in Wine

4–6 servings
Serve with fried meats or fish.

60 g (2 oz) lard, bacon fat or butter	2½ dl (8 fl oz) dry white wine
2 medium onions, thinly sliced	salt
1½ kg (3 lb) sauerkraut	freshly ground pepper
	4 tsps sugar

Heat the lard in a heavy saucepan. Cook the onions in it until they are soft and golden; do not brown. Rinse the sauerkraut under running cold water and squeeze out all excess moisture.

Add the sauerkraut and wine to the onions, mixing well. Do not press the sauerkraut down too hard, but keep it loose with a fork. Season with salt and pepper to taste and stir in the sugar. Simmer, covered, over low heat for about 1 hour. If necessary, add a little more wine to keep the sauerkraut moist, but it must not be soupy. This sauerkraut may be reheated.

Northern Italian Savoy Cabbage and Rice Soup

6–8 servings
If a thicker soup is wanted, increase the rice up to three times the amount given here.

4 tbsps salt pork, blanched and cut fine
30 g (1 oz) butter
3 large, ripe tomatoes, peeled and chopped, or 1 medium tin Italian tomatoes
2 garlic cloves, crushed
4–5 tbsps finely chopped parsley
1 tsp dried thyme

1 small Savoy or other cabbage weighing rather less than 1 kg (2 lb), trimmed and shredded
1¾ l (3 pts) beef stock or water
salt
freshly ground pepper
75 g (scant 3 oz) rice
freshly grated Parmesan cheese

Put the salt pork and the butter in a soup pot. Cook over medium heat, stirring constantly, for about 3 minutes. Add the tomatoes, the garlic, the parsley and the thyme. Cook, covered, stirring frequently, for about 5 minutes. Add the cabbage and mix well. Cook over low heat, stirring frequently, for about 10 to 15 minutes. Add the stock, taste and season with salt and pepper. Reduce heat to low. Simmer, covered, for 30 to 45 minutes, stirring occasionally. Add the rice and cook for 10 to 15 more minutes or until the rice is tender. Serve with plenty of freshly grated Parmesan cheese.

Cabbage and Tomatoes

6 servings

60 g (2 oz) butter
1 small onion, chopped
1 small cabbage, weighing about
  1 kg (2 lb), trimmed and
  shredded
1 tbsp flour
500 g (1 lb) fresh tomato pulp
  (strain peeled tomatoes through
  a sieve or purée in a blender)

3 tbsps finely chopped parsley or
  fresh basil leaves
2–3 tbsps soured cream or
  yoghurt
salt
freshly ground pepper

Heat about half the butter. Cook the onion in it for 2 to 3 minutes, or until soft. Add the cabbage and water to cover. Cook over high heat, stirring constantly, for about 3 minutes or until the cabbage is quite tender but still crisp. Remove from heat. In a small saucepan, heat the remaining butter. Stir in the flour and cook for 1 minute. Add the tomato pulp and the parsley. Cook over medium heat, stirring constantly, for about 3 minutes or until the purée begins to thicken. Stir in the soured cream. Combine the tomatoes and the cabbage and mix well. Season with salt and pepper. Cover the saucepan and simmer over low heat for about 10 minutes, stirring frequently.

French Cabbage Soup

8 servings
The soup can be made in advance and reheated.

500 g (1 lb) potatoes, peeled and
  chopped
500 g (1 lb) lean bacon or
  ham, in one piece
3½ l (5 pts) water
1 medium cabbage weighing
  approximately 1 kg (2 lb),
  trimmed and chopped
6 whole peppercorns, crushed
6 parsley sprigs
1 bay leaf

1 tsp thyme
½ tsp marjoram
2 garlic cloves, crushed
2 onions
2 carrots, quartered
2 stalks celery, sliced
2 peeled turnips, chopped
  (optional)
250 g (½ lb) cooked red or white
  beans
salt

Vegetable Cookery

Place the potatoes and the bacon in a soup pot. Add the water. Bring to boiling point. Add all other ingredients except beans. Simmer, covered, for 2 hours or until meat is tender. Skim as needed. Remove meat and slice it into serving pieces. Skim off any excess fat from the soup. Return the meat to the soup. Add the beans. Season to taste with salt. Heat thoroughly. Serve with French bread.

Carrot

(Daucus carota)

The fleshy, orange carrot that we know today is a far cry from its wild ancestor, a small, tough, pale-fleshed, acrid tap root said to have originated in Middle Asia and the Near East. Carrot seeds from about 2000–3000 B.C. have been found in the remains of the lake dwellings of central Switzerland, but there are no signs that the vegetable was cultivated. Most likely they were used for medicinal purposes. The Greeks of the first century B.C. valued carrots as a stomach tonic.

The wild vegetable was developed and improved in the Mediterranean countries, but how and when is unclear; it even seems that the Romans did not always distinguish it from its cousin the parsnip. The first clear description of carrots not unlike our own cultivated ones comes in the twelfth century, when an Arab writer in Spain, citing a still older work, wrote of two kinds of carrot. One he called red, juicy and tasty – we think these were actually purple, since orange-red carrots appear at a later date. The other one was green blending into yellow and coarser than the red. The carrots were eaten with olive oil, vinegar and salt, and with other vegetables. By the thirteenth century carrots were known in Italy, and by the fourteenth century in France, Germany and the Netherlands. England may have known carrots in the fifteenth century but it was in the reign of Elizabeth I that Flemish refugees first grew them in quantity, mainly in Kent and Surrey. As time went on, yellow carrots gradually superseded the purple kind. Some white carrots were grown in France and the Netherlands at a later date. The first written evidence of orange carrots is from the Netherlands in the eighteenth century, when four types were known, but seventeenth-century Dutch paintings already show orange carrots.

Carrots, which belong to the same botanical group as the lovely Queen Anne's lace of our gardens, are one of the most popular vegetables. They are extremely healthy, they store well and combine well with other foods. They are also one of the vegetables that most children will eat with pleasure.

How to buy

Buy firm, smooth, clean, well-shaped, bright orange-gold carrots with fresh green tops. The smaller carrots tend to be more tender and sweet, but the large winter carrots have far more true flavour. Avoid wilted, flabby, soft or shrivelled carrots with a dim colour. Avoid cracked, rough or forked carrots, and carrots with wilted tops.

How to keep

Remove the green tops and store the unwashed carrots in plastic bags in the refrigerator. Raw, on refrigerator shelf: 1 to 2 weeks. Cooked and covered, on refrigerator shelf: 2 to 3 days.

Nutritive values

Carrots are one of the richest sources of vitamin A, necessary for good eyesight and bone formation. They also have some vitamin C, and contain a good supply of minerals. Raw: 42 calories; cooked and drained: 31 calories (per 100 g/3½ oz).

Marinated Carrots

4–6 servings

8 large carrots, trimmed and cut into strips	1 tsp dried thyme
	salt
boiling water or chicken bouillon	freshly ground pepper
1 dl (4 fl oz) olive oil	lettuce
1 dl (4 fl oz) white vinegar	juice of 1 large lemon
1 small onion, thinly sliced	2 tbsps minced parsley or dill
2 garlic cloves, crushed	

Put the carrots into a saucepan and cover with boiling water. Cook without a cover, stirring frequently, for about 3 minutes or until the carrots are barely tender. Drain. Combine the oil, vinegar, onion, garlic, thyme, salt and pepper in a bowl (do not use aluminium). Add the carrots. Toss with two forks to coat the carrots with the dressing. Cover and refrigerate overnight. Drain the carrots and remove the garlic. Pile in a bowl lined with lettuce. Sprinkle with the lemon juice and the parsley.

Sugar-Browned Carrots

4 servings
A standard Danish recipe.

4 large or 6 medium carrots, trimmed	60 g (2 oz) butter
	2 tbsps granulated sugar
boiling water	salt

Scrape the carrots and cut them into thin strips. Wash and drain. Put them in a saucepan and add just enough boiling water barely to cover them. Cook, covered, for about 3 to 4 minutes or until just tender; the carrots must remain crisp. Drain. Heat the butter in a frying pan. Stir in the sugar. Cook over low heat, stirring constantly, until the sugar has melted and is golden. Add the carrots. Cook, stirring constantly with a fork, until the carrots are golden on all sides. Do not scorch. Sprinkle with salt. Serve very hot.

Flemish Carrots

6 servings
This is a rich dish which can be served by itself as a first course or as the sole accompaniment to roast meats.

8 medium carrots, cut into strips	1 tsp sugar
boiling water	2 egg yolks
1 dl (4 fl oz) boiling water	1½ dl (¼ pt) double cream
60 g (2 oz) butter	2 tbsps fresh lemon juice
salt	2 tbsps finely chopped parsley
freshly ground pepper	

Plunge the carrots into a saucepan full of boiling water. Cook them for 2 to 3 minutes. Drain. Put the carrots into a buttered casserole, preferably one that can go to the table. Add the 1 dl (about 4 fl oz) boiling water, and the butter, salt, pepper and sugar. Bring to boiling point and reduce heat to lowest possible. Cook, covered, for 5 to 10 minutes or until just tender and dry. Stir or shake the casserole every few minutes to prevent sticking; if necessary, add 1 tablespoon of water at a time to prevent scorching. But if the carrots are soupy, cook without a cover to reduce the cooking liquid. Remove from heat. Beat together the egg yolks and the cream. Add to the carrots and mix. Return to low heat and cook only long enough to heat through. Remove from heat and stir in lemon juice and parsley. Serve very hot.

Carrots Cooked in Orange Juice

4 servings

4 large or 6 medium carrots, trimmed	grated rind of ½ orange
30 g (1 oz) butter	grated rind of ½ lemon
1 tbsp light brown sugar	⅛ tsp ground mace
4 tbsps fresh orange juice	salt

Cut the carrots into thin slices. Combine all the other ingredients and bring to boiling point. Lower heat to low. Add the carrots. Simmer, covered, stirring frequently, for about 5 minutes. If necessary to prevent scorching, add a little more orange juice, 1 tablespoon at a time. There should be just a little sauce in the finished dish.

Cauliflower

(Brassica oleracea var. *botrytis)*

This member of the cabbage family is a cultivated low plant with a single stalk, bearing a large, round, tightly packed mass of white or creamy flower buds, called 'curd' because that is what it looks like. The curd is protected by inner and outer surrounding leaves, which in the summer variety stand open and in the winter ones are wrapped over the curd. Cauliflower is cut before the buds open, which happens when the buds are no longer tightly joined but begin to segment.

Though cabbage has been used by man since antiquity, the origins of cauliflower and broccoli (its brother or sister vegetable) are rather vague. There are second-century Roman writings which do not make it clear whether cauliflower or broccoli is meant, nor is it clear how cauliflower spread from its Mediterranean and Asia Minor homeland. We do know that the French grew it in 1600, and that it was sold in London vegetable markets in the early seventeenth century. Gerard's *Herbal* (1596) mentioned it as 'cole flower' even before that. But it has only become a popular vegetable during this century – even in the nineteenth century it was scarce and considered 'delicate'.

How to buy

Buy clean, firm, creamy-white heads with compact curd and fresh, juicy, green leaves.

Vegetable Cookery

Avoid heads with spotted, speckled or bruised curd. Smudgy and speckled surfaces indicate aphid insects (plant lice). Avoid granular-looking heads, or heads with spreading clusters.

How to keep

Refrigerate, unwashed, in a plastic bag. Use as soon as possible: old cauliflower acquires a strong taste and odour. Uncooked, on refrigerator shelf: 3 days. Cooked and covered, on refrigerator shelf: 1 to 2 days.

Nutritive values

Cauliflower is a good source of vitamins C and A, and a fair source of iron and other minerals. Raw: 27 calories; cooked: 22 calories (per 100 g/3½ oz).

How to use

Trim off the tough outer leaves and cut off the woody base. Fresh and tender-looking leaves may be cooked with the cauliflower or trimmed off and cooked as a separate vegetable. The head may be left whole, or separated into flowerets. The flowerets may be sliced lengthwise or chopped. Wash thoroughly and drain. Cook, covered, in 3 to 5 cm (1 to 2 inches) of boiling, lightly salted water. Cook only until just tender and still crisp. A whole head takes 15 to 25 minutes, flowerets 5 to 9 minutes, sliced or chopped 3 to 5 minutes. Cooking time also depends on the age and size of the vegetable. Drain.

One or 2 tablespoons of milk or ½ tablespoon of lemon juice added to cooking liquid helps preserve the white colour.

Do not overcook cauliflower or it will become mushy, discoloured and strong flavoured. When cooking cauliflower for salad or later use, drain and then plunge immediately into ice water to stop the cooking. Drain again, cover with plastic wrap and chill in refrigerator. The flowerets lend themselves very well to the Chinese quick stir-fry method.

Serve hot cauliflower with melted butter and lemon juice, or herb butter, or a creamy cheese or hollandaise sauce. Alternatively, dress cooked cauliflower with French dressing for a salad, to be served at room temperature. Young, tender cauliflower may be separated into flowerets and served raw as an appetizer for dipping, or used, with or without French dressing or mayonnaise, as a relish or a salad.

Cauliflower Mayonnaise

4 servings

1 medium cauliflower	1 dl (4 fl oz) mayonnaise
1 dl (4 fl oz) French dressing	1 tbsp drained capers
1 tbsp Dijon mustard	

Trim the cauliflower and separate it into flowerets. Wash and drain. Cook in 3 to 5 cm (1 to 2 inches) boiling salted water for 5 minutes or until barely tender. Drain. While still warm, place in a serving dish and toss carefully with the French dressing. Cool. Stir the mustard into the mayonnaise. Coat the cauliflower thinly with the mayonnaise. Sprinkle with the capers and chill.

Cauliflower in Cheese Sauce

4 servings
Serve as a main dish for lunch or supper.

Cheese sauce:	1 tsp Dijon mustard
30 g (1 oz) butter	salt
1 tbsp flour	freshly ground pepper
3 dl (½ pt) single cream or milk	dash of Tabasco sauce (optional)
60 g (2 oz) grated Gruyère cheese	
1 medium cauliflower	paprika

In the top of a double boiler, heat the butter and stir in the flour. Cook for 1 minute. Stir in the cream or milk. Cook over low heat, stirring constantly, for about 3 to 4 minutes or until smooth and thickened. Stir in the cheese and the mustard. Taste and, if necessary, add a little salt and pepper. Stir in the Tabasco sauce. Cook, stirring constantly, for about 3 to 4 minutes or until the cheese is melted and the sauce is smooth. Keep warm over hot water in the bottom part of the double boiler. Trim the cauliflower and separate it into flowerets. Wash and drain. Cook in 3 to 5 cm (1 to 2 inches) boiling salted water for 3 to 4 minutes or until almost tender. Drain. Place in a buttered shallow baking dish. Cover with the cheese sauce. Sprinkle with the paprika. Cook in a preheated hot oven (Gas 6, 400° F, 210° C) for 5 minutes or until the top is golden brown.

Celeriac

(*Apium graveolens* var. *rapaceum*)

A variety of celery grown for its enlarged roots rather than for the stalks and leaves of ordinary celery. Only the root is eaten. This root is usually of an irregular roundish shape, 5 to 10 cm (2 to 4 inches) across, with a rough brownish skin and whitish flesh. It is eaten raw in salads, or cooked as a hot vegetable or in soups and stews. The flavour is an intensive celery one, with smoky overtones.

Celeriac apparently originated in the Mediterranean area. It was first described by a Neapolitan and a Swiss writer in the early seventeenth century. A century later it was popular in Italy, France and Germany, where it is still the most popular form of celery, our bunch celery being unknown and only the leaves being used as a herb, much like parsley. In England it was known by the mid eighteenth century.

How to buy

Buy firm, clean roots. Press the top of the root to be sure it is firm since a soft spot on top means internal decay. Choose smaller rather than larger heads since the latter may be woody.

Avoid soft, wilted-looking roots with unduly large crevices and knobs on the skin.

Vegetable Cookery

How to keep

Remove and throw away top leaves and root fibres. Wrap in plastic wrap and refrigerate. Use within a week of purchase. Cooked and covered, on refrigerator shelf: 3 to 4 days.

Nutritive values

Celeriac is a minor source of minerals. Raw: 40 calories per 100 g (3½ oz).

How to use

Celeriac must be peeled before being eaten raw or cooked. Since it darkens when cut, have a bowl of acidulated water ready (2 tablespoons lemon juice or vinegar for each litre or quart of water) into which to drop the prepared pieces to prevent discolouring, or rub them with half a lemon. If the roots are small and not woody, and are to be used for salad, peel quickly and cut into slices, sticks or dice. Place in a bowl and sprinkle with a little lemon juice, then dress with French dressing, mayonnaise or *rémoulade* sauce, check the seasoning and refrigerate.

If celeriac is to be used cooked, cook it either whole, without peeling, or peeled and prepared as above. To cook whole, scrub the root with a vegetable brush and cut off the leaves and rootlets. Cook in boiling salted water to cover for about 20 to 30 minutes, or until just tender. Do not overcook since celeriac tends to go mushy. Peel when cool enough to handle and cut as desired. Cook peeled slices, sticks or dice, or shredded celeriac, in 3 cm (about 1 inch) boiling, lightly salted water. A little lemon juice in the cooking liquid will help keep the celeriac white. Cover the pot and cook for 3 to 10 minutes, depending on the size of the pieces, or until just tender. Drain and use as in recipe. If the celeriac is to be cooked further in the recipe, cook it the first time only until half tender.

Danish Celeriac Salad

4 servings
In this salad, the celeriac is not cooked.

3 medium-to-large celeriacs
a bowl of acidulated water
1 dl (4 fl oz) double cream
1 dl (4 fl oz) mayonnaise
1 tsp Dijon or other prepared
   mustard

salt
freshly ground pepper
lettuce
2 tbsps finely chopped parsley

Peel the celeriacs until only the white part shows and drop into the acidulated water. Taking out one celeriac at a time, cut it into very thin slices. Cut the slices into slivers the size of a kitchen match. As you've finished with them, drop all the pieces into the acidulated water. In a salad bowl, whip the cream. Fold in the mayonnaise, the mustard, the salt and pepper and mix well. Drain the celeriac pieces and dry them between layers of kitchen paper. Fold into the dressing and toss with two forks. Pile in a salad bowl lined with lettuce and sprinkle with the parsley.

Purée of Celeriac and Potatoes

4 servings
Serve with pork or game. The purée should be of the consistency of mashed potatoes.

2 large celeriacs
2 very large potatoes
boiling salted water
60 g (2 oz) butter, at room
   temperature

salt
freshly ground pepper
4–6 tbsps double cream
2 tbsps finely chopped parsley
   (optional)

Trim and peel the celeriacs. Quarter and cut into eighths as you would an apple. Cut off any woody core. Peel the potatoes and cut them into pieces the same size as the celeriac pieces. Wash and drain the celeriac and the potatoes. Put into a saucepan and add boiling salted water to cover. Cook, covered, over medium heat until the vegetables are tender. Drain and reserve the cooking liquid for soups. Strain the vegetables through a sieve or a food mill (do not purée in a blender since this affects the texture). Beat in the butter. Season with salt and pepper. Beat in the cream. Return to heat and beat until hot and fluffy. Serve immediately, sprinkled with the parsley.

Celery

(Apium graveolens var. *dulce)*

Leaf celery or bunch celery, as we know it, is the cultivated version of a wild plant native to wet places in temperate Europe from Asia Minor to England. This original version is inedible, being tough with a rank, bitter, horrid juice. There are ancient Roman writings about a celery-like plant, but they do not identify it as a food plant; very likely it was used as medicine, as a blood purifier, nerve tonic and stimulant: as 'smallage' this wild variety was put to much the same uses throughout the Middle Ages. In the sixteenth century celery began to be cultivated in Italy for eating and became increasingly milder in flavour. The first definite notice of celery as a food plant comes from France in 1623, when it was used to flavour soups, meats and stews. The leaves and stalks were also eaten with oil and pepper. In England celery does not seem to have been used until the later seventeenth century – in fact the name itself is first recorded as late as 1664. Nobody is quite sure of the origin of the name but it sounds more or less the same in English, 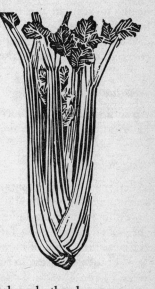 German, French, Italian, Danish, Dutch and other languages.

Most celery is blanched to give its stalks their light, whitish, golden-green colour and yellow-green leaves; blanching means excluding the light from the plant by covering it up. Celery comes to the market in trimmed bunches, with an average length of between 25 and 30 cm (1 foot or just over).

Vegetable Cookery

As a vegetable, celery has many advantages. It is inexpensive, crisp, flavourful, good raw or cooked and, perhaps best of all, totally edible.

How to buy

Buy celery with firm, crisp, glossy stalks that snap easily and fresh leaves.

Avoid soft, spongy, wilted or loose stalks which have tired, yellow leaves.

How to keep

Rinse the bunch under running cold water and shake dry. Do not separate the stalks from the root. Place in plastic bag and close it firmly to keep in the moisture celery needs. Refrigerate. The bunch can also be placed upright in a jar or glass with a little cold water. Raw, on refrigerator shelf: 1 to 2 weeks. Cooked and covered, on refrigerator shelf: 3 to 4 days.

Nutritive values

An indifferent-to-fair source of vitamins and minerals. Raw: 17 calories; cooked and drained: 14 calories (per 100 g/3½ oz).

How to use

When ready to use, separate the stalks from the bunch. Trim the leaves and base off the stalks. Remove strings as much as possible by pulling off with a knife. Use the outer stalks for cooking and the tender, inner stalks for salads and for eating raw. To make celery hearts, trim off outer stalks and all but the smallest leaves and slice lengthwise into two parts. Wash and drain the trimmed celery. Do not waste the leaves; fresh or dried (see below), their concentrated flavour adds greatly to soups, stews and salads.

To cook celery, cut into thin, thick or slanted slices, or cut into strips, or chop. Cook covered in 3 cm (1 inch) boiling, lightly salted water for about 3 to 8 minutes or until just tender but still crisp, and dress with butter, herb butter, white sauce or cheese sauce or some other kind of sauce. Cooking time depends on the size of the pieces. Cook celery hearts in boiling salted water to cover for about 10 minutes or until just tender and crisp. An excellent way of cooking celery is to use bouillon instead of water.

To dry leaves: Cut them off neatly, wash and dry them well between layers of kitchen paper. Place the celery leaves on a shallow baking sheet. Dry in a very slow oven (Gas ¼, 240° F, 120° C); the leaves must be very dry. Store whole in a covered container, or rub through a sieve to make a powder and store.

Celery Rémoulade

4–6 servings

1 dl (4 fl oz) soured cream
1 dl (4 fl oz) mayonnaise
1 tbsp chopped capers
2 tbsps chopped spring onions
1 clove garlic, crushed
1 tbsp chopped fresh dill

1 tsp fresh lemon juice
1 tbsp chopped parsley
¼ tsp salt
large bunch celery, sliced
3 dl (½ pt) chicken stock

In a medium bowl, combine the soured cream, the mayonnaise, the capers, the spring onions, the garlic and dill, the lemon juice, the parsley and salt. Mix well. Cover and let it stand for at least 1 hour to blend the flavours. Cook the celery, covered, in the chicken stock for 10 minutes or until tender but still firm. Drain and add to the sauce. Mix well. Chill for 1 hour before serving.

Braised Celery

3–4 servings
Serve with pork.

1 large bunch celery
boiling salted water
2 tbsps olive oil
4 slices *prosciutto* or ham, finely
  chopped
1 small onion, chopped
2 tbsps finely chopped parsley
500 g (1 lb) tomatoes, peeled and
  chopped

salt
freshly ground pepper
dash of Tabasco sauce (optional)
1 tbsp capers, drained, or about
  half a dozen stoned olives,
  chopped

Vegetable Cookery

Trim the celery and remove the tough outer stalks and the leaves. String the other stalks with a vegetable peeler. Cut into 7-cm (3-inch) pieces. Cook in boiling salted water to cover for 3 minutes or until half tender. Drain. Heat the olive oil in a saucepan. Add the *prosciutto*, the onion and the parsley. Cook, stirring constantly, for about 3 minutes. Add the tomatoes and cook for 3 minutes longer. Add the celery. Season with salt and pepper and the Tabasco sauce. Simmer, covered, until the celery is tender. Check occasionally for moisture; if too dry, add a little hot water. Stir in the capers or the olives.

Chard, Sea-kale (Beet), Spinach Beet

(*Beta vulgaris* var. *cicla*)

Chard is a member of the beet family (see page 65); it is grown for its large glossy green leaves and thick white stalks, and does not develop the usual bulbous root. It is the oldest type of beet known to have been used as a vegetable. There is confusion as to exactly what vegetable, chard or beets, is meant in Roman writings of the third and fourth centuries B.C.: the two appear to have been far more similar than they are now. It also appears that for centuries the roots were used rather than the leaves, while in today's chard, the leaves have been developed at the expense of the roots. On the other hand, those who gather wild sea-kale prize its broad white leaf stalks the most, and often eat them separately. It is far more popular on the Continent than in the United Kingdom where it was not cultivated until well into the eighteenth century. William Curtis, founder of the *Botanical Magazine*, wrote a pamphlet on its propagation in 1799. In small plots, chard has the advantage of being sturdy and producing much and for a long time. You harvest it by leaf which replaces itself all summer, whereas you pull out the whole spinach plant and that is the end of it.

How to buy

Buy thick, juicy-looking, white or reddish stalks with tender, fresh leaves. Avoid wilted stalks and faded leaves.

Vegetable Cookery

How to keep

Trim, wash and shake dry. Refrigerate in a plastic bag. Raw, on refrigerator shelf: 1 to 2 days. Cooked and covered, on refrigerator shelf: 2 days.

Nutritive values

Both leaves and stalks are high in vitamins A and C and a good source of iron, other minerals and vitamin B.

How to use

Chard may be called two vegetables in one, since the leaves may be cooked as greens (all spinach recipes apply) and the white stems like asparagus or celery. The vegetable is really better steamed rather than boiled and must be cooked for a short time only or it will lose its flavour.

Trim off root ends. If the vegetable is large and mature, cut off the leaves. Cut the stalks into large pieces. If the leaves are very large, cut them up. Wash thoroughly. Cook the stalks in 3 to 5 cm (1 to 2 inches) of boiling salted water for 5 to 10 minutes. Cook the leaves in 3 cm (1 inch) boiling salted water for 5 minutes. Cook both in covered saucepans. Drain thoroughly and season with butter and lemon juice or with herbs, or serve with cheese or hollandaise sauce. Stalks and leaves can also be sautéed in hot melted butter over a low heat for 2 to 3 minutes, then covered and simmered for 5 to 10 minutes or until tender. Do not overcook.

Chard with Oil and Lemon

4 servings
A Roman way of eating this green.

1 kg (2 lb) chard, trimmed and washed	2 tbsps fresh lemon juice
boiling salted water	salt
4 tbsps olive oil	freshly ground pepper

Cut the stalks of the chard and the leaves (if they are large) into bite-sized pieces. Wash in several changes of water and drain. Cook, covered, in 3 cm (1 inch) boiling salted water to cover for 3 to 5 minutes or until barely tender and still crisp. Drain thoroughly and squeeze dry with the back of a spoon or with the hands. Turn the chard into a deep serving dish. Mix together the oil, lemon juice, salt and pepper. Pour over the chard, toss and serve hot, lukewarm or chilled.

Chard with Tomato Sauce

4 servings

1 kg (2 lb) chard, trimmed, washed, cooked and drained	350 g (¾ lb) tomatoes, peeled and chopped
4 tbsps olive oil	salt
2 garlic cloves, sliced	freshly ground pepper
3 anchovies, drained and chopped finely	2 tbsps drained capers

Coarsely chop the chard and set aside. Heat the olive oil in a heavy saucepan. Add the garlic and cook until browned; discard the garlic. Add the anchovies and cook, stirring constantly, for 2 minutes. Add the tomatoes and the salt and pepper. Cook, covered, over medium heat for 5 to 10 minutes. Add the chard, mix well and cook for 10 more minutes, stirring frequently. Stir in the capers before serving.

Chestnut

(genus *Castanea*)

Chestnuts are the edible nuts of several varieties of a tree of the same name, which is related to the oak family. They are an important food crop in many parts of the world, especially in southern Europe, in China and in Japan.

The European chestnut, *Castanea sativa*, has nuts with dark mahogany-brown shells. It has long been a staple food in southern  Europe, where it was cultivated for centuries to use fresh or dried as a fruit, or made into a meal that often served for bread. It is still used in these ways in France and most Mediterranean countries. The ancient Greek writer Theophrastus tells us that Mount Olympus, the home of the gods, was thick with chestnut trees. The Romans imported chestnuts from Kastana in Asia Minor, which gave the tree and its fruit the botanical name as well as most of its names in the various European languages. In English the spelling was 'chesnut' until the early nineteenth century, when it rather inexplicably acquired its 't'. In my Roman childhood, in the autumn we used to gather chestnuts that grew in profusion in the thick forests of the Roman hill towns. Now the frequent forest fires of Italy have decimated the century-old trees.

There are many cultural varieties of the Japanese and Chinese chestnut, *Castanea crenata*. The nuts of the Japanese are less sweet than the Chinese and smaller. These varieties are either totally or nearly immune to the chestnut blight which completely destroyed the American chestnut forests in 1904, and from which the European varieties at times suffer severely as well.

Chinese water chestnuts belong to a different species, see page 132.

Chestnuts deserve a far larger use as a vegetable than they currently have. Mashed or braised whole, they combine beautifully with red cabbage, mushrooms, Brussels sprouts, onions and carrots.

How to buy

Fresh chestnuts: Buy plump, glossy, fresh-looking nuts, free from blemishes, which are heavy for their size. Avoid dried-out, shrivelled, cracked or blemished nuts that are light for their size.

Tinned chestnuts and chestnut purée, both available either unsweetened or sweetened, are used like cooked fresh chestnuts. Most of them come from France, as do the sugar-glazed chestnuts, called *marrons glacées*, which need not concern us here.

Shelled dried chestnuts can be reconstituted in water and used like fresh ones. They have less flavour.

How to keep

Keep fresh chestnuts in a cool, dry place; they dry out easily. Cover opened tins or jars and refrigerate. Keep shelled dried chestnuts as you would beans or lentils, in a covered container in a cool dry place. Fresh, unshelled, on kitchen shelf: 1 week. Fresh, shelled, cooked and covered, on refrigerator shelf: 3 to 4 days. Tinned, preserved, opened but covered, on refrigerator shelf: 1 week. Dried, on kitchen shelf, uncooked: 2 months. Dried, cooked and covered, on refrigerator shelf: 3 to 4 days.

Nutritive values

Chestnuts are high in carbohydrates and a moderate source of protein and minerals. Fresh: 194 calories; dried: 370 calories (per 100 g/3½ oz).

Vegetable Cookery

How to use

Before they can be eaten the chestnuts' hard outer shells and the thin, brown, bitter inner peel must be removed. This is usually done by boiling or roasting.

To cook and shell chestnuts: Make a horizontal slash in the flat side of the chestnut using a sharp, pointed knife. Place the chestnuts in a saucepan with ample cold water to cover. Bring to boiling point and boil for 3 minutes. Remove from heat. With a slotted spoon, scoop 2 or 3 chestnuts at a time from the hot water. With the same sharp pointed knife remove the outer shell and the inner skin, taking care to keep the chestnuts whole. This is easier said than done; invariably many of the chestnuts break and have to be used with other vegetables, in stuffings or mashed. Keep the unpeeled chestnuts in the hot water to wait their turn or the inner skin won't come off. If the water gets cold, boil it up once more.

To roast chestnuts: Slash the flat side as described above. Place on a baking sheet in a hot (Gas 6, 400° F, 210° C) oven for 15 to 20 minutes, stirring occasionally. Serve piping hot, with a glass of wine. To roast chestnuts over an open fire, punch rows of holes into a large flat tin like a metal lid or large pie pan. Prepare the chestnuts as above and place on a grill over white coals. This is the method of the street chestnut vendors.

To purée chestnuts: Cook and shell the nuts. Depending on the recipe chosen, cook them further until tender in boiling water, milk or stock to cover. Do not overcook them or they will fall apart. Cover the pot and use low heat. Drain and mash like potatoes, or strain through a sieve, or whirl in the blender with a little of the cooking liquid. Season and use as in recipe.

To reconstitute dried chestnuts: Soak overnight in water to cover. Then simmer, covered, in about 10 cm (4 inches) of water until the chestnuts puff up and are tender. Use as fresh cooked chestnuts.

Purée of Chestnut Soup

6 servings

500 g (1 lb) chestnuts, peeled
1 medium carrot, chopped
1 small onion, chopped
2 bay leaves
1½ l (2½ pts) chicken stock
salt

freshly ground pepper
3 dl (½ pt) cream
30 g (1 oz) butter
1 tart apple, peeled, cored and
   thinly sliced
2 tbsps finely chopped parsley

Combine the chestnuts, the carrot, the onion, the bay leaves and
the stock in a large saucepan. Bring to boiling point and lower the
heat. Simmer, covered, until the chestnuts are very soft and
falling apart. Remove the bay leaves. Strain through a sieve or
purée in a blender. Check the seasoning; if necessary, add a little
salt and pepper. Stir in the cream. Return to lowest possible heat,
or place on an asbestos mat, and keep hot. Heat the butter in a
small frying pan. Quickly sauté the apple slices in it until they are
golden. Float them on the soup just before serving and sprinkle
with the parsley.

Braised Chestnuts

4–6 servings

3 dl (½ pt) chicken stock
3 tbsps dry white wine or dry
   sherry
500 g (1 lb) chestnuts, peeled
60 g (2 oz) butter

1 bay leaf
salt
freshly ground pepper
1 tbsp flour

Combine the stock and the wine in a saucepan. Bring to boiling
point and lower the heat. Add the chestnuts, half of the butter
and the bay leaf. Simmer, covered, over lowest possible heat for
about 15 to 20 minutes or until the chestnuts are tender. Remove
the bay leaf. Taste; if necessary, add a little salt and pepper.
Knead together the remaining butter and the tablespoon of
flour. Drop in pea-sized pieces into the chestnut liquid, stirring
carefully in order not to break the chestnuts. Serve hot.

Variations: (1) Add 500 g (1 lb) cooked Brussels sprouts to the finished braised chestnuts and heat together. (2) Add 110 g (4 oz) diced lean ham or *prosciutto* to the braised chestnuts or braised chestnuts with Brussels sprouts and heat through.

Chick Pea

(*Cicer arietinum*)

Chick peas are the seed of a branching, bush annual which is well adapted to arid and semi-arid regions. It is a very nutritious legume, widely cultivated in Mexico and Latin America, as well as in India, where as Bengal gram it is the chief pulse crop, used split and separated from the husk to make the typical and basic pulse dish of *dhal*.

The chick pea is also a native of the Middle East and southern Europe and a very old crop, being known to the Egyptians, Hebrews, Arabs, Greeks and Romans who all eat quantities of chick peas to this day. There are black, white and red varieties, all known to the herbalists of the sixteenth, seventeenth and eighteenth centuries though the white chick pea is the most commonly used kind. The red varieties are only grown in the East and the black is now a curiosity. Occasionally chick peas are eaten fresh, but most commonly they come to the market dried and are cooked like dried beans. They have a rich nutty flavour that lends itself to soups and stews, to salads and to appetizers like the 'hummus' made popular by England's many Greek and Cypriot cafés. Actually, *hummus* is the Arab word for chick pea; *garbanzo* is the Spanish, *ceci* the Italian. Our own name comes from the French and was 'chich pease' (*pois chiche*) for three centuries until it began to be misspelled.

How to buy

Dried chick peas are sold both in bulk and in 1-lb packages. Italian and Spanish chick peas are also tinned like beans and ready to use. Buy full, clean chick peas. Avoid shrunken, blemished ones.

One measure dry chick peas makes approximately 2½ measures cooked and drained.

Vegetable Cookery

How to keep

Keep dry chick peas in a covered container in a cool dry place. Dry, on kitchen shelf: 1 year. Cooked or tinned, opened but covered, on refrigerator shelf: 1 week.

Nutritive values

Chick peas are an excellent source of proteins and carbohydrates, iron and thiamine and a fair source of other minerals. Dry: 360 calories per 100 g ($3\frac{1}{2}$ oz).

How to use

Wash in several changes of water. Soak overnight in plenty of water. Using the same water, place in saucepan, bring to boiling point and simmer over low heat for about $1\frac{1}{2}$ hours or until tender. It is almost impossible to overcook them; they will lose neither shape nor flavour easily. Alternatively, place washed chick peas (without soaking) in large saucepan with water to cover plus 5 or 6 cm (a good 2 inches). Bring to boiling point. Remove from heat and cover. Let it stand for 1 to 2 hours. Then bring to boiling point again, cover and simmer over low heat until tender, adding more hot water if necessary. Never use this quicker method for old peas: only overnight soaking will liven them up at all. Unless you are making soup and need the cooking liquid, drain and use as in recipe. If the cooked chick peas are to be stored, pour a little of their cooking juice over them to keep them moist. If they are to be puréed in a blender, also use a little of the cooking liquid.

Hummus bi Taheeni

4–6 servings
Serve as a dip, with raw vegetables or flat Arab bread (pitta).

110 g (4 oz) dried chick peas,
  cooked
3–4 tbsps sesame paste (*taheeni*)
3 tbsps vegetable oil
4–6 tbsps fresh lemon juice
1 garlic clove, crushed (preferably
  in a pestle and mortar) or very
  finely chopped

salt
lettuce
2 tbsps finely chopped parsley or
  chopped fresh mint

Press the chick peas through a food mill or a sieve. Stir in, alternately, the sesame paste, the oil and the lemon juice, to taste. Stir in the garlic and season lightly with salt. The purée should be smooth, with the consistency of double cream. If too thick, stir in a little water, 1 tablespoon at a time. Pile on a plate lined with lettuce and sprinkle with the parsley or mint. Chill before serving.

Note: This may be made in a blender, though the texture will be rougher because the chick pea skins are blended in. To make, blend together the sesame paste, the oil, the lemon juice and the garlic. Add the chick peas. Cover and blend at high speed. If too thick, add a little water, 1 tablespoon at a time. Then proceed as above.

Sautéed Chick Peas

4–6 servings
Serve with roast meats.

2 tbsps olive oil
250 g (½ lb) dried chick peas,
  cooked and drained
1 large tomato, peeled, seeded
  and chopped

2 tbsps finely chopped fresh basil
  or 1 tbsp dried basil
1 tsp dried thyme
salt
freshly ground pepper

Heat the olive oil in a deep frying pan. Add the chick peas. Cook, stirring constantly, for 3 minutes. Add all the other ingredients. Cook, covered, over medium heat for 5 to 10 minutes. Serve hot.

Roman Chick Pea Stew

6–8 servings

*This is a heavy and utterly delicious stew, which I take along on picnics
and reheat to lukewarm on the site. To make a meal, have some tomato
salad, bread, cheese and fruit.*

2 dl (6–7 fl oz) olive oil
3 large garlic cloves, chopped
   fine
8 anchovy fillets, cut up
60 g (2 oz) chopped parsley
about 500 g (1 lb) dried chick
   peas, cooked, or two 500-g
   (1-lb) tins chick peas, drained

4 large tomatoes, peeled, seeded
   and chopped
1 tbsp dried rosemary, crumbled
1 l (scant qt) water
500 g (1 lb) elbow macaroni
salt
freshly ground pepper
freshly grated Parmesan cheese

In a large pan, combine the olive oil, the garlic, the anchovies and
the parsley. Cook over low heat, stirring constantly, for about 5
minutes. Add the chick peas, the tomatoes, the rosemary and the
water. Simmer, covered, over low heat for about 30 minutes,
stirring occasionally. Cook the macaroni until just done (*al dente*)
while the soup is simmering. Add to soup. Check the seasoning;
if necessary, add a little salt and pepper. Simmer, covered, for
5 to 10 minutes, stirring occasionally. Serve with plenty of freshly
grated Parmesan cheese.

Chicory

(*Cichorium intybus*)

There are three sorts of chicory. One is used for greens (see Endive), one is grown for its large roots which are dried and made into a coffee supplement, and there is one whose roots are forced to produce a compact cluster of blanched leaves. This latter form, used as a salad green and a cooked vegetable, is what concerns us here.

Witloof, a Flemish word meaning 'white shoots', was first discovered by chance around the middle of the last century, when some coffee chicory roots that had been lying around in the dark were found to have sprouted whitish leaves. An enterprising head horticulturist of the Brussels Botanical Gardens, M. Brezier, took up the challenge and grew the first chicory, as we now know it, in the cellars of the Botanical Gardens, along with mushrooms. In 1872 the first *witloof* went to Paris, and from then on it conquered the world. It is still obtained principally from its native country to this day, for attempts to grow it outside Belgium have not been successful.

There are two distinct processes in *witloof* farming. The first is the growing of the rootstock, the second the growing of the leaf vegetable. Since the chicory farms are usually tiny, growers with large tracts of land in other parts of Belgium sow and raise the chicory in the open air and harvest it just before the frosts set in. The plants are uprooted, the leaves discarded and the chicory farmers take home the roots to plant on their farms. This is tight planting indeed; the roots are planted deep, in furrows, each root set against the next, and the furrows are extremely close together. When the roots are securely covered with the rich, soft, crumbly black earth, little Quonset huts are placed over them to shut out light and cold. The huts are lined with straw to protect the delicate plants against sudden changes of temperature. When a crop is needed, underground pipes are heated, and the roots sprout leaves. It takes twenty days or so for shoots to pierce the earth above them and to nudge their heads against the straw. Thanks to the darkness in the huts, the *witloof* achieves its pure, creamy colour. When the chicory measures at least 7 cm (3 inches), it is ready for digging with a special four-pronged fork.

How to buy

Buy crisp, firm, tightly closed chicory, which should be creamy white, with pale yellowish-green tips, free from stains and blemishes.

Avoid those with loose leaves, or leaves that are browning at the ends or have brown stems or are soft and wilted.

How to keep

Refrigerate in a plastic bag or in vegetable drawer. Raw, on refrigerator shelf or in vegetable drawer: up to a week. Cooked and covered, on refrigerator shelf: 1 or 2 days.

Nutritive values

There is not much nutrition in chicory, but since it is very low in calories, tastes good and is filling, it is valuable diet food. Raw: 12 calories per 100 g (3½ oz).

How to use

Remove any wilted leaves and trim off stem. For salads, either separate leaves or cut into slices. Wash, drain and dry between layers of kitchen paper or with a kitchen towel. Place in plastic bag or dry towel and refrigerate to crisp further. To cook, prepare as above but leave whole, or cut into halves lengthwise.

Braised Chicory

4 servings
Serve with roast pork or fowl.

60 g (2 oz) butter
750 g (1½ lb) small chicory heads, trimmed and washed
1½ dl (¼ pt) chicken stock or water

¼ tsp salt
freshly ground pepper
2 tbsps fresh lemon juice

Grease a shallow casserole or baking dish with a little of the butter. Lay the chicory in it in a single or double layer. Combine the stock, the salt, the pepper and the lemon juice and pour over the chicory. Dot with most of the remaining butter. Cover tightly with a lid or with tied-on aluminium foil. Cook over low heat for about 10 minutes. Uncover and cook for about 5 to 10 minutes longer or until the chicory is tender but keeping its shape. The pan juices should be reduced to 2 or 3 tablespoons. For a golden effect, dot with the last remaining butter and put briefly under the grill.

Chicory and Ham au Gratin

4 servings

8 large chicory heads, trimmed and washed
2 tbsps fresh lemon juice
½ tsp salt
water
30 g (1 oz) butter
2 tbsps flour
3 dl (½ pt) milk

110 g (4 oz) grated Gruyère or Parmesan cheese
1 egg yolk
salt
freshly ground pepper
8 slices boiled ham or *prosciutto*

Put the chicory into a saucepan with the lemon juice, the salt and just enough water barely to cover. Simmer, covered, over low heat for about 10 minutes or until the chicory is just tender; cooking time depends on the size. Drain and dry between layers of kitchen paper or the final dish will be watery. Heat the butter in a saucepan and stir the flour into it. Cook, stirring constantly, for about 2 minutes. Stir in the milk. Cook, stirring all the time, until the sauce is smooth and thickened. Stir in all but about a tablespoon of the grated cheese. Remove from the heat and stir until the cheese is melted. Beat in the egg yolk. Season with salt and pepper. Wrap 1 ham slice around each chicory head. Place seam-side down side by side in a shallow buttered baking dish. Pour the cheese sauce over the vegetables and sprinkle with the remaining cheese. Bake in a preheated moderate oven (Gas 4, 350° F, 180° C) for about 15 minutes or until browned and bubbly.

Note: This dish may be made ahead of time, refrigerated and browned in the oven before serving. Do not leave too long in the oven or the dish will be watery.

Chicory and Beetroot Salad

4–6 servings
One of the best winter salads. Combine the vegetables just before serving or the beetroots will colour the chicory red.

4 large, firm chicory heads,
    trimmed and washed
2 medium beetroots, cooked and
    peeled
4 tbsps French dressing, to which
    2 tsps Dijon mustard have been
    added

lettuce
2 tbsps finely chopped parsley

With a sharp knife, cut the chicory into long, thin strips. Cut the beetroots into strips as well. Combine the vegetables in a kitchen bowl and toss carefully with the French dressing. Transfer the salad to a bowl lined with lettuce and sprinkle with the parsley.

Chinese Cabbage

(*Brassica chinensis*, *Brassica pekinensis*)

East Asia, notably China, has produced among other distinctive forms of vegetables several so-called cabbages, which differ from the European varieties but nevertheless belong to Brassica, the cabbage family. In China, they were cultivated before the Christian era, but until fairly recently they have remained almost unknown in other countries. In the United States, with its large Chinese population, two varieties have been cultivated extensively for sale in oriental markets. Now, these Chinese cabbages are increasingly found in other markets, and their use is no longer limited to oriental cooking only. They both are confusingly called 'Chinese cabbage'.

1. Pak-choi, Bok Choy, *Brassica chinensis.* This vegetable consists of a long (25 to 50 cm, 10 to 20 inches) cluster of thick, broad-based, white or greenish-white stalks with loose, broad, dark-green leaves, resembling sea-kale rather than an ordinary cabbage. It does not form a heart. Some varieties have tuberous roots, which are cooked and eaten like turnips, but these are never sold here.

How to buy

Choose fresh-looking, crisp, firm heads and avoid limp, yellow-leaved vegetables.

Vegetable Cookery

How to keep

Refrigerate, unwashed, in a plastic bag for 1 to 3 days.

Nutritive values

Pak-choi is a good source of vitamin A, calcium and other minerals. Raw: approximately 14 calories per 100 g (3½ oz).

How to use

Pak-choi has a light, delicate flavour and a delightful crisp texture. It must be cooked quickly or both are lost. If mature, cook stalks and leaves separately since the stalks will take a longer time. Or cut into bite-sized pieces and stir-fry to add to any mixed meat and vegetable or vegetable combinations or wherever some crisp texture is desirable in a dish.

2. Pe-tsai, Wong Bok, *Brassica pekinensis*. These two vegetables look somewhat like a pale head of cos lettuce, with broad-ribbed, whitish-green, strong-veined, wavy and somewhat crinkled leaves (the main distinction between the two kinds is the varying sharpness of the 'teeth' of the leaf edges). The heart is pure white and used as a delicacy.

How to buy

Buy heads with crisp outer leaves; avoid very large or very firm heads which have a strong flavour.

How to keep

Refrigerate, unwashed, in a plastic bag for 1 to 3 days.

Nutritive values

Raw: 14 calories per 100 g (3½ oz).

How to use

Pe-tsai has a more delicate flavour than other cabbages and practically no odour in cooking. Cook as you would any cabbage.

Sautéed Chinese Cabbage

4 servings
This is my favourite way with any cabbage. Speed is of the essence, though non-Chinese cabbages may have to cook a few moments longer. If desired, add 1 tablespoon crushed fennel or aniseed to the cooked cabbage.

30 g (1 oz) butter or vegetable oil
1 small Chinese cabbage, trimmed and shredded

salt
freshly ground pepper

Heat the butter in a deep frying pan. Add the cabbage. Cover and cook over medium heat for 3 minutes, stirring three times. Remove from heat and season with salt and pepper.

Instant Kimchi

4 servings
Kimchi is a national Korean relish. It can be extremely hot and elaborate, ripening for weeks, or, faute de mieux, it can be quick. I prefer this less powerful version. Use it as you would coleslaw.

1 Chinese cabbage, trimmed
2 garlic cloves, crushed
1 tsp hot pepper sauce or flakes
1–2 tbsps soy sauce

1 tsp vinegar
1 tbsp salt
1 tbsp sugar

Chop the cabbage into small pieces. Wash and drain. Combine the cabbage and all the other ingredients and mix well. Taste and if necessary, adjust the flavour with more pepper, soy sauce or vinegar. Cover and let stand at room temperature for about 1 hour.

Chinese Water Chestnut, Pi-tsi

(*Eleocharis dulcis*)

The edible tuber of a rush-like plant of the Sedge family that grows in shallow waters at the edges of lakes and in marshes, used widely in oriental cookery. Water chestnuts are roundish, with a brown or blackish skin and a firm white flesh. Since their flavour is delicately nutty though rather bland, their main virtue is that of giving crispness to a dish. The Chinese water chestnut, here under discussion, must not be confused with the nut-like fruit of another aquatic plant, *Trapa natans*, which is also called water chestnut or caltrops and is used in the same manner. Both plants are natives of the Far East, where they have been cultivated as food plants for centuries.

How to buy

Chinese water chestnuts are generally available tinned in water, imported from Hong Kong, Taiwan and Japan.

Nutritive values

Raw: 79 calories per 100 g (3½ oz).

How to use

Chinese water chestnuts should be thinly sliced, quartered or diced and immersed about 2 minutes in boiling salted water, then drained and cooled in cold water before further use.

Sliced, diced, halved or quartered, Chinese water chestnuts may be added to any salad or cooked dish, improving it with a deliciously crunchy texture.

Stir-Fried Pork and Water Chestnuts

4 servings

3 tbsps vegetable oil
1 garlic clove, crushed
6 spring onions, white and green parts, chopped fine
110 g (¼ lb) lean boneless pork, cut in small, thin strips
4 tbsps soy sauce

1 tbsp sugar
2 tbsps lemon juice
500-g (16–19-oz) tin water chestnuts, thinly sliced
salt
freshly ground pepper
shredded lettuce

Heat the oil in a wok or a large frying pan. Cook the garlic and the onions, stirring constantly, until they are turning golden brown. Add the pork. Stir-fry until the pork is browned on all sides. Stir in the soy sauce, the sugar and the lemon juice. Stir-fry for 1 minute. Lower the heat, cover and simmer over low heat for 5 minutes. Add the water chestnuts and salt and pepper. Stir-fry for 2 more minutes. Pile on shredded lettuce and serve immediately.

Collard, Collard Greens

(*Brassica oleracea* var. *acephala*)

Collards are a humble but very healthy member of the cabbage family. They do not form a head, but are cultivated for their dark-green, smooth, rather thick, broad, curly-edged leaves which grow in a kind of loose rosette on top of a tall stem. Today's plants vary in size, growing to a height of a metre or more (3 to 4 feet). Collards are a close relative of kale, with which they are sometimes confused. Together they are the most primitive members of the cabbage group, originating in the eastern Mediterranean or Asia Minor, and not much changed from the wild forms of cabbage eaten by prehistoric man. The Greeks and Romans ate collards and it is thought that the latter introduced them into northern Europe. Their English name is a seventeenth-century development of 'colewort', the original designation for any kind of cabbage which later became restricted to the non-hearting varieties.

Collards are a hardy vegetable, withstanding heat and drought to a far greater extent than cabbages; like kale, cold weather and even a light frost improves their quality. They are largely cultivated as a winter vegetable, and are very easy to grow even in the smallest of gardens as a quickly maturing crop.

How to buy

Buy fresh, crisp, green, tender young leaves that are free from insect injuries. Avoid wilting, yellowing, blemished leaves.

How to keep

Remove wilted leaves and wash and shake dry thoroughly before refrigerating in a plastic bag. Uncooked, on refrigerator shelf: 3 to 5 days. Cooked and covered, on refrigerator shelf: 3 to 4 days.

134

Nutritive values

Collards are a superior source of vitamins A and B and contain heavy amounts of calcium, phosphorus and other minerals. Raw: 40 calories; cooked and drained: 33 calories (per 100 g/3½ oz).

How to use

Cook like spinach, chard, cabbage or kale. Wash thoroughly in several changes of cold water to remove sand and earth. Trim off the stems that are tough and the midribs of the leaves. Cut large leaves into pieces for cooking, or shred like cabbage. Cook, covered, in 2 or 3 cm (1 inch) of boiling salted water for 5 to 10 minutes, or the shortest possible time for tenderness. Drain, season, and add butter. When collards are cooked with some form of pork, the resulting juice is an extremely nutritious broth which can be eaten or sopped up with bread.

Southern Collard Greens

4–6 servings
A recipe from the southern United States, where it would be served with corn bread. The long cooking is essential for the typical flavour.

1½ l (2½ pts) water
1 ham hock or 250 g (½ lb) salt pork
2 kg (4 lb) collard greens, washed and prepared for cooking

½ tsp flaked or chopped hot pepper, or to taste (optional)
3 tbsps vegetable oil
salt
freshly ground pepper

Put the water and the ham hock in a pot with a tight fitting lid and large enough to hold the collards. Bring to boiling point, then turn the heat to very low and simmer, covered, for 30 minutes. Add the collards and the hot pepper flakes. Simmer, covered, for about 2 hours, stirring occasionally. Add the oil and simmer, covered, for 30 more minutes. Check the seasoning; if necessary, add a little more salt and some pepper.

Collards all'Italiana

4 servings
Serve with pork chops.

3 tbsps olive oil
1 medium onion, thinly sliced
250 g (½ lb) tomatoes, peeled
  and chopped
salt
freshly ground pepper

½ tsp dried marjoram
1 kg (2 lb) collard greens,
  trimmed and prepared for
  cooking
30 g (1 oz) freshly grated
  Parmesan cheese

Heat the oil in a saucepan large enough to hold the collards. Add the onion and cook, stirring constantly, until soft. Add the tomatoes and cook for 5 minutes longer. Season with salt and pepper and marjoram. Add the collards. Simmer, covered, over low heat for about 15 to 20 minutes or until tender. Stir frequently and check the moisture; if necessary, add a little water, 2 tablespoons at a time. Sprinkle with Parmesan cheese and serve hot.

Corn, Maize, Mealies

(Zea mays)

Corn, the only cereal of American origin, is one of the most widely cultivated food plants, exceeded in acreage only by wheat. It grows under a variety of conditions, in temperate as well as in tropical zones, below sea level and high up in the Andes, in arid or rainy regions, and in short or long growing seasons. The edible grain serves as food for humans or is easily dried and stored as livestock fodder, and the whole plant is used for forage. Its products, such as starch and oil, have given rise to large industries.

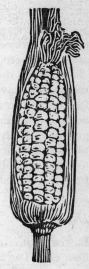

Its proper name is maize, a word of Indian origin, understood throughout the world. Calling the vegetable corn is an exclusively Anglo-American practice. The word 'corn' has a common Teutonic origin, meaning small particles which have been 'worn down' by threshing or milling. The early American settlers planted it as the Indians showed them and saw that it flourished whereas their wheat did not. Columbus is said to have brought the first corn to Europe, but oddly enough, in countries such as Austria and Hungary, maize is also known as 'Turkish' corn, because when the Turks invaded Europe in the sixteenth and seventeenth centuries, they brought many novelties, and corn was thought to be one of them.

Corn is a grass that had been domesticated and cultivated long before the white man arrived in the New World; it has never been found in a wild state. The grass probably originated in the lowlands east of the Andes and was carried to Peru, where various varieties have been found in Inca tombs. From there it went north to become part of the Maya and Aztec civilizations.

137

Vegetable Cookery

The corn of the past was a small, primitive form of the vegetable, very unlike our own which is derived from constant and ancient hybridization of the wild forms. Corn to this day intercrosses so rapidly that where two or more kinds are grown in the same field, a single ear may have two classifications of kernels on it. Numerous mutations produced different forms of corn suited to various purposes, such as field corn, flint corn and others. The one that concerns us here is sweet corn, of which more than 200 varieties are now being grown, almost all of which are hybrids.

The mythology of corn, and its religious significance to the Incas, Mayans, Aztecs and the American Indians of the Southwest, the Plains and the northern parts, have filled many volumes. Corn was the basic food of these peoples, corn was the deity that made them live, to be propitiated with gifts and dances. In Christian times in Mexico, some religious images were huge, life-size statues, mainly made of cornstalks. In the Central and South American corn civilizations, the Indians' use of corn went further than food. It was used as currency, and the husks, wrapped around tobacco, made simple cigars.

In Europe, the use of fresh corn as human food is comparatively recent. In Italy and eastern Europe, where it is an important feed crop, corn meal plays an important part in the diet, though no one would dream of eating a fresh ear. Since no table corn is grown, the only way of finding a tender ear is to pluck a very unripe ear of field corn. Its cultivation in England is largely due to William Cobbett, who advocated its use strongly after his return from the United States in the early nineteenth century.

How to buy

Buy ears with fresh, snug, green husks with dark-brown silk at the husk end. The kernels should be firm, plump and juicy-looking, and large enough to leave no spaces between the rows. Ears should be filled to the tip, with no rows of missing kernels. The stem ends should not be too discoloured or dried out. Medium-size kernels are preferable. Avoid soft, tired-looking ears with spots, signs of decay or worm damage. Avoid tiny soft kernels, which mean that the corn is immature, and very large, tough kernels which indicate over-maturity.

How to keep

Use as quickly as possible; the best fresh corn is that cooked as soon as picked. The sooner used the sweeter and more tender: flavour and texture are lost within the first 24 hours after picking and the sugar content turns quickly into starch at higher temperatures. To store, wrap the whole, unhusked ear in damp paper towels and store in the coldest part of the refrigerator. Large amounts of corn are frozen on the cob, or as kernel corn, or tinned as kernel or cream corn. Fresh, on refrigerator shelf: use as soon as possible. Fresh and cooked, or tinned, covered, on refrigerator shelf: 2 to 3 days.

Nutritive values

Fresh corn contains mostly agreeable carbohydrates, as well as a fair amount of vitamin A, and some vitamin C, protein and minerals. Kernels, cooked on cob: 91 calories per 100 g ($3\frac{1}{2}$ oz).

How to use

To husk fresh corn, remove the outer husk and the silk; a small vegetable brush is helpful for silk-removing. Rinse in cold water.

For fresh whole kernels, cut lengthwise from the cob with a sharp knife, scraping well to get all the milky juice.

For fresh cream-style corn, with the point of a sharp knife slit through the centre of each row of kernels. Press out the pulp and the juice with the blunt edge of the knife.

To boil fresh corn, husk and place in a large pan of rapidly boiling water. Do not salt the water as salt toughens, but if you like add 1 tablespoon of sugar for sweetness. After the water reaches boiling point again, cover and cook for 3 to 5 minutes. Do not overcook. Drain and serve immediately with butter, salt and pepper.

To roast fresh corn, pull back the outer husk, remove the silk, smooth the husks back into place and tie with string. Then *either* soak the prepared corn in salted cold water for 5 minutes, drain and place in a shallow baking dish, and roast in a preheated moderate oven (Gas 4, 350° F, 180° C) for 30 minutes, *or* roast without first soaking. The corn may also be grilled over an open fire for 10 to 15 minutes, or roasted buried in hot coals for 10 to 15 minutes. Unhusked corn wrapped in heavy aluminium foil can be roasted in a preheated moderate oven (as above) or over hot coals for 10 minutes. Another method is to husk the corn, spread the kernels with melted butter seasoned with soy sauce, curry or other spices, wrap in heavy aluminium foil and roast in hot coals for 10 to 15 minutes.

Cook fresh kernels in a covered saucepan in a small amount of water, milk or single cream for 3 to 5 minutes or until just tender and season with salt and pepper and butter.

Corn Frittata

4 servings

4 slices bacon	30 g (1 oz) grated Parmesan
1 small onion, finely chopped	cheese
4 ears corn, cut off the cob	salt
4 eggs	freshly ground pepper
3 tbsps water	¼ tsp dried thyme

In a large frying pan, cook the bacon until it is crisp. Drain the bacon on kitchen paper, crumble and reserve. Pour off all but 2 tablespoons of the bacon fat. Cook the onion and the corn in the bacon fat for about 3 to 5 minutes or until tender. Beat together all the remaining ingredients and stir in the crumbled bacon. Pour the mixture over the corn. Cook over low heat, without stirring, but shaking the frying pan to prevent sticking for about 5 minutes or until set. Cut into four wedges. Turn each wedge over with a large spatula. Cook until set. Or place the frying pan under the grill and cook until the top is set. Serve hot or luke-warm.

Fresh Chili Pepper Cornbread

110 g (4 oz) flour
110 g (4 oz) corn meal
½ tsp baking soda
2 tsps baking powder
¾ tsp salt
2 eggs, beaten
2 ears corn, cut off the cob

2½ dl (8 fl oz) sour milk
1 dl (⅕ pt) water
3 tbsps hot, green peppers, seeded and diced
60 g (2 oz) butter or bacon fat or dripping, melted butter

Sift together the flour, corn meal, baking soda, baking powder and salt. Stir in the eggs, corn, sour milk, water and hot peppers. Mix only until all the ingredients are moistened; do not overmix. Stir in the butter. Generously grease a deep, square baking tin (about 20 to 25 cm, 8 to 10 inches). Place briefly on direct heat to heat the tin. Turn the batter into the hot baking tin. Bake in a preheated hot oven (Gas 7, 425° F, 220° C) for about 30 minutes or until the bread shrinks away from the sides of the pan. Serve hot with butter.

Fresh Corn Salad

6 servings

8 ears corn, husked
8 tbsps olive oil
4 tbsps cider vinegar
1 tbsp fresh lemon juice
2 tsps Dijon mustard
salt
freshly ground pepper
3 tbsps finely chopped parsley
2 tbsps chopped fresh basil leaves
  or 2 tsps crumbled dried basil
  or 1–2 tbsps chopped fresh
  tarragon leaves

2 large tomatoes, peeled, seeded and chopped
1 small green pepper, peeled and cut into strips
4–6 spring onions, chopped fine
lettuce

Fill a large pan with water and bring to boiling point. Add the corn and cover the pan. Bring back to boiling point. Remove from the heat and let stand for 5 to 10 minutes. Drain and cool. Cut the kernels off the cobs. Combine the olive oil, vinegar,

lemon juice and mustard. Mix well. Taste; add salt and pepper.
Add the parsley and the basil or tarragon and mix well. Add the
corn and toss. Add the tomatoes, the pepper and the spring
onions and toss again. Line a salad bowl with the lettuce and pile
the corn salad on the lettuce.

Corn Salad, Field Salad

(*Valerianella olitoria*)

A spring and summer salad green that springs up wild in fields of corn and on the banks and walls of arable ground. The plant is 10 to 15 cm (4 to 6 inches) tall, with leaves that, depending on the variety, are spoon-shaped or round, smooth-edged or slightly toothed, growing in compact rosettes. Their texture is quite firm and their flavour bland and vaguely lettuce-like.

Corn salad is easily cultivated in most home gardens. On the Continent it is extremely popular, grown accordingly, and widely sold in bunches. Corn salad is the *mâche* that appears on French menus but it is also called *doucette* and *salade du chanoine*. In England, it is also known as lamb's lettuce, and the thought of baby lambs grazing on it in the spring is a pretty one. There is a longer-leaved, somewhat hairy Italian variety, which I know under its Roman name of *insalatina* (little salad) though doubtless, as with so much Italian food, it is known under different names in different regions.

Corn salad is very perishable and should be treated as other perishable salad greens. It may also be cooked briefly, like spinach.

Courgette, Zucchini

(*Cucurbita pepo*)

Courgette is a variety of narrow summer squash developed in Italy, cylindrical in shape and almost straight, the base a little wider than the top. The average size is 10 to 20 cm (4 to 8 inches) long and 2 to 5 cm ($\frac{1}{2}$ to 2 inches) across. The colour is a moderately dark green over a yellowish ground colour which gives the vegetable a striped appearance further emphasized by the faint

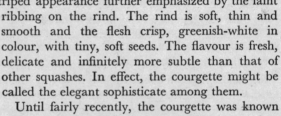

ribbing on the rind. The rind is soft, thin and smooth and the flesh crisp, greenish-white in colour, with tiny, soft seeds. The flavour is fresh, delicate and infinitely more subtle than that of other squashes. In effect, the courgette might be called the elegant sophisticate among them.

Until fairly recently, the courgette was known only to people of Mediterranean descent, and to the French, but during the last few years it has become a fashionable vegetable, prepared in far more diverse ways than its close relation, the vegetable marrow.

How to buy

Buy firm, well-rounded courgettes, with tender, glossy, unblemished rinds. Buy preferably small courgettes, from 7 to 15 cm (3 to 6 inches) in length and 2 to 3 cm (1 inch) across. Avoid soft courgettes, with torn rinds and dark spots.

How to keep

Buy in small amounts and use as soon as possible. Raw, on refrigerator shelf or in vegetable drawer: 3 to 4 days. Cooked and covered, on refrigerator shelf: 2 days.

Nutritive values

Courgette contains only a moderate amount of nutrients. Raw: 17 calories; cooked and drained: 12 calories (per 100 g/3½ oz).

How to use

Wash and trim off blossom and stem end. Do not peel or scrape if the rind is clean; if necessary, scrape off or cut off any blemished spots. Cut into strips, slices or dice. Cook as quickly as possible, with a minimum amount of water or preferably in just enough butter to keep them from sticking to the pan: courgettes are watery and quickly make more than enough cooking liquid of their own.

Sautéed Courgettes

4–6 servings

3 tbsps olive oil
2 garlic cloves, sliced
750 g (1½ lb) courgettes, thinly
   sliced
salt

freshly ground pepper
1 tbsp cider vinegar or to taste
3 tbsps finely chopped fresh basil
   or parsley

Heat the olive oil in a deep frying pan. Cook the garlic slices until they are just beginning to turn golden. Add the courgettes and season with the salt and pepper. Cook over medium heat, stirring with a fork, for 3 to 5 minutes or until the courgettes are tender but still crisp. Stir in the vinegar and the basil and cook 30 seconds longer.

Courgette and Tomato Casserole

6 servings

3 tbsps olive oil
1 small onion, chopped fine
1 garlic clove, chopped fine
4 large courgettes, cut into slices
2 tbsps finely chopped fresh basil leaves or 2 tsps dried basil
60 g (2 oz) freshly grated Parmesan cheese

4 large tomatoes, peeled and sliced
salt
freshly ground pepper
60 g (2 oz) fine dry breadcrumbs
30 g (1 oz) butter, melted

Heat the olive oil in a frying pan. Cook the onion and the garlic in it, stirring constantly, for about 3 to 4 minutes or until the onion is soft. Add the courgettes. Cook over medium heat, stirring constantly with a fork, for about 3 to 5 minutes, or until the courgettes are turning golden but are still firm. Place a layer of courgette in a buttered 1½ litre (or quart) baking dish. Sprinkle with a little of the basil and the Parmesan cheese. Top with a layer of tomatoes and sprinkle these with a little salt and pepper. Repeat the process. Combine the breadcrumbs and the melted butter and sprinkle over the vegetables. Bake without a cover in a preheated moderate oven (Gas 4, 350° F, 180° C) for about 20 minutes or until golden brown.

Cold Marinated Courgette

6 servings

8 medium courgettes
olive oil for frying
2½ dl (8 fl oz) mild vinegar
1¼ dl (4 fl oz) olive oil
1 garlic clove, crushed
2 tbsps finely chopped fresh basil or 1 tsp dried basil

salt
freshly ground pepper
salad greens
4 tbsps finely chopped parsley

Trim the courgettes and scrape them lightly with a knife to remove any waxy coating. Wash and dry them. Cut the courgettes into thick slices. Heat about ½ cm (¼ inch) olive oil in a heavy frying pan until the oil is hazy. Carefully fry a few slices at a time for about 2 minutes on each side, turning once. The courgettes should be golden but still crisp. Drain on kitchen paper and cool. In a small saucepan, combine the vinegar, olive oil, garlic, basil, salt and pepper. Simmer over medium heat for 5 minutes. Cool to lukewarm. Meantime, line a salad bowl with salad greens. Pile the fried courgettes in orderly rows on the greens. Pour the marinade over them and sprinkle with the parsley. Serve immediately.

Note: If the courgettes are to be refrigerated after frying, do not pile them on the salad greens because these would wilt under the marinade. Put the fried courgettes carefully into a bowl, pour the marinade over them and refrigerate. At serving time, pour off any excess marinade, pile the courgettes on salad greens and sprinkle with parsley.

Cucumber

(Cucumis sativus)

Cucumbers, which belong to the squash–gourd family Cucurbitaceae, are one of the most widely cultivated vegetables and one of the oldest, going back some 3,000 years. Some botanists say that the cucumber originated in India, others that it came from Malaysia from where it began its triumphal spread both East and West. The Chinese have known cucumbers for at least 2,000 years, and the ancient Egyptians, Greeks and Hebrews mention them in their writings. The Romans liked them in their salads or braised, and the Emperor Tiberius, known for his dubious personal life, was so fond of cucumbers that he had to eat them every day, wherever he was, so that they were grown in special movable frames. Charlemagne grew cucumbers in his gardens in the ninth century, and the English did in the fourteenth century. Large-scale cultivation apparently did not take place here until the advent of glasshouses. In the eighteenth century 'cowcumbers' established themselves as a middle-class delicacy.* Since then, however, the popularity of the cucumber, fresh or pickled, has become immense. In Germanic and Slavic countries it may be considered, alongside cabbage, as the national vegetable.

The New World owes cucumbers to Columbus, who had them planted in Haiti in 1494. The Spaniards re-introduced them to the Indians on the Atlantic coast, and the English grew them in their settlements in Virginia in 1609 and Massachusetts in 1629.

* Dr Johnson, of course, disagreed: 'A cucumber should be well sliced, and dressed with pepper and vinegar, and then thrown out, as good for nothing.'

The cucumber, which strictly speaking is a fruit though used as a vegetable, grows on a trailing vine – a graceful plant that singly has been known to yield 25 to 125 cucumbers. There are many varieties, which, however, may be formed into three main groups; the large, smooth, greenhouse-green, English cucumber grows to as much as 60 cm (2 feet) in length and has flesh more delicate and tender than the field-grown or garden-grown cucumber and the small, pickling varieties. The latest thing is seedless cucumbers which grow at the same rate to the same size so that they can be harvested mechanically.

Besides being very low in calories, inexpensive and widely available, cucumbers have healing and cosmetic virtues. Rubbed on the skin, cucumber will keep it white and soft, and soothe sunburn and other irritations. Cucumber juice is said to get rid of, or at least soften, freckles. Especially in France, soap and other cosmetic products made from cucumbers are thought of very highly.

How to buy

Buy cucumbers that are fresh, firm and well-shaped. They should be bright green in colour. Avoid soft, rubbery, dull cucumbers, or very large ones.

How to keep

Do not peel or slice until ready to use. Cucumbers, especially cut cucumbers, whether raw or cooked, in any form, give off a strong odour that other refrigerated foods will rapidly absorb. Put whole, unpeeled cucumbers in the vegetable drawer of the refrigerator. Cover any cut or cooked cucumbers very tightly with plastic wrap or aluminium foil before refrigerating. Do not freeze. Unpeeled, on refrigerator shelf: 1 week. Made into salad or cooked, and covered: 3 to 4 days.

Vegetable Cookery

Nutritive values

Cucumbers are 95 per cent water. They have small amounts of vitamins and minerals and are very low in calories. Raw, peeled: 15 calories per 100 g ($3\frac{1}{2}$ oz).

How to use

Wash, trim ends and slice, cut into strips or dice. Peel if the skin is tough or heavily waxed. If lightly waxed, try to remove the wax under hot water; some of it may come off. Do not peel young cucumbers with a tender skin. To flute for decorative slices: Score the skin lengthwise with a fork before slicing. For shells: Peel or not, cut into halves lengthwise and scoop out the seeds with a sharp spoon or the tip of a knife. To crisp: Cut into thin or thick slices or strips. Refrigerate in salted ice water for 1 to 2 hours. Drain thoroughly. To prepare for salads: Thinly slice cucumbers. Place in a bowl and sprinkle with salt – about 1 to 2 tablespoons per cucumber. Cover and weigh down with a weight such as a tin of food. Let stand at room temperature for 30 to 60 minutes. Drain and rinse out salt under running cold water. Drain again and squeeze dry with hands. Dress with sour cream, yoghurt, or vinegar and sugar. These are the German, Scandinavian and Russian ways of making cucumber salad.

Cucumbers make an excellent vegetable when cooked, sautéed, deep-fried or stuffed. To cook: Peel and cut into thick slices or large strips or quarters. Cook, covered, in a couple of cm (1 inch) boiling water for 3 to 5 minutes; do not overcook. Drain and serve with butter, lemon juice or herbs. To sauté: Cut into $\frac{1}{2}$-cm ($\frac{1}{4}$-inch) slices or sticks. Dip in flour and sauté in hot butter for 2 to 3 minutes. To deep fry: Dip thicker slices or strips in beaten egg and breadcrumbs or flour and drop into hot oil ($375°$ F, $190°$ C on frying thermometer) and fry until golden-brown. Serve immediately, with lemon wedges.

Note: When cooking cucumber, do not add salt until it is cooked and ready. It is a watery enough vegetable and salt, during cooking, draws out even more water.

Cold Cucumber Soup

6 servings
This soup should not be buttery, because cold buttery soup is not attractive. The cream will add the needed richness. Remember that thorough chilling always takes more time than one thinks.

30 g (1 oz) butter
2 leeks, chopped, white parts only, or 1 medium onion, chopped
1 bunch spring onions, white and tender green parts (remove coarse outer leaves), chopped
2–3 cucumbers
1 bunch watercress leaves or 110 g (4 oz) parsley leaves

2 medium potatoes, peeled and chopped
1½ l (2½ pts) chicken stock
salt
freshly ground pepper
½ tsp dry mustard or ground cardamom
2½ dl (8 fl oz) double cream
1 bunch radishes, finely chopped (optional)

Heat the butter in a deep pan. Over low heat, stirring frequently, cook the leeks and the spring onions in the butter until the vegetables are tender. Do not let them brown. Peel the cucumbers, cut them lengthwise into quarters and scrape off the seeds. Chop the cucumbers. Add the cucumbers, the watercress or parsley, the potatoes, the chicken stock, salt and pepper to taste, and the mustard or cardamom to the onion mixture. Simmer, covered, over low heat for about 20 minutes or until the potatoes are tender. Strain through a fine sieve or blend in a blender. Check the seasonings. Pour into a bowl; tightly cover the bowl with aluminium foil or plastic wrap. Chill the soup thoroughly. Stir in the cream before serving, and sprinkle with the chopped radishes.

Sautéed Cucumbers

4 servings

3 large cucumbers
4 tbsps flour
½ tsp salt
⅛ tsp freshly ground pepper

60 g (2 oz) butter
1 tbsp grated onion
4 tbsps finely chopped parsley

Wash and peel the cucumbers. Cut them into halves lengthwise. Split each half lengthwise, scrape out the seeds with a spoon and cut into 3-cm (1-inch) pieces. Dry the pieces with a clean kitchen towel. In a paper bag, mix together the flour, the salt and the pepper. Add the cucumbers. Shake to coat the pieces and shake off excess flour. Heat the butter in a deep frying pan and cook the onion for about 1 minute. Add the cucumbers. Cook over medium-to-high heat, stirring constantly with a fork, for about 4 to 5 minutes or until crisp and golden. Do not overcook or the cucumbers will be soggy. Drain on kitchen paper. Serve in a hot serving dish sprinkled with the parsley.

Soured Cream Cucumber Salad

4 servings
Good with curries or other hot or strong-flavoured dishes.

2 or 3 medium cucumbers	¼ tsp sugar
1 tbsp salt	salt
1½ dl (¼ pt) sour cream	freshly ground pepper
1–1½ tbsps white vinegar	3 tbsps finely chopped dill or
2 tbsps vegetable oil (do not use olive oil)	parsley

Trim the cucumbers. Slice them as thinly as possible. Sprinkle with salt, mix and let stand at room temperature for 1 hour. Drain and rinse under running cold water to remove the salt. Squeeze dry. Combine the sour cream, vinegar, oil, sugar, salt and pepper. Pour over the cucumbers. Cover and chill for 1 hour or more. Sprinkle with the dill or parsley before serving.

Scandinavian Pickled Cucumbers

4 servings

1 dl (4 fl oz) white vinegar	2–3 tbsps sugar
2 or 3 tbsps water	3 tbsps chopped dill
salt	2 large cucumbers
freshly ground pepper	

Combine all the ingredients except the cucumbers and mix well. Slice the cucumbers as thinly as possible – they should be almost transparent. Place in a serving dish. Pour the dressing over the cucumbers. Cover and refrigerate 3 or more hours. Check the seasoning and drain before serving.

Dandelion

(*Taraxacum officinale* agg.)

The dandelion is a weed that exasperates those who care for beautiful lawns, but pleases others who like a fresh-tasting, pungent green on their tables. The name seems to come from the French *dent de lion*, lion's tooth, describing the jagged edges of the leaves. The name of the vegetable in France is not as romantic: *pissenlit* refers to the dandelion's diuretic effects, as do a variety of local names in English: mess-a-bed, schoolboy's clock, wet-weed.

A native of Eurasia, dandelions have been a popular green since the days of the Romans in all of Europe and a good part of the orient. The young leaves of the plant can be eaten raw in salads and all the green leaves may be cooked like spinach, or as a potherb. The flowers of this adaptable plant have long been used for home-made wines and the roots, dried, roasted and ground, serve as a coffee substitute. Dandelion teas, from the leaves or the roots, have been famed for centuries for their therapeutic, blood-purifying uses. All the medieval herbals list them for their health-giving properties. Well-manured, and with the spreading leaves covered with earth to blanch them, the plants produce spectacular results practically all year long. Several kinds of large-leaved dandelions are now grown commercially, especially in France and in the United States. Interestingly, a Russian variety yields a latex (wild rubber) juice.

How to buy

Cultivated dandelions, gathered in bunches, appear only sporadically in our markets. They are lighter green in colour and less bitter than the wild ones on which most of us have to rely.

Gather fresh, tender, crisp and comparatively large green leaves. If the roots are left attached, the leaves stay juicier longer. Avoid wilted, flabby and yellowed leaves, and leaves that are very dirty and have insect damage.

How to keep

Trim away damaged or yellowed leaves. Wash thoroughly and shake dry. Wrap in plastic wrap and refrigerate. Raw, on refrigerator shelf: 3 to 5 days. Cooked and covered, on refrigerator shelf: 3 to 4 days.

Nutritive values

Dandelions are an excellent source of vitamin A and a good source of iron and other minerals. Raw: 45 calories; cooked: 33 calories (per 100 g/3½ oz).

How to use

To cook: Cut off roots, wash leaves and shake dry. Cut or tear into pieces of about 5 cm (2 inches). If young, use no water, but cook, covered, like spinach, in the water that clings to them, for 5 minutes or until just tender. If older leaves, cook, covered, in a little boiling salted water. Drain and season to taste.

Use the small tender leaves for salads, whole or chopped. Blanching them will take most of the bitterness out.

Cooked Dandelion Greens

4 servings

6 slices bacon, cut into strips
750 g (1½ lb) dandelion greens,
  prepared for cooking

4 tbsps vinegar
½ tsp sugar
salt

Cook the bacon in a deep frying pan until crisp. Drain off all but 3 tablespoons of the fat. Add the dandelion greens, the vinegar, the sugar and a little salt. Mix well. Cover and simmer until the greens are soft. Stir frequently and taste; if necessary, add a little more vinegar to flavour the greens. Serve hot.

Dried Beans

Dried beans, in many varieties, have been and still are a staple food of a large part of mankind. Apart from their high protein content and their tastiness, another of their advantages is that dried beans are easy to store and long lasting. Many dried beans are ground into flours and used as diet supplements or in allergy diets. These bean flours are particularly important in Far Eastern cooking.

In England only broad beans are a really old cultivated crop; other beans were introduced at different times, some quite late. 'Beanes are harde of digestion and make troblesum dreams' is a line of thought still all too often subscribed to.

The varieties of dried beans that concern us most here belong to the *Phaseolus vulgaris* group, known in French generally as *haricots*. They are probably of South American origin, but most of them have long been grown almost worldwide. For purposes of identification and use, they are perhaps best treated by appearance, especially colour.

Light green beans, small and oval, have been known in England since the late nineteenth century by their French name, *flageolet*. In Italy they are called *fagiolini*. Under either name, and from either country, they come to us in tins, in bottles or dried. Of all the beans, they have the most delicate flavour.

Small white beans are usually either what the French call *haricots blancs sec* (the Americans call them navy beans) or pea beans. Both kinds are used extensively for stews: if cooked slowly (especially in the oven) they keep their shape for a long time where larger, darker beans tend to go mushy more quickly. *Haricots blancs* are the classic ingredient of cassoulets; pea beans have gained fame, and notoriety, as (Boston) baked beans.

Large white beans are white kidney beans, known also by their Italian name, *canellini*. They are available here either tinned or dried. Fleshier and therefore mealier (and more easily overcooked) than their smaller cousins, they are at their best used in salads – straight from the tin or cooked as briefly as necessary to make them just tender but still firm.

Black beans, usually fairly small (though not as minute as black grams – see page 182), have white flesh beneath their dark skins. They are still mostly of Mexican origin, and in their native country they are often combined with rice. The colour combination is pretty enough, but there is another, more subtle, reason for those beans-and-rice combinations so popular throughout the West Indies: the digestion time of rice is very short, that of beans much longer.

Speckled beans are either a pale pink or light brown. The latter are known to gardeners as '*Deuil Fin Précoce*'; the pale pink variety (getting to be known also under their American name of pinto beans) is another Mexican sort: as *frijoles* they form the basis of the national dish of 'refried beans'. In practical terms this means they split their skins very easily and cook to a mush without losing too much of their flavour.

Brown beans found here are usually the large 'Canadian Wonder' variety, better for soups than for use separately: they cook to mush very quickly and in that state are classic inducers of what is politely known as flatulence. The Egyptian brown bean (*ful medames*), easier to keep firm and of a more subtle taste, is the basis of a number of Middle Eastern dishes.

Red beans have about the largest number of varieties in the family. Red kidney beans are the ones best known here; chili beans are of a darker hue. Both purée easily, even through an ordinary sieve, but with careful cooking they can be kept whole and then have a robust taste which perfectly matches their full fleshiness. Chili con carne, a beans-and-meat stew, is their classic appearance.

Other dried beans (and peas) can be found under their own headings: Black-eye Pea, Broad Bean, Butter Bean, Chick Pea, Grams (for adzuki, mung and urd), Lentil, Pea and Soy Bean.

How to buy

Buy beans that are clean, all the same size (for even cooking) and quality, with a bright, uniform colour. If the colour is dull, the beans have lost their freshness. Avoid beans which are shrivelled, cracked or blemished or which have insect pinholes.

How to keep

Keep beans in a clean, covered container in a dry place. Dried, on kitchen shelf: 1 year or more. Cooked and covered, on refrigerator shelf: 1 to 4 days.

Nutritive values

Dried beans are the highest source of protein after animal proteins, though their protein quality is inferior to that of meats and dairy foods. They contain a fair amount of thiamide and are a very good source of iron. Cooked: about 120 calories per 100 g ($3\frac{1}{2}$ oz).

How to use

Packaged dried beans, though clean looking, should be rinsed under running cold water before using. Bulk beans should be sorted over carefully and broken or defective beans discarded; they should then be washed in several changes of cold water until the water is clear. Most recipes call for dried beans to be soaked before cooking. There are two methods of doing this.

For the overnight method, measure the beans in a cup measure and place them in a deep bowl. Add $2\frac{1}{2}$ to 3 cups water for each cup of beans. Soak overnight. If at all possible, use the nutritious soaking water for cooking the beans or in the recipe. For the quick method, measure beans in a cup measure and place in a deep pan. Add $2\frac{1}{2}$ to 3 cups water for each cup of beans. Bring to boiling point and boil for 2 minutes. Remove from heat, cover pan and let stand at room temperature for 1 to 2 hours.

Cooking time varies considerably for the different kinds of

beans, from approximately 45 minutes for small whites to $1\frac{1}{2}$ or 2 hours for some brown and red beans. Always cover beans when cooking. They may be cooked on top heat or in the oven: long, slow cooking in the oven makes the best beans. Do not cook beans quickly or over high heat because this breaks their skins. Simmer over low heat to keep them whole and flavourful. Do not over-cook beans.

Salt beans only when cooked; salt slows their cooking because it toughens them. Acids, like wine, vinegar, tomatoes and lemon juice, also slow down the softening process. Add them only when the beans are almost cooked.

A ham bone, sliced or cut-up bacon, chopped onion, garlic, celery, green pepper, carrots, herbs, in reasonable quantities, added to the beans when cooking, will add flavour to them.

When making a salad of cooked dried beans, add the dressing to the drained, *hot* beans. This adds greatly to the flavour of the salad.

Cooked beans and bean dishes freeze well. Left-over beans can also be reheated or made into soup.

One measure of raw dried beans will make about 2 to $2\frac{1}{2}$ measures cooked.

Flageolet Bretonne

6 servings
This dish may be made with flageolet *beans or any small white beans. It is an excellent accompaniment for lamb and pork dishes.*

500 g (1 lb) dried *flageolet* beans, soaked and ready to cook
1 onion, stuck with 1 clove
1 medium carrot, scraped
$\frac{1}{2}$ a celery stalk
a *bouquet garni* ($\frac{1}{2}$ tsp dried thyme, 3 sprigs parsley, 1 bay leaf) tied together in a small piece of cheesecloth

water
30 g (1 oz) butter
1 large onion, chopped fine
250 g ($\frac{1}{2}$ lb) tomatoes, peeled and chopped
$\frac{1}{2}$ tsp dried thyme
salt
freshly ground pepper
2 tbsps finely chopped parsley

Put the beans into a large saucepan. Add the onion, the carrot, the celery and the *bouquet garni*. Add water to cover plus 7 cm

(3 inches). Bring to boiling point. Lower the heat and simmer, covered, for 45 minutes to 1 hour or until the beans are tender. Remove the onion, the carrot, the celery and the *bouquet garni*. Drain and reserve the cooking liquid. Heat the butter in a casserole. Add the second onion and cook, stirring constantly, until it is golden; do not brown. Add the tomatoes and the thyme. Cook for 5 more minutes, stirring frequently. Add the beans and a little of their cooking liquid, beginning with 2 tablespoons. Season with salt and pepper. Stir gently with a fork to mix well. Simmer, covered, over low heat for 10 to 15 minutes. Check for moisture; if necessary, add a little more of the bean liquid. Sprinkle with the parsley and serve very hot.

Tuscan Beans

4–6 servings
The dish should be well flavoured with sage.

350 g (12 oz) dried white beans, soaked and ready to cook	salt
water	freshly ground pepper
30 g (1 oz) butter	4 tbsps fresh tomato pulp
3 tbsps olive oil	
2–3 tbsps finely chopped fresh sage or 1–1½ tsps dried or ground sage	

Cook beans in boiling water to cover plus 7 cm (3 inches) for 45 minutes to 1 hour or until the beans are tender. This must be done over very low heat to prevent the beans from bursting open. Do not salt or the beans will be tough. Drain the beans. Heat together the butter and the olive oil. Add the beans, the sage and salt and pepper to taste. Cook over medium heat for about 3 minutes, stirring with a fork so as not to break the beans. Add the tomato pulp and cook for 3 minutes longer or until sauce and beans are very hot.

Black Beans

6 servings

500 g (1 lb) dried black beans
1½ l (2½ pts) water
1 medium onion, chopped
2 garlic cloves, chopped
1 tsp ground cumin (optional)
1 tsp ground thyme

500 g (1 lb) ham hocks or slab
bacon, in one piece, soaked
overnight
salt
freshly ground pepper
sour cream

Wash and drain the beans. Put them into a large casserole of a size that will go into the oven. Add the water, the onion, the garlic, the cumin, the thyme and the hocks. Cover and cook in a slow oven (Gas 1, 290° F, 145° C) for about 8 hours or until the beans are tender. At serving time, remove the meat. Skim off as much fat as possible. Or chill, skim off fat and reheat slowly in the oven. Season with salt and pepper. Serve with sour cream on the side.

Ranch Style Speckled Beans

4–6 servings

500 g (1 lb) dried speckled beans,
soaked and ready to cook
water
2 large tomatoes, peeled and
chopped
1 medium onion, chopped
2 garlic cloves
½ hot chili pepper, peeled, seeded
and chopped or Tabasco sauce
to taste

½ tsp ground cumin
2 tbsps olive oil
juice of 1 lemon
salt
freshly ground pepper

Put the beans into a large saucepan. Add water to cover plus 7 cm (3 inches). Bring to boiling point. Lower the heat and simmer, covered, for about 1 hour or until the beans are almost tender. Drain and reserve the cooking liquid. Return the beans to the saucepan and add the tomatoes, the onion, the garlic, the chili pepper, the cumin, the olive oil and the lemon juice. Simmer,

covered, over low heat, stirring frequently, until the beans are
tender. Season with salt and pepper. Check for moisture; if
necessary, add a little of the cooking liquid to prevent scorching.
Serve very hot.

Red Beans in Red Wine

6 servings

500 g (1 lb) dried kidney beans,
soaked and ready to cook
1 onion, stuck with 1 clove
1 garlic clove
a *bouquet garni* (1 tsp dried
thyme, 3 sprigs parsley, 1 bay
leaf) tied together in a small
piece of cheesecloth

110 g (4 oz) lean bacon, in one
piece
6 dl (1 pt) dry red wine
6 dl (1 pt) water
salt
freshly ground pepper
30 g (1 oz) butter

Put the beans into a large casserole. Add the onion, the garlic, the
bouquet garni, the bacon, the wine and the water. Bring to boiling
point and lower the heat to very low. Simmer, covered, for 1 to 2
hours or until the beans are tender. Remove the onion and the
bouquet garni and throw away. Remove the bacon. Drain the
beans and season with salt and pepper. Turn into a heated serving
dish and keep hot. Cut the bacon into small dice. Heat the butter
in a small frying pan and cook the diced bacon for 2 to 3 minutes.
Add the bacon to the beans and mix well. Serve very hot.

Endive

(Cichorium endivia)

Endive is a variety of chicory which grows in a loose head, with crisp, narrow, white or rose-tinted ribs with ragged-edged leaves which curl at the end. It has a pleasantly bitter flavour and is used as a salad green and potherb. The long, fleshy taproot, which tastes somewhat like parsnip, can be boiled or braised like any other root vegetable.

Endive is a weed, originating probably in China or other parts of Asia, but native also to the Mediterranean and found wild in other parts of Europe. Both wild and cultivated it has been used for centuries for human food and animal fodder. It is described as a salad green and potherb in ancient Roman writings, and was known as such in England during the Middle Ages but probably was not cultivated before the sixteenth century. The English Navy used to grow 'succory' in pierced barrels for salading.

Two types are grown commercially. The curly-leaved one is the earlier of the two; the sturdy batavias, with broader leaves, are a winter vegetable. Both are usually blanched by shutting the grown plant off from the sunlight for its last weeks in the ground. The broad-leafed variety, also known as escarole, is more often used as a cooked vegetable than its curly cousin, and the recipes given here for its use in cooking are southern European ones.

The very pretty, red-tinged and broad-leafed Italian variety, much appreciated for salads on the Continent, is hard to come by in England but as 'Red Verona' is easy to grow in home gardens.

How to buy

Buy clean, tightly-packed heads with crisp, bright and unblemished greens. Avoid wilted or flabby heads and greens with blight spots or insect damage.

How to keep

Treat like any fresh greens and use as soon as possible. Refrigerate unwashed greens in a plastic bag. Uncooked, on refrigerator shelf: 2 days. Cooked and covered, on refrigerator shelf: 1 to 2 days.

Nutritive values

Fresh endive is an excellent source of vitamin A, a fair one of iron. Raw: 20 calories per 100 g ($3\frac{1}{2}$ oz).

How to use

For salad use, trim and wash the endive as any other fresh salad greens. Large leaves may be torn into smaller pieces. Dry well and chill before using.

To cook as a vegetable, trim and wash the endive. Drop into boiling salted water, cook for 1 minute and drain. This removes the bitterness and may be repeated. Serve with melted butter, lemon or herbs, as any other leafy green vegetable. Alternatively, put the washed and trimmed endive in a pan with a little butter. Cook, stirring constantly, for about 2 minutes. Season with salt and pepper and simmer, covered, for 5 minutes. Check the moisture; if necessary, add a tablespoon of water at a time.

Add cut endives to soups, stews or casserole dishes: the slightly bitter flavour improves these dishes.

Stir-Fried Endive

4 servings

4 slices bacon
30 g (1 oz) sesame seeds
 (optional)
4 to 6 spring onions, thinly
 sliced
60 g (2 oz) mushrooms, thinly
 sliced

1 medium head endive, trimmed,
 washed and coarsely shredded
salt
freshly ground pepper

Cook the bacon in a large frying pan until crisp. Drain and

crumble. Cook the sesame seeds in the bacon fat, stirring constantly, until they are golden. Add the onions, the mushrooms and the endive. Season with salt and pepper. Cook over high heat, stirring constantly, for 3 minutes or until the endive is tender but crisp. Sprinkle with the bacon and serve very hot.

Roman Braised Endive

4 servings

3 tbsps olive oil	2 heads endive, coarsely chopped
1 large garlic clove, sliced	and washed
6 anchovy fillets, chopped, or 2	salt
tbsps anchovy paste	freshly ground pepper
3 medium tomatoes, peeled and	hot water or beef stock
chopped	

Heat the olive oil in a deep frying pan. Cook the garlic in it until it is brown; discard the garlic. Add the anchovy and cook, stirring constantly, for about 2 minutes. Add the tomatoes and cook for 2 minutes more. Add the endive and mix well. Check the seasoning; if necessary, add a little salt and pepper. Simmer, covered, over low heat for about 10 minutes or until the vegetable is cooked, but still crisp. Stir frequently and check for moisture; if necessary to prevent scorching, add a little hot water or stock, 2 tablespoons at a time.

Endive and Rice Soup

6 servings

1 dl (4 fl oz) olive oil	2 l (3½ pts) hot chicken stock or
1 garlic clove, sliced	water
1 medium tomato, peeled and	2 tsps salt
chopped	250 g (8 oz) long-grain rice
1 large head escarole, trimmed,	freshly grated Parmesan cheese
washed and coarsely shredded	

Heat the olive oil in a soup pot. Brown the garlic in the oil and discard. Add the tomato and the escarole. Cook, stirring constantly, for about 3 to 4 minutes or until the escarole is soft. Add the stock or water and the salt. Bring to the boil and add the rice. Lower the heat. Simmer, covered, stirring frequently, for about 10 to 15 minutes or until the rice is cooked. Serve with plenty of freshly grated Parmesan cheese.

Fennel

(Foeniculum vulgare)

The common fennel, to translate its botanical name, is an aromatic plant native to the Mediterranean and even to the cliffs of southern England and Wales. It is a tall perennial, grown for its fine feathery leaves, which are used to flavour foods as dill weed is used, and for its very aromatic seeds, which are also used as flavouring in the way dill seeds are used. Fennel oil is used

medically and for soaps and perfumes. The stalks, fresh and dried, are used as fuel for grills since they flavour grilled foods such as fish deliciously.

The cultivated variety, *Foeniculum vulgare* var. *dulce*, also known as sweet or French or Florence fennel, is the one that concerns us more, as a salad plant and a vegetable. This fennel is a bulbous vegetable, composed of broad leaf stalks which overlap each other at the base of the stem, forming a bulb which is firm, white, crisp and 7 to 10 cm (3 to 4 inches) across. The stalks end in feathery bright-green leaves which can grow to a height of about 60 cm (2 feet). Since there are several leaf stalks to each bulb, fennel looks somewhat like a hand with feathery fingers. The flavour of the bulb and the leaves is reminiscent of that of liquorice or of anise, but the plant has nothing else in common with the herb anise (*Pimpinella anisum*) which produces the seed used in baking and sweets.

Throughout the centuries fennel was used not only for eating, but to cure eye trouble, draw poison and increase the milk supply of nursing mothers. It was held in the highest esteem in England. Poor folk used fennel to still the pangs of hunger and to make food palatable, or, for a treat, they coated fennel seeds with sugar and ate them like sweets. In Shakespearean England, fennel stood for flattery; in Italy, the word *finocchio*, applied to a man, means that he is a homosexual.

How to buy

Buy firm, crisp bulbs with no more than one coarse outer branch and with at least 20-cm (8-inch) tops which ensure succulence. The colour of the bulb should be a very pale greenish-white with fresh-looking green tops. Avoid soft, coarse bulbs with brownish-edged bases and stalks and wilted tops, and discoloured or cracked bulbs.

Allow one medium bulb for two servings.

How to keep

Wrap bulb and stalks in plastic bag and refrigerate. Raw, on refrigerator shelf: 3 to 4 days. Cooked and covered, on refrigerator shelf: 2 days.

Nutritive values

All fennel is rich in vitamin A and a good source of potassium and calcium. Raw: 28 calories per 100 g ($3\frac{1}{2}$ oz).

How to use

Fresh fennel leaves or the leafy tips are used for garnishes and, chopped, to add flavour to salads, stews and other dishes, in the manner of dill weed.

Fennel seeds are used to spice soups, stews, sauces and especially fish dishes, as well as pies, buns and breads; they are also one of the spices used in Indian curries and for pickling.

Fennel is eaten raw as an appetizer or as a salad, or is cooked as a vegetable. Do not cut off the feathery tops until the fennel is used. To prepare, cut off feathery tops and remove the tough outer stalks. Wash and drain. Cut off hard base. If it is to be used for an appetizer or a salad, cut into slices, cutting with the grain. Place on a serving dish, sprinkle with salt and pepper, and dribble over it a little olive oil and, if desired, a little lemon juice or vinegar. If the fennel is to be cooked, cut it into halves or quarters lengthwise, according to size. Place in a saucepan and add boiling salted water or stock to cover. Cook, covered, for 5 minutes or until tender but still firm. Dress with butter and serve.

Fennel à la Grecque

4–6 servings
Serve as an hors d'œuvre or with cold roast chicken.

1 bottle dry white wine
4 tbsps olive oil
2 tbsps tomato paste
grated rind of 1 lemon
1 bay leaf
8 coriander seeds, or more to taste

½ tsp dried thyme
salt
freshly ground pepper
4 large heads fennel, trimmed and cut into quarters

Combine all the ingredients except the fennel in a heavy casserole. Bring to the boil. Reduce heat to very low and add the fennel. Simmer, covered, for 15 to 20 minutes or until the fennel is tender but still firm, then transfer it to a deep serving dish. Over high heat, cook the pan liquid until it is reduced by a third; this intensifies the flavour. Pour over the fennel and chill before serving.

Fennel au Gratin

4 servings
Serve with grilled meats.

4 large or 6 medium or 8 small heads fennel, trimmed
boiling salted water or chicken stock
salt

freshly ground pepper
110 g (4 oz) butter, melted
60 g (2 oz) freshly grated Parmesan cheese

Cut large or medium fennel heads into quarters lengthwise; cut small ones into halves lengthwise. Cook in boiling water or stock to cover for about 5 minutes, or until barely tender. Drain thoroughly. Place half of the fennel in a buttered shallow baking dish. Sprinkle with a little salt (the cheese is salty) and pepper, half of the butter and half of the grated cheese. Top with the remaining fennel, butter and cheese (no more salt is needed). Cook in a preheated hot oven (Gas 6, 400° F, 210° C) for about 10 minutes or until the top is golden brown.

Fennel and Mushrooms

4–6 servings
Instead of fennel, you could use 2 medium artichokes, thinly sliced.

2 large heads fennel, trimmed
30 g (1 oz) butter
2 tbsps olive oil
1 garlic clove
1 large tomato, peeled and chopped

500 g (1 lb) mushrooms, sliced
3 tbsps hot chicken stock
salt
freshly ground pepper
½ tsp dried thyme

Cut the fennel into thin slices lengthwise. Heat the butter and the olive oil in a saucepan. Cook the garlic in it until browned; discard. Add the tomato and the fennel. Simmer, covered, stirring frequently, for 5 minutes or until the fennel is half tender. Add the mushrooms and the stock, and season with salt and pepper and the thyme. Simmer, covered, over low heat for about 10 minutes or until the vegetables are tender but still firm. There should be just a little sauce in the dish since mushrooms release water during cooking; you may have to simmer it without a cover to reduce the cooking liquid.

French Bean, Snap, String or Green Bean, Runner Bean

(Phaseolus vulgaris, Phaseolus coccineus)

French beans, of which there are many varieties, are the most popular of fresh beans. Snap beans, which grow on low or tall bushes, apparently originated in tropical Central America and spread to both North and South America long before the white man came; they had been cultivated there before the Toltecs (seventh to eleventh centuries A.D.). Early North American explorers found that climbing beans were generally planted along with corn all over America. The first drawing of a bush bean was made as early as 1542, looking very much like varieties found today.

Green beans were, and still are, known as string beans, for reasons which may seem obvious but all the same bring pain to their growers who have spent a great deal of time and money to make them as stringless as possible (the first so-called stringless beans appeared in 1894). In Britain the scarlet runner is the most popular climbing bean; it was introduced into Britain as a decorative plant during the first half of the seventeenth century (the 'scarlet' in its name refers to its very pretty flower, not to the bean). Not until the latter half of the nineteenth century did it become a common food plant, a perennial which is usually grown as an annual. The beans grow easily in home gardens, especially the popular dwarf varieties ('Hammond's Dwarf' has either scarlet or white flowers). The most exquisite of all green beans are the little, sliver-like, dark-green beans found in France and Italy.

How to buy

Buy smooth, crisp pods that snap easily and which are free from blemishes and spots. The pods should be well filled but with immature seeds.

Avoid flabby or wilted pods, discoloured, blemished pods and thick, fibrous pods which are too mature.

How to keep

Put unwashed beans into plastic bags and refrigerate. Use as soon as possible, because time toughens and discolours the beans. Raw, on refrigerator shelf: 3 to 4 days. Cooked and covered, on refrigerator shelf: 1 to 3 days.

Nutritive values

Cooked for a short time in a small amount of water, snap and green beans are a fair source of vitamins A and B, and rate 25 calories per 100 g ($3\frac{1}{2}$ oz).

How to use

The way beans are cut affects their flavour and their cooking time. When ready to use, wash beans well in cold water. Snip off stems and tops. Beans may be left whole, snapped, cut straight across in convenient pieces, or cut Chinese-style in long slanting slices or French-style in thin slivers. Green beans may be cooked in quantities of boiling salted water (the French way), drained, rapidly rinsed in cold water and drained again before being finished as in recipe directions. Alternatively, cook small or cut beans in about 3 to 5 cm (1 to 2 inches) water with about $\frac{1}{2}$ teaspoon salt per pound of beans. Bring to the boil, cook vigorously without a cover for 2 to 4 minutes to retain the colour, then cover tightly and cook until barely tender. Young, cut beans may take as little as 3 minutes, large, mature ones as much as 15 or more minutes. Cooking time depends on the variety, the age and the size of the beans.

Cook beans for the shortest possible time, only until just tender but still crisp and bright green. Overcooked beans are mushy and flavourless.

Cook frozen green beans according to package directions, but in many cases the recommended cooking time is too long and overcooks the beans. Reheat tinned beans quickly in a little of their own liquid, just enough to prevent scorching.

Green Beans Lyonnaise

4 servings

1 kg (2 lb) green beans, trimmed and washed	½ tsp dried thyme
	salt
60 g (2 oz) butter	freshly ground pepper
1 large onion, chopped fine	2 tbsps finely chopped parsley

Cook the beans in boiling salted water until tender but still crisp. While the beans are cooking, heat the butter in a frying pan. Add the onion. Cook, stirring constantly, for 3 to 5 minutes or until the onion is tender and golden. Drain the beans and add them to the frying pan. Stir in the thyme and salt and pepper. Cook over medium heat for about 3 to 4 minutes, stirring with a fork to coat the beans with the onion. Sprinkle with parsley and serve hot.

Green Beans with Cheese

4 servings

1 kg (2 lb) green beans, trimmed and washed	salt
	freshly ground pepper
60 g (2 oz) butter	
110 g (4 oz) grated Gruyère or other hard cheese	

Cook the beans in boiling salted water until tender but still crisp. Drain. Heat the butter in an oven-to-table frying pan or in a

shallow baking dish placed on an asbestos mat to prevent crack-
ing. Add the beans. Cook over medium heat, stirring constantly,
for about 3 to 5 minutes. Sprinkle with the cheese and add a little
salt (the cheese is salty) and pepper. Mix well. In a moment,
there will be a golden crust at the bottom of the pan and the beans
are ready to serve.

Green Beans Provençale

4 servings

1 kg (2 lb) green beans, trimmed and washed	salt
	freshly ground pepper
2 tbsps olive oil	3 tbsps finely chopped fresh
30 g (1 oz) butter	basil or 1–2 tbsps dried basil
1 large onion, very thinly sliced	3 tbsps finely chopped parsley
1 garlic clove, crushed	
2 large tomatoes, peeled, seeded and chopped	

Cook the beans in boiling salted water for 5 minutes. Drain and
plunge into a bowl of cold water. Drain again. Heat the olive oil
and the butter in a frying pan. Add the onion and the garlic and
cook for 5 minutes until the onion is soft. Add the tomatoes, salt,
pepper, the basil and the parsley. Cook, stirring frequently, for
about 5 minutes. Add the beans and mix well. Cook, covered,
for 3 to 5 minutes or until the beans are just tender.

Garlic

(Allium sativum)

This most pungent and famous of all flavourings is a plant that, together with chives, onions, leeks and shallots, belongs to the lily family. Its edible part, like that of the onion, lies underground, consisting of a compound bulb made up from an unpredictable number of white or purplish almond-shaped segments called cloves which are enclosed in a thin common skin. Each of the

cloves is also enclosed in its own skin. The garlic flowers, a tiny mass of white blooms at the end of a stem that can reach the height of 90 cm (3 feet), do not produce seeds suitable for propagation: this has to be achieved by planting the cloves. The bulbs are harvested when

the tops are beginning to dry out, and often the dried tops are left on to be plaited into garlands or tied into bunches, a decorative and practical way of storing garlic, popular in French and Italian kitchens.

Garlic has been cultivated in both temperate and hot climates for thousands of years. Its origin is obscure, but it appears to have originated in southern Asia and the Mediterranean. The slaves who built the pyramids of ancient Egypt are said to have lived on garlic and onions. The Israelites in the Wilderness spoke about a lack of garlic to Moses (Numbers XI:5), Homer makes it part of the entertainment Nestor served to Machaon, and the Romans, who did not like its smell but believed in its strength, fed it to their soldiers and labourers. In thirteenth-century China, Marco Polo observed that the higher classes ate their meat preserved in several spices whereas the poor ate theirs steeped in garlic juice. Throughout the centuries, garlic served medicinal purposes. Ancient and medieval herbals speak of its power to cure toothache, dog bites, poisoned-arrow wounds, the plague and skin diseases, to mention just a few disorders and illnesses, and the belief in garlic's power to repel evil has been strong since antiquity.

Garlic has long been an essential in Mediterranean and some Far Eastern cooking. It would be impossible to think of the cookery of Provence or of some Italian cooking without the presence of the potent bulb. In England it has never been all that popular, at least partly because of pure misuse. Even the *Oxford English Dictionary* attributes to garlic 'a very strong smell, and an acrid, pungent taste', but neither is necessarily true. Its power varies according to the ways in which it is used. Peeled, raw garlic, crushed in a garlic press, is indeed unbearable; it might be said that the garlic press was invented for just this purpose: to bring out the 'acrid, pungent taste' any lover of garlic objects to. If raw garlic is to be crushed, it is best done with whole cloves in a pestle and mortar. Add a little salt if the bits are too lumpy (but remember to use less salt in your recipe later). If garlic is to be used only to flavour butter or oil, it is best sliced for maximum effectiveness. On no account should the oil be too hot: gentle cooking gives a gentle taste. When garlic is cooked – that is, boiled, steamed, sautéed or roasted with food – it will be a different thing. Peeled garlic, unbruised so as not to release its volatile oils, and cooked whole, assumes a sweet, nut-like flavour. These cooked cloves may be crushed or left whole in the dish they belong to. They will leave no odour on your breath. Dishes containing forty garlic cloves or more sound terrifying, whereas in practice they are often subtle gourmet fare.

Large quantities of garlic are processed into flakes, powders and salts, to be sold as fresh-garlic substitutes; but, however great their convenience, they are no match for the real thing, and they will always have the same synthetic flavour.

How to buy

Buy firm, plump bulbs which are heavy for their size. Their skins should be clean, dry and unbroken. Buy small amounts at a time unless you can buy strings of French garlic shortly after the harvest. Avoid soft bulbs with broken skins, dried out, dirty or shrivelled bulbs, or bulbs that are sprouting.

How to keep

Keep garlic away from other foods. Place in a small open pot or basket and keep in a cool, dry, well-ventilated place. Do not refrigerate. Cool, dry place: 1 month.

Nutritive values

Garlic contains only a negligible amount of minerals. Raw, unpeeled, about 3 bulbs: 137 calories (which sounds more than it is as this quantity breaks up into at least two dozen fair-sized cloves).

How to use

Peel garlic just before using. Rub a salad bowl with a peeled, cut garlic clove. Drop a peeled clove into French dressing for 24 hours (then remove, since it will deteriorate). Add peeled garlic cloves to soups, stews and casseroles and, if desired, remove with a slotted spoon before serving. If a large quantity of garlic is to be peeled, drop unpeeled bulb into boiling water and cook for 2 minutes. Drain and peel. For sauces, cook a few cloves of blanched garlic in butter over low heat for 10 minutes or until very tender. Crush and add to sauces. Never allow garlic to brown or it will be bitter.

The following three garlic sauces are all 'more-or-less' cookery.

Bagna Cauda

A sauce or dip from Piedmont, meaning literally 'hot bath'. Use it as a dip for raw vegetables, or as a sauce for plain, hot, cooked vegetables, boiled fish or meats. The sauce must *never* brown nor boil.

110 g (4 oz) butter
4 tbsps olive oil
6 garlic cloves, sliced paper thin,
  or to taste

60 g (2 oz) anchovy fillets,
  chopped fine

Over lowest possible heat (use an asbestos mat), cook together the butter, the olive oil and the garlic for 15 minutes. Stir in the anchovies. Cook, stirring constantly, until the anchovies have dissolved. Keep hot over a candle-warmer or chafing-dish lamp.

Pesto

This Genovese basil sauce is commonly used as a pasta sauce: the quantity given here will make 6 to 8 helpings for a main course. However, a tablespoon ladled into a dish of hot soup, preferably vegetable soup, improves the soup immensely. The basil *must* be fresh. The sauce can also be made in larger quantities and stored in a jar topped with a closing layer of olive oil.

3–5 garlic cloves
110 g (4 oz) fresh basil leaves
60 g (2 oz) grated Parmesan
  cheese

4–6 tbsps olive oil
60 g (2 oz) pine nuts
salt

Pound the garlic and the basil together in a mortar. Pound in the grated cheese, turning always in the same direction, together with a drop or two of oil to make the mixture stick together. Pound in the nuts and a little more oil. Stir in the remaining oil, a few drops at a time, until you have used 4 tablespoons. If a thinner sauce is wanted, stir in the remaining oil. Check seasoning, and add salt if necessary.

The sauce may be made in a blender almost as satisfactorily, but a blended sauce has a different consistency from one made in a mortar. For the blender sauce: Combine all the ingredients and 4 tablespoons of the oil in a blender. Purée and scrape down the sides with a rubber spatula. If too thick, add the remaining oil and purée again.

Aïoli

The famous garlic mayonnaise of Provence is used as a dip for fresh or cooked vegetables and as an accompaniment for roast meat. It should not be made in a blender, because blender mayonnaise does not have the thick, silken consistency that is its great virtue. Use a stone mortar and a wooden pestle and have the egg yolks and the oil at room temperature; this is important. Or make the mayonnaise in the traditional way, in a bowl, with a wooden spoon.

4–6 large garlic cloves, peeled
¼ tsp salt
2 egg yolks, lightly beaten
about 5 dl (a scant pint) olive
   oil, or half olive oil and half
   groundnut oil (the mixture
   makes for a lighter aïoli)

lukewarm water
juice of 1 lemon

Pound the garlic cloves and salt to a smooth paste. Add the egg yolks. Mix with the pestle, always turning in one direction, until the garlic and eggs have assimilated and are just beginning to get pale. While beating the garlic and the eggs, add about 4 tablespoons of the oil very, very slowly, drop by drop, in a steady stream, never stopping turning the pestle in the same direction. The mixture should be thick. Add 1 teaspoon of water and 1 teaspoon of lemon juice and continue turning the pestle, adding the oil in a very thin stream. When the mixture gets too thick again, add 1 more teaspoon each of lukewarm water and lemon juice. Repeat until the desired consistency is reached and the oil has been used.

If the mayonnaise separates, all is not lost. Put the mayonnaise into a clean bowl. Wash and dry the mortar and pestle. Add a garlic clove, a pinch of salt, 1 teaspoon of lukewarm water and 1 egg yolk. Crush and mix together. Add the separated mayonnaise, a teaspoon at a time, to the mortar, turning the pestle constantly in the same direction.

Garlic Chicken

6 servings

In spite of the large number of garlic cloves, this dish is fragrant rather than offensive.

3 tbsps salad oil	freshly ground pepper
1 large onion, diced	juice of 2 lemons
2 large carrots, sliced	20–30 garlic cloves, peeled but
4 celery stalks, sliced	left whole and unbruised
1½–2 kg (3–4 lb) chicken, cut into pieces	6 slices buttered toast or fried bread
salt	

Heat the oil in a frying pan. Cook the onion, the carrots and the celery in it, stirring constantly, until they are soft. With a slotted spoon, transfer the vegetables to a casserole with a tight-fitting lid or to a clay pot. Remove any fat from the chicken pieces and, if desired, skin them. Lay the chicken pieces on top of the vegetables. Sprinkle with the salt, the pepper and the lemon juice. Put the garlic around and on the chicken pieces. Cover tightly; *this is essential*, because the chicken must cook in its own juices. Cook in a preheated moderate oven (Gas 4, 350° F, 180° C) for 1 hour. Do not uncover during cooking and until ready to serve. Serve each diner with some of the garlic and a slice of buttered toast. The diner can spread the toast with the garlic: it has a gentle flavour, and will neither repeat nor stay on the breath.

Grams

The word gram came into English usage very early in the eighteenth century, probably from the Portuguese *grão*. Originally it was used only for the chick pea, but it was soon extended to various other 'exotic' beans which began to be imported around the same time.

Red grams, also known as cajans in the eighteenth century, are now usually called by their Jamaican name of pigeon peas (see page 253).

Green grams are mung beans (*Phaseolus aureus*). Black grams (*Phaseolus mungo*, to confuse the issue) are also known by their Indian name, *urd*. Both mung and urd, as well as the small adzuki bean (*Phaseolus angularis*, ranging from dark red to black in colour), are among the oldest and most widely cultivated food crops of Asia – the adzuki doing particularly well in the north (Korea, Japan), the grams in the south and east. The black gram is now also grown in Africa and the West Indies.

All of these beans are highly nutritious, especially because of their high protein content. Mung beans are widely used for sprouting (see page 62). All are available here in dried form, and can be used much as other dried beans. They are especially good in soups and stews, or combined with rice.

Hearts of Palm

These are the edible inner portion of the Sabal palmetto palm tree, also known as cabbage tree. To obtain them, the outer husks of palms are stripped off and the inner layers chopped off until the edible part is reached. This is immediately placed in water to avoid darkening. Hearts of palm are off-white in colour, reasonably firm and vaguely reminiscent of artichoke in their flavour. They reach us, tinned, from Brazil or Florida. They are used as a delicate salad vegetable, in sauce or deep fried. Since they are rather bland, they need to be well seasoned any way that they are prepared.

Hearts of Palm in Lemon Butter

4–6 servings
Palm hearts are packed in tins of different sizes, but this does not matter in the following recipe: decrease or increase the butter and lemon juice depending on the amount of vegetable. It is good with fish and seafood.

60 g (2 oz) butter
500-g (16–19-oz) tin palm
   hearts, drained, thinly sliced
1 tsp grated lemon peel
1½ tbsps fresh lemon juice

salt
freshly ground pepper
1 tbsp chopped chives
1 tbsp chopped parsley

Heat the butter in a large frying pan; do not let it brown. Add the palm heart slices. Cook over very low heat, stirring carefully with a fork so as not to break the slices, until the vegetable is coated with the butter and very hot. Do not brown. Stir in the remaining ingredients and serve very hot.

Jerusalem Artichoke

(Helianthus tuberosus)

The edible parts of this native North American plant are the underground tubers, which resemble small knobbly potatoes or, even more, root ginger. These tubers vary in shape from oblong to elongated, they may be branched, their skin is very thin, with either yellowish, brown or pinkish tinges, and the flesh is white and crisp with a sweetish flavour all its own.

Jerusalem artichokes are no relation whatsoever of the globe artichoke. Why they were called so I do not know, except that their flavour resembles vaguely that of globe artichokes. Nor have they anything to do with Jerusalem; their name is an adaptation of the Italian *girasole* (sunflower), which is not surprising since the Jerusalem artichoke plant is indeed a 2- to 3½-metre (7- to 12-foot) tall sunflower which 'turns to the sun' as the Italian name says.

Jerusalem artichokes had been cultivated for centuries by the North American Indians before the plant was introduced to Europe around 1616. It always has been cultivated much more extensively in France than in this country; Parkinson records in 1629 that 'the French brought them first from Canada into these parts'. He calls them 'potatoes of Canada', a name which later made way for 'girasol' after the original Italian.

How to buy

Buy firm tubers that are free from mould, have a clean skin and are heavy for their size. Avoid soft, wrinkled, blemished tubers.

How to keep

Store in a cool, dry, well-ventilated place, or refrigerate in a plastic bag. Raw, in a cool, dry place or on refrigerator shelf. 1 week. Cooked and covered, on refrigerator shelf. 2 days.

Nutritive values

Jerusalem artichokes contain few nutrients. Their sweetness is due to insulin, a sugar which can be eaten by diabetics. Their caloric values change from approximately 7 calories for 100 g (3½ oz) of freshly-harvested tubers to approximately 75 calories for the same amount of long-stored tubers.

How to use

Jerusalem artichokes can be served raw as appetizers or salad; when raw they have a sweet, nut-like taste. Or they can be served cooked as a vegetable. To prepare, scrub with a vegetable brush or peel with a vegetable peeler. Do not worry about any skin that remains between the knobs because when cooked it will be like the skin of new potatoes. Jerusalem artichokes, when cut, discolour easily. Drop cut pieces into cold water as you work. Cook them whole, or slice, dice or cut them into strips, or bake them in their jackets.

Cook cut-up Jerusalem artichokes, covered, in 2 to 3 cm (1 inch) boiling salted water for 5 to 8 minutes. Do not overcook or the vegetable will be mushy. Season with salt and pepper and dress with butter and lemon juice.

Cream of Jerusalem Artichoke Soup

4–5 servings

1 kg (2 lb) Jerusalem artichokes, peeled and sliced
2 medium onions, sliced
60 g (2 oz) butter
6 dl (1 pt) hot water or chicken stock
salt

freshly ground pepper
4½ dl (¾ pt) milk, heated
2½ dl (8 fl oz) single cream, heated
⅛ tsp ground cardamom (optional)
30 g (1 oz) slivered toasted almonds

Combine the Jerusalem artichokes, the onions and most of the butter in a saucepan. Cover tightly and cook over low heat, stirring frequently, for about 8 to 10 minutes. Add the hot water or stock and salt and pepper to taste. Cook 10 minutes longer.

Purée in a blender or strain through a sieve. Return to the saucepan. Stir in the milk, the cream, the remaining butter and the cardamom. Heat through, but do not boil. Sprinkle with toasted almonds before serving.

Jerusalem Artichokes à la Crème

4 servings

6 dl (1 pt) water	1 tbsp olive oil
juice of 1 lemon	1½ dl (¼ pt) double cream
1 tbsp flour	salt
500 g (1 lb) Jerusalem artichokes	freshly ground pepper
60 g (2 oz) butter	⅛ tsp ground nutmeg, or to taste

Combine the water, the lemon juice and the flour in a saucepan. Bring to boiling point and lower the heat to medium. Scrub, wash and drain the Jerusalem artichokes. Drop into the water and cook for about 10 minutes or until almost tender. Drain. Heat the butter and oil in a frying pan. Add the Jerusalem artichokes and cook, stirring with a fork, for about 3 to 4 minutes or until they are well coated with the butter. Stir in all but about 2 tablespoons of the cream. Season with the salt and pepper and the nutmeg. Cook, shaking the pan to prevent sticking, until the cream has thickened and reduced to about half. Stir in the remaining cream and heat through briefly. Turn into a heated dish and serve immediately.

Jerusalem Artichokes Polonaise

4 servings

8 large Jerusalem artichokes, cooked and peeled	60 g (2 oz) butter
salt	60 g (2 oz) fine, dry, white breadcrumbs
freshly ground pepper	1 tbsp finely chopped parsley

Cut the Jerusalem artichokes into slices or strips. Season with salt and pepper to taste. Heat the butter in a frying pan. Cook the breadcrumbs, stirring constantly, until they are golden. Add the

Jerusalem artichokes and toss until heated through. Serve in a hot dish, and sprinkle with the parsley.

White Beans and Jerusalem Artichokes

6 servings

1 kg (2 lb) Jerusalem artichokes, prepared for cooking
salted water
2 tbsps olive oil
1 garlic clove, chopped
4 tbsps parsley, chopped
2 tsps dried basil

250 g (½ lb) chopped fresh tomatoes or tinned tomatoes, drained
salt
freshly ground pepper
500 g (1 lb) cooked white beans (haricot beans)

Place the Jerusalem artichokes in a saucepan with salted water to cover. Bring to boiling point and lower the heat. Simmer, covered, for about 5 minutes or until they are easily pierced with a knife. Drain and cool. Cut into thick slices. Heat the oil in a large, deep frying pan. Cook the garlic, parsley and basil in it for 2 minutes. Add the tomatoes and season with salt and pepper. Cook over medium heat, stirring frequently, for about 5 to 10 minutes. Add the beans and the Jerusalem artichokes. Mix together gently with a fork and simmer until thoroughly heated through.

Kale

(Brassica oleracea var. *acephala)*

Kale and collards are the members of the cabbage family which most closely resemble cabbage in its wild form. Unlike cabbage, kale does not form a head, but consists of a bunch of coarse, loose leaves with curly or crisped edges. It is a prolific and extremely healthy vegetable, which improves after a frost has hit it, with a robust flavour that does not appeal to all. 'Kale' as a word is a northern equivalent of 'cole', originally the generic name for the whole cabbage group, later applied mostly to the non-hearting ones. The Scottish version of the word, 'kail', by extension simply means dinner.

Kale and collards are ancient vegetables, known for some 2,000 years in the Mediterranean world where they originated, and taken from there to the other parts of Europe, where they became popular in cool countries such as Germany. The first English mention of the variety called curly kale, which is the most popular nowadays, dates from the early eighteenth century and uses the name 'borecole' derived from Dutch *boerenkool* meaning 'peasant's cabbage'.

How to buy

Buy crisp leaves with a good dark-green colour. Avoid wilted, bruised or crushed leaves.

How to keep

Use as soon as possible. Refrigerate unwashed in plastic bag or vegetable drawer. Raw, on refrigerator shelf: 2 to 3 days. Cooked and covered, on refrigerator shelf: 2 to 3 days.

Nutritive values

Kale is valuable for an extremely high content of vitamin A and a good supply of calcium and other minerals. Raw, leaves and stems: 38 calories; cooked: 28 calories (per 100 g/3½ oz).

How to use

Remove tough outer leaves and thick midribs. Cut large leaves into pieces. Wash thoroughly and shake dry. Cook, covered, in a little boiling salted water for 5 to 10 minutes; do not overcook or kale will be mushy and lose flavour. Season with salt and pepper and melted butter. The robust flavour of kale goes well with foods like sausages and bacon.

Creamed Kale

4 servings
A Danish recipe, to serve with pork.

1 kg (2 lb) kale	2½ dl (8 fl oz) single cream
1 tsp salt	salt
water	freshly ground pepper
60 g (2 oz) butter	⅛ tsp ground nutmeg or more to
4 tbsps flour	taste
2½ dl (8 fl oz) milk	

Cut off the tough stalks and cut the kale leaves into bite-sized pieces. Wash and drain. Put the kale into a saucepan and sprinkle with the teaspoon of salt. Add just enough water to cover. Bring to the boil and cook, covered, for about 5 to 10 minutes or until just tender. Drain well and chop the kale. Heat the butter and stir in the flour. Cook, stirring constantly, for about 2 minutes. Stir in the milk and the cream. Cook over low heat, stirring all the while, for about 5 minutes. Cook for a further 5 minutes, stirring frequently, to remove the raw taste of the flour. The sauce should be smooth and thick. Season with the salt and pepper and stir in the nutmeg. Add the kale. Heat through thoroughly.

Colcannon

4–6 servings

A tasty Irish dish, traditionally eaten on Hallowe'en. The kale and the potatoes must be cooked separately and, preferably, be freshly cooked.

500 g (1 lb) potatoes, peeled and cut into quarters
boiling salted water
750 g (1½ lb) kale, trimmed, shredded, washed and drained
1½–2½ dl (5–8 fl oz) milk or single cream

2 leeks, trimmed, sliced, washed and drained
salt
freshly ground pepper
⅛ tsp ground mace
110 g (4 oz) butter, melted

Cook the potatoes in boiling salted water to cover for 10 minutes or until quite soft. Drain, mash and keep warm. While the potatoes are cooking, cook the kale in boiling salted water for 10 minutes or until soft. Drain and chop fine. Keep warm. Heat together the milk and the leeks; the milk should just cover the leeks. Cook, covered, over very low heat until the leeks are very soft and mushy. Beat the milk and the leeks into the potatoes the way you make mashed potatoes. Stir in the kale. Beat until the mixture is light green and fluffy, and has the consistency of mashed potatoes. Season with salt and pepper and mace. Turn the colcannon into a heated deep serving dish. Make a well in the centre and pour in the melted butter. Serve the vegetable with a spoonful or two of the melted butter poured over it.

Panned Kale

4 servings

750 g (1½ lb) kale, trimmed and shredded
4 slices lean bacon, cut into strips
1 medium onion, chopped fine

1 bay leaf
salt
freshly ground pepper
½ tsp dried marjoram

Wash the kale, but do not shake it dry. In a deep frying pan cook the bacon until limp. Add the onion. Cook over low heat, stirring frequently, until the onion is soft. Add the kale, the bay leaf, the salt and pepper and the marjoram and mix well. Cook, covered, over medium heat, stirring frequently, for about 10 minutes or until the kale is tender. Check the moisture; if necessary, add 1 to 2 tablespoons of water to prevent scorching.

Kohlrabi

(Brassica oleracea var. caulo-rapa)

Kohlrabi is a member of the cabbage family and a native of northern Europe. Its name, taken from the German, means 'cabbage turnip' which, like the earlier English 'turnip-rooted cabbage', describes the vegetable quite accurately. The turnip-like globe of the kohlrabi is not a root but the oblong, swollen base of the stem, sprouting leaves like any normal stem. Kohlrabi

may get as big as a grapefruit, but it is eaten before fully grown, when about the size of an orange. The texture is somewhat crisp and the flavour more delicate than that of a turnip. There are two kinds of kohlrabi, green and purple.

Kohlrabi is much more popular on the Continent than in England. It was first described by a European botanist in the middle of the sixteenth century. By the end of the century it was known in Germany, in the Mediterranean area and in England, where Gerard included it in his *Herbal* but where it was never cultivated particularly widely. Kohlrabi may not be a vegetable that appeals to small children, but steamed and buttered it makes an excellent accompaniment to grilled and roast meats, while young and tender kohlrabi is a good ingredient for a mixed salad.

How to buy

Buy small kohlrabi with fresh tops and a thin rind that can easily be pierced with a fingernail. Avoid large heads which are tough and woody, and heads with cracks or other blemishes.

How to keep

Do not trim before using. Store in a cool, dry, well-ventilated place or refrigerate in plastic bag. Raw, in a cool, dry area or on refrigerator shelf: 1 week. Cooked and covered, on refrigerator shelf: 2 to 3 days.

Nutritive values

Kohlrabi is a fair source of vitamin C and minerals. Uncooked: 29 calories; cooked and drained: 24 calories (per 100 g/3½ oz).

How to use

Both the bulb and the leaves that shoot from it are good to eat. Cut off the leaves and stems, and chop the stems. Wash and drain. Cook separately or with prepared bulb.

If the kohlrabi bulb is very young and tender, it need not be peeled. Peel more mature bulbs to remove tough outer skin. Slice, dice or cut into strips. Serve in salads or steamed with butter.

Kohlrabi Improved

4–6 servings

750 g (1½ lb) kohlrabi	freshly ground pepper
30 g (1 oz) butter	4 tsps flour
½ tsp sugar	2½ dl (8 fl oz) double cream
2½ dl (8 fl oz) chicken stock	3 tbsps finely chopped parsley
salt	

Peel the kohlrabi and cut into small cubes. Wash and drain, but do not shake dry. Heat the butter in a large saucepan. Stir the sugar into it and cook, stirring constantly, until the sugar has melted. Add the kohlrabi. Cook over medium heat, stirring constantly, for about 2 minutes. Add the stock. Season lightly with salt and pepper. Simmer, covered, over low heat, stirring frequently, for about 10 minutes or until tender. Stir the flour into the cream. Add the mixture to the kohlrabi and mix well. Stir in the parsley. Simmer over very low heat, stirring constantly, until the cream has thickened and is of sauce consistency. The dish should be heated through thoroughly.

Leek

(Allium ampeloprasum var. *porrum)*

Leeks, which belong to the onion family, are shaped like cylinders, with a thickened, blanched, white base and flat, compactly-rolled leaves that go from white to dark green at the top. Their average length is 20 to 30 cm (8 to 12 inches) and they are 3 to 5 cm (1 to 2 inches) across. Leeks have a mild onion flavour and they are used as a vegetable or potherb. With the exception of the roots and the tough part of the leaves, the whole leek serves in cooking.

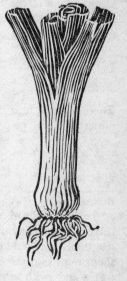

Leeks probably originated in the eastern Mediterranean area, where wild leek is still native as it is on the subtropical islands of the Atlantic. In the Middle East they have been cultivated for at least 3,000 years. Greeks and Romans prized them as a delicacy. Leeks were known throughout the Middle Ages, a common crop which remained popular especially with the poor. This association with the lower classes was expressed by Shakespeare (in *Henry V*) in the phrase 'to eat one's leek', meaning to swallow an insult without protesting. Today they are an important crop and a favourite vegetable in almost all of Europe. Their legendary connection with Wales may go back much farther than the victory of King Cadwallader over the Saxons in A.D. 640: it is thought that Phoenicians trading in Welsh tin brought them north.

Vegetable Cookery

How to buy

Buy leeks which are well blanched 5 to 10 cm (2 to 4 inches) from the base and which have tightly-rolled leaves with fresh, green tops. Small or medium leeks are more tender. Avoid leeks that are soft or have soft spots, or that have bruised, wilted, yellowish tops, flabby, fibrous bases and unduly loose leaves.

How to keep

Cut off rootlets and the unusable upper part of the leaves. Do not wash until ready to use. Refrigerate in a plastic bag or in the vegetable drawer of the refrigerator. Do not leave unwrapped leeks in the vicinity of other refrigerated foods because these will absorb some of the leeks' oniony flavour. Raw, on refrigerator shelf or in vegetable drawer: 3 to 5 days. Cooked and covered, on refrigerator shelf: 1 or 2 days.

Nutritive values

There is little nutrition in leeks, except for a small amount of minerals. Raw: 52 calories per 100 g ($3\frac{1}{2}$ oz).

How to use

Because of the way leeks grow, dirt is found between the layers of the leaves. Trim off the rootlets and remove any tough outer leaves. Cut off any unusable upper part of the leaves. Split leeks lengthwise and hold under running cold water to remove dirt. Or slice or cut into pieces, place slices and pieces in a bowl with cold water and swish around. Repeat the operation until there is no dirt in the bottom of the bowl. Drain.

Cook cut or whole leeks, covered, in about 2 to 3 cm (1 inch) boiling salted water or stock for 3 to 10 minutes, depending on size. Do not overcook or leeks will be mushy. Chill and serve with French dressing. Or braise in a covered saucepan with butter and very little water for about 5 minutes, depending on the size; then season and serve.

Leek Hors d'OEuvre

4–6 servings

12 medium leeks
1 dl (4 fl oz) olive oil
3 dl (½ pt) water
4½ dl (¾ pt) dry white wine
salt
freshly ground pepper
250 g (½ lb) black olives, stoned and halved

60 g (2 oz) seedless raisins or currants, plumped in warm water and drained (optional)
3 large onions, cut into thick slices
4 tbsps finely chopped parsley

Trim the leeks and remove all but 5 cm (2 inches) of the green tops. Cut into longish pieces. Wash in several changes of water to remove all sand. Drain. Heat half of the olive oil in a large, deep frying pan. Add the leeks and cook, stirring with a fork, for 3 minutes. Add the water and the wine and season with salt and pepper, remembering that the olives may be salty. Cover and simmer over low heat for about 10 minutes or until the leeks are tender but still firm. Add the olives and the raisins and simmer for 5 more minutes. Drain the leeks and reserve the cooking liquid. Transfer leeks, olives and raisins to a serving dish. Heat the remaining oil in the frying pan. Cook the onion rings in it until they are soft and golden. Stir carefully with a fork in order not to break the slices. With a slotted spoon, put the onions on top of the leeks. Drizzle a little of the reserved cooking liquid over the vegetables and sprinkle with the parsley. Cover and chill before serving.

Cold Vichyssoise

6 servings

30 g (1 oz) butter
4 medium potatoes, thinly sliced
4 medium white onions, thinly sliced
4 leeks, white parts only, thinly sliced, or 2 bunches spring onions, white parts only, thinly sliced
1 large garlic clove, crushed

1 l (1¾ pts) chicken stock
2½ dl (8 fl oz) milk
2½ dl (8 fl oz) double cream
salt
freshly ground pepper, preferably white
2 tbsps finely chopped chives or parsley

Heat the butter in a large, heavy saucepan. Add the potatoes, the onions, the leeks, the garlic and a quarter of the chicken stock. Simmer, covered, over very low heat until the vegetables are very soft. Stir frequently. Add the remaining stock. Simmer, covered, for 10 more minutes. Add the milk and the cream. Bring to boiling point but do not boil. Cool. Season with salt and pepper to taste. Purée the soup in a blender. If too thick, thin with a little cold milk. Chill very thoroughly. Check the seasoning before serving and sprinkle with the chives.

Leeks au Gratin

4–6 servings
Serve as a main dish, with rice and a green salad.

12 medium to large leeks
3 dl (½ pt) beef or chicken stock
2½ dl (8 fl oz) dry white wine
60 g (2 oz) butter
4 tbsps flour

110 g (4 oz) grated Gruyère or Parmesan cheese
salt
freshly ground pepper

Trim the leeks and cut off all but 5 cm (2 inches) of the green leaves. Wash thoroughly in several changes of water. Drain. Combine the stock and the white wine in a saucepan. Bring to boiling point. Lower the heat and add the leeks. Simmer, covered, over low heat for about 5 to 7 minutes or until the leeks are barely tender. Drain and reserve the cooking liquid. There should be about 4½ dl (¾ pint); if not, add enough stock to make that amount. Place the leeks in a buttered shallow baking dish. Heat the butter and stir in the flour. Cook, stirring constantly, for about 3 minutes; do not brown. Stir in the leek liquid. Cook, stirring all the time, until thickened and smooth. Stir in all but about 2 tablespoons of the cheese. Taste and if necessary season with salt and pepper. Cook until the cheese is melted. Pour the sauce over the leeks. Sprinkle with the remaining cheese. Place under the grill or in a preheated hot oven (Gas 7, 425° F, 220° C) and cook until the top is golden brown.

Lentil

(Lens culinaris, Lens esculenta)

Lentils are the small, round seeds of a small, shrubby plant believed to have originated in the eastern Mediterranean area and the Near East. They are one of the oldest leguminous crops, known to the ancient Egyptians and the Greeks. To this day they are one of the staple foods of India and the Near East and they are widely used throughout Europe. The Bible often speaks of lentils, the most famous reference being that to Esau who sold his birthright for bread and a 'pottage of lentils' (Genesis 25:29–34).

There are two distinctive varieties of lentils. One is the common French kind which is brown or greyish, sold with the seed coat on. The other is the Egyptian or Syrian kind, which is red or orange, smaller and rounder, without a seed coat and split, which means that it cooks much more quickly. Lentils are never used fresh, but when fully ripe they are dried.

How to buy

Lentils are usually sold in 1-pound packages, but can also be found, much cheaper, in bulk.

How to keep

Store in original package or tightly covered container, in a dry place. Raw, on kitchen shelf: 6 to 8 months. Cooked and covered, on refrigerator shelf: 1 week.

Nutritive values

Lentils are a good source of carbohydrates, a good source of phosphorus and iron, and have fair amounts of vitamins and

minerals. Their protein content is very high. Cooked: 106 calories
per 100 g (3½ oz).

How to use

Pick over lentils. Wash and drain. Lentils generally need no
soaking, but if they are to be soaked, place in a bowl, cover with
water and soak for 8 hours. Or bring to the boil in a saucepan,
boil for 2 minutes, remove from heat, cover and let stand for 1
hour. Cook lentils in the water in which they were soaked. Or
add the liquid called for in the recipe to the measured lentils.
Lentils may be cooked in water or in stock. Place the lentils in a
heavy saucepan, add the liquid, cover and bring to the boil.
Reduce heat to simmer and cook for about 1 hour or until tender
but still retaining their shape (orange lentils cook to a mush
fairly quickly; the grey ones retain their shape long after they
have become tender). Lentils in soup should be cooked until they
mash readily. Drain and season cooked lentils with salt and
pepper; like beans, if they are salted in cooking they may be
tough. Use as directed in recipe. All lentil dishes should be well
seasoned.

One measure dried lentils makes 2 to 2½ measures cooked.

Lentil Soup

4–6 servings

500 g (1 lb) dried lentils	2 tbsps bacon fat
2 l (3½ pts) cold water	2 tbsps flour
110 g (4 oz) bacon, in one piece	2 tbsps vinegar
2 large onions, finely chopped	salt
1 large carrot, finely chopped	freshly ground pepper
1 celery stalk, finely chopped	

Wash the lentils under running cold water. Pour the water into a
large pan and bring to the boil. Add the lentils, the bacon, 1
onion, the carrot and the celery. Cover partially and simmer over
low heat for 30 minutes. Heat the bacon fat in a large, heavy
frying pan. Add the other onion and cook, stirring constantly,

until the onion is golden brown. Stir in the flour and cook, stirring all the time, until the flour is golden brown. Put a soup-ladleful of the lentil soup into the frying pan and stir thoroughly until the mixture is smooth and thickened. Stir in the vinegar. Turn the whole contents of the frying pan into the lentil soup, scraping the bottom with a rubber spatula. Season with salt and pepper. Stir thoroughly. Simmer over low heat, covered, for 30 more minutes or until the lentils are tender. Before serving, remove the bacon and cut it into small cubes; return to soup, and check the seasoning.

Lentils, Rice and Spinach

6–8 servings
Serve as a meatless main dish with a cucumber salad.

3 tbsps olive oil
2 large onions, thinly sliced
250 g (½ lb) lentils
12 dl (2 pts) water
110 g (4 oz) long-grain rice
salt

freshly ground pepper
250 g (½ lb) spinach, trimmed and coarsely chopped
⅛ tsp allspice
juice of 1 lemon

Heat the olive oil in a frying pan. Cook the onions, stirring constantly, until they are golden brown; do not scorch. Put the lentils into a large saucepan. Add the water and bring to boiling point. Lower the heat, cover the saucepan and simmer for about 15 minutes, stirring frequently. Add the rice and season with salt and pepper. Simmer, covered, for 10 minutes. Add the spinach and half of the cooked onions. Mix well. Cook, stirring frequently, until the rice is tender. Stir in the allspice. Turn into a serving dish. Spread with the remaining onions and sprinkle with the lemon juice. Serve hot or cold.

Lentil Salad

4–6 servings
Serve with hot or cold roast meats or ham.

750 g (1½ lb) lentils
water
1 large onion stuck with 2 cloves
2 garlic cloves
1 medium carrot, cut into 2
  pieces
1 celery stalk, cut into 2 pieces
2 bay leaves

6 spring onions, white and green
  parts, thinly sliced
lemon French dressing (see below)
salt
freshly ground pepper
tomato wedges
3 tbsps minced parsley

Put the lentils into a large saucepan. Add water to cover plus about 7 cm (3 inches). Bring to the boil and turn heat to very low. Add the onion, the garlic, the carrot, the celery and the bay leaves. Simmer, covered, for about 30 minutes or until the lentils are tender but not mushy; they must retain their shape. Drain the lentils and remove the vegetables. Turn the lentils into a bowl while they are still hot. Add the spring onions and the French dressing. Mix well. Taste and season with salt and pepper. Cool the lentils. Then cover the bowl and refrigerate for 2 hours to blend the flavours. At serving time, mix again then drain off any excess dressing. Turn into a flat serving dish, garnish with the tomato wedges and sprinkle with freshly ground pepper and the parsley.

Lemon French Dressing

Combine 4 tablespoons olive oil, 2 to 3 tablespoons fresh lemon juice (to taste), 1 crushed garlic clove, ¼ teaspoon dried thyme, salt and pepper. Stir and mix well before using.

Lettuce

(Lactuca sativa)

Cultivated lettuce, the world's most popular salad plant, is descended from wild forms of lettuce often said to be native to the Mediterranean area and the Near East, but occurring in some form or other all over the globe. As a cultivated vegetable it is not as old nor as widely cultivated as other garden crops, possibly because all sorts of other tender wild leaves may serve the same culinary purpose. The milky juice exuded by lettuce gave it its name, the Latin root of which is *lac*, milk, from which come the French *laitue* (that is, milky) and the English lettuce.

Primitive lettuce, like primitive cabbage, was a loose-leaved and sometimes stemmy plant. Lettuces with firm heads are a later development of the plant which hybridizes easily. Several varieties were known in antiquity. Persian kings ate lettuce around 550 B.C., according to Herodotus, and a century later Hippocrates confirmed that it was good for people. According to many other Greek and Roman writers, lettuce was known in a number of varieties, including blanched ones, which speaks of its great popularity. We know that lettuce was an English crop from Chaucer, who in 1387, in his Prologue to the *Canterbury Tales*, writes, 'Well loved he garlic, onions and lettuce.' The French became acquainted with cos lettuce, probably an Italian variety, in the middle of the sixteenth century. How this and other firm-headed lettuces developed we do not know, but sixteenth- and seventeenth-century European writings describe a number of curly-leafed varieties in various colours.

Today lettuces are classified as 'cabbage' lettuce (var. *capitata*) or 'cos' lettuce (*varroriana* or *longifolia*).

Cabbage lettuces have round heads, composed of soft, delicately-flavoured leaves that often bruise easily. Softest of these are the Dutch lettuces, crispest is the famous 'Webb's Wonder' (originally 'Webb's Wonderful'). Modern plant breeding has performed wonders in creating varieties that withstand mechanical harvesting and long-distance transport but they still need the protection of glasshouses to grow in wholly unsuitable climates like our winters.

Cos lettuces, which the Americans call romaine after the botanical name which records their supposed Italian origin, have longer leaves forming elongated heads either by being tied up or, again, through the marvels of scientific breeding. They are coarser than the round-headed lettuces but also crisper, and are better suited to cooking purposes.

How to buy

Buy fresh, crisp, blemish-free heads. Look for a bright colour, whatever the shade of green. Avoid soft, wilted, faded heads, and check leaves for bruises, tipburn or browning of leaf edges which may indicate soft rot. Many greengrocers water their lettuces to keep them fresh in warm weather. This practice is permissible if not overdone; if the lettuces are heavily watered it means they are not fresh. Watch leaves for bruises.

How to keep

Lettuce should be refrigerated as soon as possible after buying or picking. During storage, it needs some moisture, but it must not be wet. Store in a plastic bag in the vegetable compartment of the refrigerator. Cos lettuce keeps well rolled up tightly in newspaper. On a refrigerator shelf or in the vegetable compartment: 3 to 5 days, depending on variety and condition when bought.

Use lettuce as soon as possible.

Nutritive values

Aside from some vitamin A, lettuce has few nutrients and few calories. At least 90 per cent of it is water. Raw: 13 to 18 calories per 100 g ($3\frac{1}{2}$ oz).

Vegetable Cookery

How to use

For salads, lettuce can be cut into wedges, shredded or torn apart (which prevents it from turning dark at the edges as it does when cut with a knife). For whole lettuce leaves, remove the core and let water run into the hole. Spread the leaves gently apart and gently tear off. All washed lettuce should be well drained and dried with kitchen paper or a kitchen towel, or in a salad basket which can be spun round.

Lettuce wilts easily, especially under the influence of the vinegar and salt in a salad dressing; it wilts even more easily if it was not properly dried after washing. It is best to dress a lettuce salad just before using, or even at the table. An easy method of keeping salad crisp is to make or pour the dressing in the salad bowl and pile the greens lightly on top of it, tossing only at serving time.

Salad dressings: These are more than something to dress a salad with: they are a state of mind. Personally, I think it best to keep them simple so as not to overwhelm the lettuce; I usually stick to a basic French dressing, made with different kinds of vinegar or with lemon, but invariably with a good, light olive oil, which I think the only one fit to use in salads, admitting that French walnut oil adds its own dimension, as does sesame oil – but these are for special occasions, not for everyday use. Garlic and herbs in a dressing depend on how I feel at the moment. Whatever the dressing, it must be home-made and fresh; mixed and bottled salad dressings, whatever their makers claim, are horrors that desecrate good greens.

Cooked lettuce, especially cos, lends itself to many delicious dishes, as soups, as purées or as additions to other vegetables. The tougher outer leaves, which are usually thrown away, serve very well for the purpose, not only for economy reasons, but also because they are usually more flavourful than the lighter inner ones.

Lettuce and Bacon

4–6 servings
Serve with hot roast meats, poultry or game.

3 heads cos lettuce
boiling water
250 g (½ lb) lean bacon, diced
1 large onion, chopped
1 large tomato, peeled and seeded
(optional)
salt

freshly ground pepper
sprinkling of a favourite herb
such as fresh or dried basil,
thyme or marjoram
hot chicken stock or water (if
necessary to prevent scorching)

Trim the lettuce heads but leave them whole. Dip into a sink with several changes of cold water until no sand remains. Shake dry. Plunge the lettuce into a large saucepan filled with boiling water and blanch for about 2 minutes. Do not overcook; the lettuce must remain firm. Drain and lay in a strainer to allow the lettuce to drip off excess moisture. Dry with kitchen paper. In a heavy pan, cook the bacon until crisp. Pour off about two thirds of the fat in the pan. Add the onion and the tomato, and cook, stirring constantly, until the onion is tender. Add the lettuce. Season with salt and pepper and sprinkle with the herbs. Cook, covered, over low heat for about 10 minutes. Check for dryness; if necessary, add a little hot stock or water, 1 to 2 tablespoons at a time, to prevent scorching. The cooked lettuce should be dry. Serve very hot.

Lettuce in Cream

4 servings
The lettuce must be very young, very tender and very fresh.

3 small round lettuces, trimmed
and washed
3 tbsps sugar
3 tbsps white vinegar

1¾ dl (6 fl oz) single cream
salt
freshly ground white pepper

Wrap the lettuces in a kitchen towel and chill for 1 hour. Tear apart and place in a glass or china bowl. Stir the sugar into the vinegar until it is melted. Stir in the cream. Pour over the lettuce and toss. Refrigerate for 5 to 10 minutes. Just before serving, pour off any excess dressing and season very lightly with a little salt and pepper. Serve immediately.

Cream of Lettuce Soup

4–6 servings

30 g (1 oz) butter	2 tbsps cornflour
1 large head cos lettuce, shredded	2 tbsps water
12 to 18 spring onions, sliced	2 egg yolks
1¾ l (3 pts) chicken stock	4 tbsps double cream
salt	butter-fried croûtons
freshly ground pepper	

Combine the butter, the lettuce and the onions in a deep, heavy saucepan. Cook over medium heat, stirring occasionally, for about 5 minutes or until the lettuce is soft. Add the stock and season with salt and pepper. Simmer, covered, over low heat for 15 minutes. Blend the cornflour and the water to a smooth paste and stir into the soup. Cook for 5 minutes longer. Purée the soup in a blender or strain through a sieve. Beat together the egg yolks and the cream. Spoon a little of the hot soup onto this mixture, stir and then stir this into the remaining soup. Heat through but do not boil. Serve hot with the croûtons.

Lettuce Custard

4 servings

A delicate, French dish. Serve with chicken or veal. Some cooks manage to turn this dish out onto a serving plate, intact. I have not always succeeded in doing this and therefore do not recommend it : if you want to make a good impression it is better to play safe and serve it in the baking dish.

4 large heads round lettuce (about 1 kg or 2 lb), trimmed and washed	2½ dl (8 fl oz) double cream
	2 tsps grated onion
boiling water	salt
4 eggs	freshly ground pepper
	⅛ tsp ground nutmeg

Plunge the lettuce into a large pan full of boiling water. Cook over high heat for 4 minutes. Drain, rinse under running cold water and drain again. Squeeze the lettuce with your hands to remove any remaining moisture; the lettuce must be very dry. Chop the lettuce. Beat together the eggs, the cream, the grated onion, the salt and pepper and the nutmeg. Stir in the chopped lettuce and mix well. Turn into a buttered 1- to 1½-litre (or -quart) baking dish. Stand the baking dish in a baking tin filled with 3 cm (1 inch) hot water. Cook in a preheated moderate oven (Gas 5, 380° F, 195° C) for about 30 to 40 minutes or until the mixture is set and firm to the touch. Serve immediately.

Lotus

(*Nelumbium nuciferum*)

Lotus is a decorative water plant belonging to the water lily family whose spectacular flowers and bell-shaped leaves rise well above the water surface on long stalks. Surprisingly to most Westerners, it is a food plant in the Orient; all the parts of the lotus (leaves, flower petals, seeds and underwater rhizomes) are eaten.

The sacred lotus of India and China reaches from the Caspian Sea to Japan, and serves both decorative and culinary purposes. The leaves are boiled as a vegetable and the ripe seeds are dried or roasted and then pickled in various ways or sweetened with soy and then ground to make lotus jam to fill Eastern pastries. The lotus roots, which are best used when young, are divided into sausage-like segments whose reddish-brown surface hides flesh that ranges from white to orangy. They can be boiled whole, scraped and mashed; dried out to make a flour; scraped and sliced and used in soups, or to stir-fry and for other Chinese dishes in the same way as water chestnuts are used. The flavour of the roots is not as pronounced as that of the seeds, which for non-orientals take some getting used to.

Lotus root is grown as a commercial crop in the Far East, especially China, and in Hawaii, from where it is shipped either sliced and preserved, at times pickled or in a sweet soy sauce, or tinned in water or brine.

Lotus Root Salad

4–6 servings

2 tbsps white vinegar
1 l (1¾ pts) water
3 medium segments lotus root
(about a 500-g or 16–19-oz
tin)
3 tbsps water

3 tbsps *sake*
3 tbsps sugar
½ tsp salt
1 green or red sweet pepper, cut
into rings

Combine the vinegar and the water in a saucepan. Scrub and peel the lotus root. Cut into thick slices. Drop the slices immediately into the vinegar water to prevent discolouring. Bring the water with the lotus slices to the boil. Cook for about 2 to 3 minutes until the slices are tender but still crisp. Drain and turn into a serving dish. Combine the 3 tablespoons of water, the *sake*, the sugar and the salt in a small saucepan. Bring to the boil. Cook, stirring constantly, until the sugar has dissolved. Pour the hot mixture over the lotus root slices and toss gently with a fork. Let stand at room temperature for 20 minutes. Drain and chill. Serve garnished with the pepper rings.

Mange-Tout, Snow Pea, Edible Pod, Chinese Pea, Sugar Pea, Pea Bean

(*Pisum sativum* var. *macrocarpon*)

Mange-tout is a firm, crisp, flattened pod which tapers at both ends and which measures about 7 cm (3 inches) in length and about 1 cm ($\frac{1}{2}$ inch) across. The colour is a very bright, almost translucent green, through which the tiny seeds are visible. The whole pod is eaten, which accounts for its French name, which means 'eat-it-all'.

They are an important vegetable both in Chinese and French cooking. Justly so for, properly prepared, they are one of the most delicious vegetables. In south-east Asia the asparagus pea or boa bean (*Psophocarpus tetragonolobus*) is used in the same way – its use in Britain has always been decorative only.

How to keep

If they are to be stored, seal the unwashed mange-tout tightly in a plastic bag to keep in their natural moisture. They must be used as soon as possible.

Nutritive values

Raw: 53 calories; cooked and drained: 43 calories (per 100 g/$3\frac{1}{2}$ oz).

How to use

Fresh mange-tout should have both tips snipped off, along with a little string, just before cooking time, then be washed and drained, and preferably dried to ensure their crispness in cooking, one of the vegetable's main virtues. The best way of cooking mange-tout is to stir-fry them for 2 minutes so that they will be tender but still very crisp. If they are to be added to other dishes, put them in for just the final 2 to 3 minutes of cooking, again to keep them crisp. The smallest amount of overcooking robs them of their delicious crisp texture.

Mange-Tout with Ham

4 servings

750 g (1½ lb) mange-tout, ready for cooking
boiling salted water
30 g (1 oz) butter
110 g (4 oz) smoked ham or lean bacon, cut fine

salt
freshly ground pepper
2 tbsps finely chopped parsley

Cook the mange-tout in boiling salted water to cover for 2 minutes. Drain and rinse quickly under running cold water. Drain. Heat the butter in a frying pan and add the ham. Cook, stirring constantly, for about 3 minutes. Add the mange-tout, salt and pepper. Over high heat, and stirring constantly, cook for 2 more minutes. Sprinkle with the parsley and serve immediately.

Marrow

(Cucurbita pepo ovifera)

Vegetable marrow is perhaps the only truly English vegetable in this book, but strangely it is of comparatively recent cultivation and even more strangely nobody seems to know just how it got here at all. A member of the large squash or gourd family, it probably originated like the rest of them in the northern parts of South America. In 1816, an article in the *Transactions of the Royal Horticultural Society* first mentions vegetable  marrows, calling them 'new in this country within a few years'. They became popular very quickly, and Victorian cottagers probably appreciated their decorative qualities as much as the addition to an, on the whole, rather meagre diet. Many a country fair even now reminds us of the passions that can be aroused by ever-larger home-grown marrows; that the poor things are inedible by the time they have bloated to such an unnatural extent seems not to matter.

To a large extent, the vegetable marrow is losing ground to its later cousin, the courgette, cultivated to be picked when small. Earlier this century the cocozelle, a close forerunner of the courgette, was popular. The cushion-shaped custard marrow, grown here for much longer than the vegetable marrow, has never achieved popularity as a food plant at all.

How to buy

Buy only firm, well-rounded marrows with glossy, unblemished rinds. Avoid soft, soggy-ended marrows, with damaged rinds or dark spots. Avoid also over-large ones.

How to keep

Raw, on refrigerator shelf or in vegetable drawer: 3 to 4 days. If too large for the refrigerator, use as soon as possible. Cooked and covered, on refrigerator shelf: 2 days.

Nutritive values

Marrows consist mainly of water and have hardly any nutrients at all. Raw: 16 calories; cooked and drained: 12 calories (per 100 g/3½ oz).

How to use

Wash, and trim off both ends. Do not peel; only scrape or cut off any blemishes on the rind. Cut into slices or lengthwise, and either steam or cook in minimum water or just enough butter to keep the marrow from sticking to the pan. Take out the seeds, especially of larger marrows, either before or after cooking (the latter method is often thought to preserve the taste better).

Fried Marrow

4 servings

1 small marrow (about 750 g or 1½ lb), washed and dried
110 g (4 oz) flour
salt
freshly ground pepper
1 l (1¾ pts) groundnut or vegetable oil

Trim off the ends of the marrow. Do not peel. Cut into quarters lengthwise and scrape out the seeds and the soft middle. Cut into small cubes, or slices about 1 cm (½ inch) thick. Combine the flour with a little salt and pepper. Dredge the cut-up marrow in the flour and shake off excess. Heat the oil in a deep saucepan to 375° F (190° C) on the frying thermometer. Add about half of the marrow. Cook, stirring all the time, for about 3 to 4 minutes or until golden and crisp. Remove with a slotted spoon and drain on kitchen paper. Cook the remaining marrow. Serve very hot, sprinkled with salt.

Baked Marrow and Eggs for Lunch or Supper

6–8 servings

The secret of this dish consists in having the marrow really squeezed free of as much of its moisture as possible, so that the finished dish won't be watery. It may be served hot or lukewarm, but never chilled. Serve with ham and tomato salad.

1 vegetable marrow (about 1 kg or 2 lb)
salt
3 tbsps olive oil
60 g (2 oz) butter
1 large onion, thinly sliced
1½ dl (¼ pt) plain yoghurt, or 3 thick slices white bread (crusts removed), soaked in milk
4 eggs, well beaten
30 g (1 oz) grated Parmesan cheese
small bunch parsley sprigs, chopped fine
3 tbsps finely chopped fresh marjoram or 2 tsps dried marjoram
freshly ground pepper
60 g (2 oz) fine, dry breadcrumbs

Wash the marrow and cut off the ends. Cut into quarters lengthwise. Scoop out most of the seeds with a knife. Cut into strips, then into 2-cm (¾-inch) pieces. Spread out a clean kitchen towel and put the pieces on it. Sprinkle them with salt, but not heavily. Tie the four ends of the kitchen towel together and hang it over the sink or put it into a colander. Let stand for about 30 minutes. The marrow will start losing its moisture. Squeeze and twist the towel to extract as much moisture as possible; you will be surprised how much there is. In a large, deep frying pan, heat the olive oil and half the butter. Cook the onion in it until it is barely golden. Add the marrow and cook, uncovered, over medium heat, stirring frequently, for 10 minutes. Cool. Stir in the yoghurt or the bread and mix well. (If you are using bread, chop it with a knife but do not squeeze it.) Stir in the eggs, the Parmesan cheese, the parsley and the marjoram, and season with pepper. Check the seasoning and, if necessary, add a little salt. Blend the mixture thoroughly. Lightly coat a 30-cm (12-inch) baking dish with olive oil and coat it with fine, dry breadcrumbs. Turn the vegetable mixture into the baking dish. Sprinkle breadcrumbs over the top and dot with the remaining butter.

Bake in a preheated moderate oven (Gas 4, 350° F, 180° C) for about 30 minutes or until set. Serve sliced.

Stuffed Marrow

6 servings
You need smallish marrows for this, as large ones break easily. Serve hot or lukewarm.

500 g (1 lb) minced beef
1 large onion, grated
60 g (2 oz) long-grain raw rice
1 dl (scant 4 fl oz) tomato juice
3 tbsps chopped dill weed
1 egg
salt

freshly ground pepper
2 small vegetable marrows (not over 30 cm or 1 foot)
60 g (2 oz) butter
3½ dl (12 fl oz) chicken stock
lemon wedges

Combine the meat, the onion, the rice, the tomato juice, the dill, the egg, and salt and pepper to taste, in a bowl. Mix well. Wash the marrows. Cut off their tops, scoop them out a little and reserve. With a long spoon or a sharp knife, scoop out each marrow, leaving a firm shell with walls of about 1 cm (½ inch). Throw away the scooped-out pulp. Fill each marrow with half the meat mixture, pushing it down gently with the handle of a spoon. When full, cover with the top end; hold it in place with toothpicks. In a tall pan (or half a double-boiler, but protect the bottom with an asbestos mat), place the marrows side by side. If any filling is left, shape it into small balls and place them in the pan as well. Dot with the butter and pour the stock around the vegetables. Cover with waxed paper or aluminium foil. Cover and cook over medium heat for about ½ hour or until the marrows are tender. Check occasionally for moisture; if necessary, add a little more stock. Transfer to a serving dish and pour the pan juices over the vegetables. Serve with lemon wedges.

Note: If finding a suitable pan proves awkward, the marrows can also be baked in a moderate oven (Gas 4, 350° F, 180° C) for about 40 minutes or until just tender. Do not put the stock in with the vegetables to start with, but use it to baste frequently during cooking.

Millet

Millet is the name given to a number of tall grasses of the Graminease (Poaceae) family, whose edible seeds are used for human consumption or as fodder. They have been cultivated in several varieties in Asia and Africa for thousands of years as important food plants. They are used to a much lesser extent for this purpose in Europe, which treats millet as fodder; and millet is

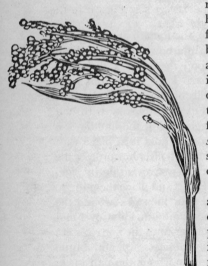

rarely eaten in this country by humans though it is widely used as fodder and bird-feed. It is, however, becoming increasingly known, liked and used in the specific form which is the basis of one of the best-known dishes of northern Africa: couscous, the name for both the granulated flour of the African millet (*Holcus spicatus*) and for the dish made by steaming this flour over the vapour of a meat broth.

Millet is high in carbohydrates and proteins. It is cooked like rice, or barley or other cereals used for porridges and pilaffs. It is available in health, speciality and oriental food-stores as whole-grain, grits or ground millet.

Nutritive values

Raw: 327 calories per 100 g (3½ oz).

Millet Casserole

4 servings

250 g (8 oz) whole-grain millet
7 dl (1¼ pts) boiling water or
   chicken stock
60 g (2 oz) butter
2 tbsps grated onion

1 tsp salt
freshly ground pepper
2 tbsps chopped fresh mint or
   parsley or dill weed

Put the millet into a heavy casserole. Over medium heat, and stirring constantly, cook for about 2 to 3 minutes or until the millet is golden brown. Add the water, three quarters of the butter, the onion and the salt and pepper. Cover tightly and simmer over low heat for about 25 minutes or until tender and dry. Stir frequently and check the moisture; if necessary, add a little more boiling water, 2 tablespoons at a time. Before serving, stir in the remaining butter and sprinkle with the mint.

Mushrooms

A mushroom is the fruiting body of certain fungi and botanically one of the simplest plants, without roots, stems or leaves. It produces no flowers or seeds and relies on spores, reproductive cells, to reproduce itself. The mushroom lacks chlorophyll and thus cannot carry out photosynthesis (manufacture its own food from sunlight). It therefore has to depend upon non-living, organic matter for its food, which makes mushroom-growing totally different from growing other food plants.

There are thousands upon thousands of mushroom species growing wild in the world, some edible, some poisonous. Many delicious edible mushrooms can be gathered all over Britain by those who know them, and the mushroom poisonings that do happen always happen to ignorant gatherers. The common mushroom (*Psalliota campestris*) and its fatter version the horse mushroom (*Agaricus arvensis*), the oyster (*Pleurotus ostreatus*), the parasol (*Lepiota procera*), the fairy-ring champignon (*Marasmius oreades*) and the many edible puff-balls are all both easy to find and relatively easy to identify. And still, in spite of the many species and varieties of mushroom, only one species (with few varieties) is cultivated anywhere at all: *Agaricus bisporus*, the French *champignon de Paris*, the one and only 'mushroom' of our dismally unadventurous greengrocer-shops.

The French, who always delighted in many kinds of mushroom, were the first to cultivate them under Louis XIV; there is a 1707 description of the various ways of cultivating them in caves. To judge from the profusion in which wild mushrooms grow under most varied conditions, one would think that growing mushrooms commercially would be easy. Far from it. Since it is not a matter of planting a seed, the spawn must be a sterile, pure-culture spawn, produced in as sterile a laboratory as a hospital operating room, to be deposited in a scientific compost from which it will draw its nourishment. Mushrooms are grown in special mushroom-houses, which can be temperature-controlled and which must be well ventilated: two all-important factors in a process so complicated that it makes one wonder why anyone would choose that field. The answer, of course, is money: production figures go into many hundreds of millions of pounds a year.

Apart from fresh and dried mushrooms, there is a large variety of tinned mushrooms, pickled mushrooms in jars, mushroom sauces and the like. All are perfectly safe, and some so good as to make one wonder why we keep bothering about the often bland and soulless cultivated *Agaricus bisporus*.

Dried mushrooms

Mushrooms are extensively dried in Europe and in the orient where they are an important part of the local cookery. They are imported into this country generally in plastic containers or plastic bags, and the most common variety to reach us is the *Boletus edulis* (*cèpe* in French or *Steinpilz* in German), but others are the chanterelle, the morel and the black mushroom of China. All of these mushrooms keep their aroma and flavour remarkably well. They are expensive, but a little goes a long way: any weight of dried mushrooms equals about five times that weight in fresh mushrooms. Buy dried mushrooms in good-sized slices, mushrooms which are thoroughly dried out and hard and clean, mushrooms free of foreign matter, though they may give off a slight dust of their own.

How to buy

Fresh mushrooms are recognized by caps closed so tightly that the gills beneath are not visible. Since they are mostly water and moisture evaporates during shipping and storage, the caps open gradually to show the brown gills. Opened mushrooms are all right for cooking, but have less flavour than closed ones. Buy firm, closed, blemish-free mushrooms. Avoid wilted, shrivelled, wide-open, slimy mushrooms, or bruised, blemished or browned ones.

Vegetable Cookery

How to keep

Refrigerate fresh mushrooms as soon as possible. Do not wash before use. Mushrooms are fragile, so they must not be crowded against other foods. They also need air to circulate around them. To keep them perfect, lay the mushrooms on a shallow tray and cover them with kitchen paper dipped in water and wrung half dry. Alternatively, place in an open plastic bag which allows ventilation. Keep refrigerated. Raw, covered, on refrigerator shelf: 3 days. Cooked and covered, on refrigerator shelf: 3 to 4 days.

Keep dried mushrooms in their own container or in a tightly covered jar in a dark, cool place. They will keep up to 1 year.

Nutritive values

Mushrooms are mostly water, but they are a moderate source of minerals. They fill without fattening, but they can absorb a surprising amount of the fats and creams with which they are cooked. Raw: 28 calories per 100 g ($3\frac{1}{2}$ oz).

How to use

There are different schools of thought on how to clean fresh mushrooms. All agree that mushrooms must never be soaked or they become waterlogged. I usually wash mine in a bowl of cold acidulated water (2 tablespoons lemon juice to 1 litre or quart water): drop the mushrooms into it, swish around quickly with hands, drain and dry with kitchen paper. Speed is of the essence, as is quick and thorough drying. The lemon juice keeps the mushrooms bright and firm and its flavour is light enough to disappear. I never peel mushrooms; much of the flavour lies in the skin. The unfortunate habit of peeling commercial mushrooms is a survival of the custom of peeling certain wild ones which have a tough skin that has to be removed before cooking.

To prepare mushrooms, trim, wash and dry only the number you are going to use; washed mushrooms, however well dried, do not keep. If you are using only the caps, leave a bit of the stem in the middle of the mushroom to prevent it from shrinking during cooking. The stems can be sliced and added to other dishes, or minced for stuffings. Mushrooms release a good deal of water during cooking which has to be accounted for in dishes that might turn watery, such as stews and sauces. It can be avoided by first blanching or sautéing the mushrooms. Mushrooms should be sautéed quickly, before they give out water. Blanched or sautéed, they are added to the dish just long enough to add to its flavour, during the last cooking period.

To blanch mushrooms: Place them in a wire basket or strainer. Plunge into a saucepan of rapidly boiling water and keep in the water for no more than 1 minute for small and 2 minutes for large mushrooms from the moment the water begins to boil again after immersion. Be sure to keep track of the time. Then, have a bowl of cold water ready and rapidly dip the mushrooms in it two or three times to reduce the heat and keep them firm.

To sauté mushrooms: Trim, wash and slice, chop or mince the mushrooms. Heat 2 measures of butter and 1 measure of salad oil in a heavy frying pan over moderate heat. Add the mushrooms. Shake the pan to coat the mushrooms with the fat. Cook, shaking the pan or stirring carefully with a fork, for about 2 to 4 minutes, depending on the size of the pieces. *Do not cover the pan or the mushrooms will give out water.*

Dried mushrooms: To reconstitute dried mushrooms, wash them first in lukewarm water to remove dust and grit. Then soak in lukewarm water barely to cover for 30 minutes to 1 hour. Use the soaking water in the dish you are cooking as additional liquid.

Mushroom and Saffron Consommé

4–6 servings

1½ l (2½ pts) well-seasoned beef
   stock
½ tsp saffron
250 g (½ lb) mushrooms,
   trimmed, washed and finely
   chopped

salt
freshly ground pepper
2½ dl (8 fl oz) dry sherry

Pour a little of the stock into a saucepan. Stir in the saffron. Add the remaining stock and bring to the boil. Lower the heat. Add the mushrooms. Simmer, covered, for 5 minutes or until just tender and thoroughly heated through. If necessary, season with salt and pepper. Have the soup very hot, without boiling it. Stir in the sherry and keep on the heat for 1 more minute or until the sherry is warmed through.

Mushroom Soufflé

3–4 servings
Serve as a first course, with fresh tomatoes.

60 g (2 oz) butter
250 g (½ lb) mushrooms, trimmed, washed and thinly sliced
1 tbsp grated onion
1 tsp grated lemon rind

3 tbsps flour
2½ dl (8 fl oz) single cream
4 eggs, separated
salt
freshly ground pepper

Heat a little of the butter in a frying pan. Add the mushrooms. Cook, stirring constantly, for about 3 to 4 minutes. The mushrooms should be firm and not watery. Stir in the onion and the lemon juice. Remove from heat and reserve. Heat the remaining butter and stir in the flour. Cook, stirring constantly, until the flour is golden. Add the cream and cook, stirring all the time, until the sauce is thick and smooth. Remove from the heat. Add the egg yolks, one at a time, stirring well after each addition. Season with salt and pepper. Add the mushrooms to the sauce and mix well. Beat the egg whites until stiff. Fold the egg whites gently into the mushroom mixture. Spoon into a buttered 2-litre or 2-quart baking dish. Bake in a preheated moderate oven (Gas 4, 350° F, 180° C) for about 30 to 35 minutes. Serve immediately.

Mushrooms Annetta

4 servings

For the white sauce:

15 g (½ oz) butter
3 tsps flour

1 dl (4 fl oz) milk
pinch of ground nutmeg

For the dish:

30 g (1 oz) butter
2 tbsps olive oil
1 medium onion, chopped fine
1 bunch parsley, trimmed and
  chopped fine
1 small garlic clove, crushed
1 tsp grated lemon rind

750 g (1½ lb) fresh, firm
  mushrooms, trimmed and cut
  into quarters
1 dl (4 fl oz) Madeira
salt
freshly ground pepper
juice of 1 lemon

To make the white sauce, heat the butter in a small saucepan. Stir in the flour. Then stir in the milk. Cook, stirring constantly, until thick and smooth. Stir in the nutmeg. Remove from the heat and reserve.

In a large saucepan, heat together the butter and the oil. Add the onion, half the parsley, the garlic and the lemon rind. Cook, stirring constantly, until the onion is soft. Add the mushrooms. Cook over medium heat, stirring frequently, for about 3 to 4 minutes. The mushrooms must remain firm and quite white. Add the Madeira. Cook over high heat, stirring constantly, for about 3 to 4 minutes. Most of the liquid in the saucepan should have evaporated, leaving about 1 dl or 4 fl oz or so of sauce. Stir in the white sauce and mix well. Cook for 2 minutes longer or until the white sauce has amalgamated with the mushrooms and their cooking liquid, and until the dish is thoroughly heated through. Season with salt and pepper. Stir in the lemon juice and the remaining parsley and remove from heat. Serve immediately.

Mushrooms Pickled in Wine

6 servings

4½ dl (¾ pt) dry white wine
2½ dl (8 fl oz) olive oil
1 medium onion, chopped
yellow rind of 2 lemons
6 whole cloves
1 tbsp dried thyme or savory
4 bay leaves

12 whole peppercorns
1 tsp salt
1 kg (2 lb) mushrooms, thickly
  sliced or quartered
2 tbsps lemon juice
small bunch parsley, trimmed
  and chopped fine

Combine the wine, olive oil, onion, lemon rind, cloves, thyme, bay leaves, peppercorns and salt in a saucepan. Bring to the boil. Turn the heat to very low, and simmer, covered, for 10 minutes. Strain into a large saucepan and bring back to simmering. Add the mushrooms. Simmer for about 5 to 10 minutes (depending on size) until they are tender but still firm. Turn into a serving dish and chill. Before serving, pour off what is left of the marinade, and stir in the lemon juice. Sprinkle with the parsley.

Mushrooms in Cream

3–4 servings
I think this simple way of cooking mushrooms one of the best.

30 g (1 oz) butter
500 g (1 lb) mushrooms, trimmed
  and sliced
1½ dl (¼ pt) double cream, hot
salt

freshly ground pepper
⅛ tsp ground nutmeg
2 tbsps finely chopped parsley or
  dill weed
buttered rice

Heat the butter in a frying pan. Add the mushrooms. Cook over medium heat, stirring constantly, for about 2 minutes. Add the cream and season with salt and pepper and the nutmeg. Cook, stirring all the time, for 2 to 3 more minutes or until the cream has thickened. Sprinkle with parsley and serve on hot buttered rice.

Fresh Mushroom Salad

4 servings

1½ dl (¼ pt) olive oil
4 tbsps fresh lemon juice
1 tsp dried thyme
1–2 tsps Dijon mustard
salt

freshly ground pepper
500 g (1 lb) mushrooms, thinly
  sliced
3 tbsps chopped parsley
lettuce

Combine all the ingredients except the mushrooms, the parsley and the lettuce and mix well. Add the mushrooms and toss with two forks. Cover and let stand at room temperature. At serving time, drain, and sprinkle with the parsley. Pile in a serving dish lined with lettuce.

Okra, Lady's Finger

(*Hibiscus esculentus*)

Okra is the finger-shaped, pointed, somewhat hairy green fruit pod of a tropical plant with a unique gooey, mucilaginous quality; it is used as a vegetable, and to thicken dishes like stews and soups. The name is of African origin, and the plant is a native of tropical Africa. It is said to have come from the region that includes Ethiopia and the eastern, higher part of the Sudan. Okra is of  considerable antiquity, but relatively little is known about its history. The first written accounts are late, as accounts of food plants go: okra was first mentioned by a Spanish Moor who visited Egypt in 1216. Very likely it came to Egypt and to the Arab countries through traders and slave-raiders working out of Ethiopia and the Sudan. The Arabs grew very fond of it, calling it *bamiya*; it is still much used in all Arab cookery.

From Arabia, okra was taken to all of North Africa and the Mediterranean area and farther east to south-western Asia. It was brought from Africa to the New World around the middle of the seventeenth century, perhaps as a crop for the Negro slaves who used it in their home countries.

In spite of the large popularity okra enjoys in India and the Arab world it is little known even in Mediterranean cooking. Okra is only beginning to come into its own in our part of the world. Many people do not know what to do with it, which is a pity, since young, tender okra (any other kind is tough and not worth eating) is an interesting vegetable, by itself or with other foods.

How to buy

Buy young, crisp, tender, small pods, free from blemishes. Mature okra pods are fibrous; it is therefore necessary to pick them when young. The ideal length is about 5 to 9 cm (2 to $3\frac{1}{2}$ inches). Avoid flabby, dull, dry, shrivelled and discoloured pods, and stiff and woody pods.

How to keep

Refrigerate in open plastic bag to permit ventilation or in refrigerator drawer. Raw, on refrigerator shelf: 4 days. Cooked and covered, on refrigerator shelf: 2 days.

Nutritive values

A mediocre source of vitamins and minerals. Cooked and drained: 29 calories per 100 g ($3\frac{1}{2}$ oz).

How to use

Okra is always eaten cooked. The most common use is as a thickener in soups and creole stews. As a vegetable, okra is stewed by itself, or combined with other vegetables; it has great affinity with corn and tomatoes. Okra is also deep fried, or used in salads. In Indian cookery, it is stuffed, though the effort hardly seems worthwhile to us. Wash and trim off the stem ends. Leave small pods whole. Cut large pods into smaller pieces. Cook, covered, in boiling salted water just to cover for 5 minutes or only until barely tender. Drain immediately, season and serve with butter and lemon juice or tomato sauce. It is important not to overcook okra since overcooking makes it slimy and dulls its colour.

Fried Okra

4–6 servings
Serve with fried fish or with an omelette.

500 g (1 lb) young, medium okra
pods
2 eggs, beaten in a bowl with
½ tsp salt

110 g (4 oz) corn meal (*not*
cornflour), in a bowl
groundnut or vegetable oil for
frying

Wash the okra and trim off the stems. Cut into thick slices. Turn into the bowl with the beaten eggs and toss with two forks until well coated with the egg. With a slotted spoon, transfer the okra to the bowl with the corn meal. Toss again until well coated with the corn meal. Heat 1 or 2 cm (about ½ inch) oil in a large frying pan. Add the okra and stir. Cover the frying pan and cook over medium heat, stirring frequently, until the okra is golden brown and crisp. Drain on kitchen paper and serve very hot.

Okra, Onion and Tomato Stew

4–6 servings
You may add 110 g (4 oz) or so of sweet corn to the stew.

6 rashers lean bacon
2 medium onions, chopped
1 large green pepper, cut into
strips
500 g (1 lb) young, medium okra
pods, trimmed and cut into
thick slices
4 medium tomatoes, peeled and
chopped

salt
freshly ground pepper
2 tsps dried basil
½ tsp hot pepper flakes, or to
taste
3 tbsps finely chopped parsley

In a large frying pan, cook the bacon until crisp. Drain, crumble and reserve. Pour off all but 3 tablespoons of the bacon fat. Add the onion and the pepper and cook, stirring constantly, until the pepper is almost soft. Add the okra. Cook, stirring all the time, until the okra is golden. Add the tomatoes, the salt and pepper, the basil and the pepper flakes. Simmer, covered, for about 10 to 15 minutes or until the okra is tender; do not overcook. Before serving, sprinkle with the bacon and the parsley. Serve hot.

Onion

(*Allium cepa*)

The familiar, dry common onion is a single underground bulb which belongs to the lily family. There are many varieties, varying in shape, size and weight, in the colour of their papery skins and in their pungency. The cause of the onion's strong smell and flavour is a volatile oil which is rich in sulphur compounds. Onions are used in the cooking of practically every country in the world; without them, most cookery would be flavourless.

The onion is a native of western Asia. It was cultivated for centuries in the Mediterranean area and the Near East. The slaves who built the Great Pyramids in the third millennium B.C. are said to have lived on onions, radishes and garlic. The Children of Israel, fleeing from Egypt, cried out bitterly when they were deprived of the onions they had enjoyed in Egypt, which they preferred to manna. From ancient times to the Middle Ages, onions were not only food but medicine as well. Hippocrates, the Greek physician known as the father of medicine, who lived around 400 B.C., declared onions bad for the body but good for the sight. Nevertheless, through the centuries, onions and their juice were used to cure all sorts of ills including earache, colds, fever, laryngitis, poor complexions and warts. Onions still play a part in contemporary folk medicine. There seems to be universal agreement that the smell of onion on the breath is unattractive. Shakespeare sums up general opinion in *A Midsummer Night's Dream*: 'Eat no onions nor garlic, for we are to utter sweet breath.'

Growing onions is not as easy as one might think since they are susceptible to light and make demands on the climate. Before they are stored and marketed, the tops and most often the roots of the onions are removed. They have to be carefully dried so that no rot enters the neck to establish itself in the moist tissues. This drying procedure is known as curing; sometimes it is done in the field, other times artificially.

Britain has never grown anything like the quantity of onions it needs for home consumption and imports four or five times as much as it produces itself – a matter of 200,000 tons a year at least. Most of these imports come from Holland, Italy and Spain. Spanish onions are usually larger and milder, but their very juiciness makes for poor keeping and storing qualities.

How to buy

Buy hard, firm, dry onions with small necks. The skins should be papery, dry and crackly, and free from blemishes. Avoid spongy, soft onions and onions with wet or very soft necks, hollow woody centres or fresh sprouts. Buy large onions for slicing, medium onions for roasting or boiling, small onions for boiling and tiny onions for pickling.

How to keep

Keep dry onions in a cool, dry, well-ventilated place, preferably in a single layer. Raw and dry, at room temperature: 3 to 4 weeks. Cooked and covered, in refrigerator: 4 days.

Nutritive values

A moderate source of vitamin C and minerals. Raw: 38 calories; cooked and drained: 29 calories (per 100 g/$3\frac{1}{2}$ oz).

How to use

If dry onions have begun sprouting and have green tops, simply cut them off. Peel onions under running water to avoid tears. Another folksy method to prevent tears is to put a piece of bread between the teeth so that it sticks out. Peel and cut onion just before using to preserve flavour; the flavouring substance in onions is a volatile oil which evaporates when exposed to the air.

To cut onions: Leave large onions unpeeled, cut into halves lengthwise and peel. Put the cut side down on a board. Slice the onion-half lengthwise into slices almost to the base. Then slice crosswise. Chop the ends.

Cut onion rings crosswise from a whole, unpeeled onion, remove dry skin from each ring and separate carefully. Chill in ice water to crisp; drain and dry.

To peel small boiling onions: Score the root end of each onion with a small cross, using a sharp, pointed knife, to keep intact. Then pour boiling water to cover over the onions and let stand for 3 to 5 minutes. Drain and peel.

For onion juice: Cut a medium onion into halves. With the edge of a spoon, or the edge of a knife, scrape the onion and catch the juice in a spoon.

To grate onion: Cut into halves and peel. Grate on the coarse side of a grater; grating on the fine side is too tedious an enterprise even to consider. Grated onion adds a more powerful flavour to a dish than chopped onion.

The mechanical chopping device advocated for chopping onions effortlessly, is in fact excellent, all the more so since the onions may be chopped together with garlic, parsley and herbs. A spring, which you push up and down, moves an arrangement of blades on the food to be chopped. Both blades and food are enclosed in plastic so that there is no spattering. I do all my chopping this way, with one large-size and one medium-size chopper.

Old-Fashioned Onion Gravy

4 tbsps meat fat and dripping, or bacon fat	salt
	freshly ground pepper
2 or 3 large onions, thinly sliced	¼ tsp dried thyme
2 tbsps flour	1 tbsp Worcestershire sauce
4½ dl (¾ pt) beef stock	2 tbsps drained capers (optional)

Heat the fat and cook the onions, stirring constantly, until soft and golden. Stir in the flour and cook for 2 more minutes. Stir in the stock. Taste (the stock may be salty) and stir in the salt and pepper, the thyme, the Worcestershire sauce and the capers. Simmer, covered, over low heat for 10 minutes: the end result should be about 6 dl (1 pint) of gravy.

The Original Basle Onion Tart

6 servings

For the pastry:

250 g (½ lb) flour
½ tsp salt

110 g (4 oz) butter
4 tbsps iced water (approximately)

For the filling:

30 g (1 oz) butter
6 large onions, thinly sliced
½ tsp salt
4 rashers back bacon, cut up
4½ dl (¾ pt) milk or single cream

3 tbsps flour
2 eggs, well beaten
250 g (½ lb) grated Gruyère
    cheese

To make the pastry, sift the flour with the salt. Cut in the butter until the particles are the size of small peas and blend with the flour. Stir in the iced water, a little at a time, to make a stiff dough. Knead the dough lightly on a floured baking board. Roll out to fit the bottom and sides of a well-buttered 25-cm (10-inch) deep pie dish. Chill.

To make the filling, heat the butter in a frying pan. Cook the onions in it until they are soft and golden. Stir in the salt and add the bacon. Cook over medium heat, stirring constantly, for 2 to 3 minutes. Remove from the heat. Stir the milk gradually into the flour in a large bowl. Beat in the eggs and the cheese. Add the onions and the bacon, including the pan juices in which they were cooked. Mix well. Pour the mixture into the pastry shell. Bake in a preheated moderate oven (Gas 4, 350° F, 180° C) for 30 minutes. Raise the temperature to hot (Gas 6, 400° F, 210° C) and bake for 5 minutes longer or until brown and bubbly. Serve hot or cold.

Onion, Orange and Olive Salad

6 servings

For all roasted or grilled meats. Crisp the onion slices by chilling them in iced water. Drain when needed.

1 bunch watercress
18 paper-thin, crisp slices mild onions
18 thin orange slices, without peel

12 large black olives, sliced
1½ dl (¼ pt) French dressing made with lemon juice (see page 203)

Pick over the watercress, remove the thickest stems, wash and shake dry. Make a bed with it in a salad bowl. Arrange the onion and orange slices on the watercress in an overlapping pattern. Top with the sliced olives. Pour the French dressing over everything. Bring to the table as it is and toss there.

Onions à la Grecque

6 servings

36 small white onions (the smaller, the better), peeled
1½ dl (¼ pt) olive oil
4½ dl (¾ pt) dry white wine
3 dl (½ pt) water
1½ dl (¼ pt) wine vinegar
2 tbsps tomato paste
2 garlic cloves, crushed

2 cloves
1 tsp each of dried tarragon, salt, coarsely ground pepper, dry mustard and mustard seed
80 g (3 oz) raisins
small bunch parsley, finely chopped

Combine all the ingredients except the raisins and the parsley in a large, deep frying pan. Bring to the boil. Lower the heat to very low and simmer, covered, for 10 minutes. Add the raisins and simmer for 5 more minutes or until the onions are tender but still holding their shape; the cooking time depends on their size. Cool and let stand at room temperature for 2 hours, then chill. Sprinkle with the parsley before serving.

Curried Onions

4 servings

60 g (2 oz) raisins
3 tbsps dry sherry
500 g (1 lb) small white onions,
   peeled
3 dl (½ pt) water
60 g (2 oz) butter
salt

freshly ground pepper
1 tbsp curry powder or to taste
approx. 1½ dl (¼ pt) single cream
   or milk
1 tbsp cornflour
juice of ½ lemon

Soak the raisins in the sherry. Put the onions into a saucepan. Add the water, half of the butter and the salt and pepper. Bring to the boil and lower the heat. Simmer, covered, for 10 minutes or until the onions are tender but still firm; cooking time depends on their size. Put the remaining butter into the top of a double boiler and stir in the curry powder. Cook, stirring frequently, over hot water for 10 minutes. When the onions are cooked, drain them into a bowl. Measure the cooking liquid and add enough cream to make 3 dl (½ pint). Stir the cornflour into the cream and stir this mixture into the curry butter. Cook, stirring frequently, until thickened and smooth. Add the onions, the raisins and the sherry in which they were soaked. Cook over hot water, stirring frequently, until the onions are thoroughly heated through. Stir in the lemon juice before serving.

Parsnip

(Pastinaca sativa)

The parsnip is the edible underground root of a plant that is a member of the ubiquitous Umbelliferae that include parsley, fennel, carrots, celery and chervil. Parsnips are ordinary vegetables, which deserve their botanical name (from the Latin *pastus* meaning food and *sativa* meaning cultivated, which spells out exactly what a parsnip is).

The parsnip originated in the eastern Mediterranean area and the Caucasus. The vegetable likes a cool climate, and even improves after a frost, which changes the starch in the root into sugar; parsnips were for centuries the vegetable of the poor in northern Europe as the potato, a New World plant, is today. In Tudor times parsnips were used as a cheap adulteration in bread, but as a vegetable they were not highly regarded and are still underrated by many people. Our cookery does not always make the best of them. Served as a vegetable in their own right rather than as a flavouring for soups and stews, they can be puréed, braised, made into fritters, deep fried – all this improves them immensely.

How to buy

Buy small to medium parsnips, no less than 3 or 4 cm (1 to 1½ inches) across, that are fairly clean and firm and well trimmed. Avoid large parsnips which are woody, soft, bruised and discoloured, and shrivelled roots suffering from insect and other blemishes.

How to keep

Refrigerate, unwashed, in plastic bag. Raw, on refrigerator shelf or in vegetable drawer: 1 to 3 weeks. Cooked and covered, on refrigerator shelf: 1 to 2 days.

Nutritive values

Chiefly carbohydrate, a poor source of other nutrients. Raw: 76 calories; cooked and drained: 66 calories (per 100 g/3½ oz).

How to use

When ready to use, trim and wash parsnips. Peel, or better, scrape. Or best, brush, boil first and then skin and prepare for recipe. Leave whole or cut lengthwise into slices, strips or dice. Have pieces the same size for even cooking. If the parsnips look woody, halve or quarter like an apple and remove woody core. Cook whole in boiling salted water for about 20 minutes, depending on size. Cover pan well, for the smell of parsnips cooking is not appetizing. Drain immediately. Or cook pieces in boiling salted water for 5 to 10 minutes. Drain, season and serve with butter. Or slice thinly and simmer, covered, in a little butter for 10 to 15 minutes. Or bake in a moderate oven in a covered baking dish for 20 to 30 minutes depending on size. It is important not to overcook parsnips which easily become mushy when cooked too long.

Braised Parsnips

4–6 servings

30–60 g (1–2 oz) butter
1 kg (2 lb) parsnips, peeled and
    cut into thin strips
1 tbsp grated onion
¾ tsp salt

¼ tsp freshly ground pepper
¼ tsp sugar
6 large outer lettuce leaves
3 tbsps finely chopped parsley

Heat the butter in a saucepan. Add the parsnips, onion, salt, pepper and sugar. Mix gently with a fork. Wash the lettuce leaves and leave them wet. Cover the parsnips with the lettuce. Cover the saucepan and simmer over low heat for 10 to 15 minutes or until the parsnips are tender. Shake the saucepan frequently to prevent sticking. Check for moisture; if necessary, add a little water, 1 tablespoon at a time. Sprinkle with the parsley before serving and serve with the lettuce leaves which will have cooked down.

Parsnips in Sour Cream

4–6 servings

1 kg (2 lb) parsnips, peeled and
    cut into cubes
boiling salted water
salt
freshly ground pepper

1½–3 dl (¼–½ pt) sour cream,
    depending on taste
¼ tsp ground mace or ground
    cardamom or ground ginger

Cook the parsnips in just enough boiling salted water to cover until tender but still firm. Drain and season with salt and pepper. Stir in the cream and the mace. Return to heat and heat through, but do not boil. Or mash the parsnips as you would potatoes and proceed as above.

Pea

(Pisum sativum)

This edible seed of a variety of herbaceous annuals is probably the most popular of all vegetables. The chief varieties are: the green-shelled garden pea, under discussion here, which is eaten fresh or dried; the field pea *(Pisum arvense)* which has small, coloured seeds and is used for making split peas and meal and as a forage and manure crop; and the sugar pea. The latter, also known as mange-tout or snow pea, has soft, edible pods, which are eaten whole (see page 212).

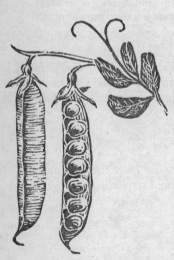

Peas are said to have originated in Middle Asia and the Near East and in the African region around Ethiopia. They certainly are a very ancient vegetable, since seeds of primitive varieties have been found in the remains of the Bronze Age lake dwellers of Switzerland (around 5000 B.C.) and in the ruins of Troy. They were cultivated by the Greeks, and by the Romans who brought them north to England and other conquered lands. However, these early peas were smaller than those we know today, and they were largely grown for dry seeds. Green peas, eaten fresh, are a later development. There is a passing twelfth-century English reference, but, by the end of the sixteenth century, German, English and Belgian botanists described different varieties with smooth, pitted or wrinkled seeds. The wrinkled-seed ones are known as marrow fats. In seventeenth-century France peas were a rare gift of the gods, on which those who could afford it gorged themselves. Louis XIV reputedly made himself quite ill on peas when they were in season. The French also refined the pea into the most desirable kind we have today: the tiny, tender, sweet *petit pois*, 'small peas', which are as delicious raw as cooked. In medieval England the best-loved peas were the Runcival ones, from Roncesvaulx in France. The field pea, still growing wild in southern Europe, was only used dried at that time, not fresh.

Today, a very large percentage of the pea crop is tinned or frozen. Although peas are among the least objectionable tinned or frozen vegetables, they do not remotely compare to freshly picked, young, green peas, one of nature's major miracles. Unfortunately, these peas are harder and harder to find, but, personally, I prefer even a more mature fresh pea to the preserved varieties.

How to buy

Buy fairly large, angular, bright-green, garden-pea pods which are well filled and which snap easily. Avoid light-coloured, swollen pods which are over-mature and contain tough seeds, or spotted, mildewed pods.

How to keep

Refrigerate unshelled peas. Use as soon as possible. Raw, on refrigerator shelf: 2 to 4 days. Cooked and covered, on refrigerator shelf: 2 to 3 days.

Nutritive values

A fair source of vitamin A and minerals. Fresh, raw: 84 calories; cooked and drained: 71 calories (per 100 g/3½ oz).

How to use

Shell peas just before using. Discard any that are beginning to sprout: though not harmful they are not worth eating. If small and tender, use raw in salads. Cook, covered, in a little boiling water for about 5 minutes or until just tender; drain. Some people add 1 teaspoon sugar to the cooking water for added sweetness. Season. (If peas are for later use, drop cooked peas into a bowl of cold water, drain immediately and refrigerate.) Serve with butter, and any desired herb such as mint, tarragon, chives or basil.

Italian Peas with Eggs

4 servings

110 g (4 oz) bacon or *pancetta*,
   cut fine
1 small onion, cut fine
2 kg (4 lb) unshelled peas, shelled
1½ dl (¼ pt) chicken stock or
   water

salt
freshly ground pepper
¼ tsp ground sage
2 small eggs, beaten
30 g (1 oz) freshly grated
   Parmesan cheese

Cook the bacon in a heavy saucepan until it is limp and transparent. Add the onion and cook, stirring constantly, until it is soft and golden. Add the peas, the stock, a little salt (the cheese is salty), pepper and the sage. Cover tightly and cook over low heat for 10 minutes or until the peas are tender but not overcooked. Stir frequently. Beat the eggs with most of the Parmesan. Stir the eggs into the peas and remove from the heat. Keep warm, but off the heat, for about 2 to 3 minutes. Sprinkle with the remaining Parmesan before serving.

Peas with Cream and Mint

4 servings
The saffron or turmeric are not strictly necessary, but they have a nice flavour and colour.

30 g (1 oz) butter
2 kg (4 lb) unshelled peas,
   shelled
4 tbsps water
salt

2 sprigs fresh mint or 1 tsp dried
   mint
⅛ tsp saffron or ground turmeric
1½ dl (¼ pt) double cream

Heat the butter in a heavy saucepan. Add the peas, the water, salt (no pepper is needed) and the mint. Simmer, covered, over low heat for about 10 minutes or until tender. If the peas look soupy, cook without a cover to allow the pan liquid to evaporate. Remove the mint from the cooked peas. While the peas are cooking, stir the saffron or turmeric into the cream. Whip just a little and fold into the cooked peas. Serve immediately.

Peas and Lettuce

4–5 servings

30 g (1 oz) butter
6 spring onions, white and green parts, thinly sliced
1 small cos lettuce, shredded fine
2 kg (4 lb) unshelled peas, shelled
4 tbsps water or chicken stock

salt
freshly ground pepper
$\frac{1}{8}$ tsp ground nutmeg
1 tsp dried thyme or 1 sprig of fresh thyme
3 tbsps finely chopped parsley

Heat the butter in a heavy saucepan which has a tight cover. Add the onions and the shredded lettuce. Stir to coat the greens with the butter. Add all the other ingredients except the parsley. Cover tightly and simmer over low heat for about 5 to 10 minutes or until the peas are tender. Sprinkle with the parsley before serving.

Variation: Sauté 250 g ($\frac{1}{2}$ lb) thinly sliced mushrooms in a little butter for 3 to 4 minutes or until tender but still firm. Add to the cooked peas and heat through. Sprinkle with the parsley before serving.

Pea Soup

4 servings
This soup may be made with tough elderly peas.

15 g ($\frac{1}{2}$ oz) butter
110 g (4 oz) bacon, cut fine
1 small onion, cut fine
2 large tomatoes, peeled and chopped
1$\frac{1}{2}$ kg (3 lb) unshelled peas, shelled

salt
freshly ground pepper
12 dl (2 pts) hot chicken stock
toasted slices of French bread
grated Parmesan cheese

Vegetable Cookery

Combine the butter and the bacon in a deep saucepan. Cook, stirring constantly, for about 2 to 3 minutes or until the bacon is limp. Add the onion and cook 2 minutes longer. Add the tomatoes and the peas and season with salt and pepper. Cook, stirring occasionally, for about 3 minutes. Add the stock. Simmer, covered, stirring occasionally, until the peas are tender. Put a slice of toasted bread into each soup plate and sprinkle with the Parmesan. Ladle the soup over the bread.

Peanut, Groundnut

(Arachis hypogaea)

Peanuts are not strictly a vegetable, but since they figure so very prominently in the diet of people in the tropics as a concentrated food they deserve a short mention here. The peanut is a legume, a pea not a nut, which ripens underground. A native of South America, it travelled at an early time to the Old World tropics. George Washington Carver (1864–1934), a black American botanist, chemist and educator, pioneered peanut cultivation and developed more than 300 products from peanuts, including foods, dyes, plastics, soap, cosmetics and medicinal oils. Since peanut agriculture enriches the soil rather than impoverishing it, it revolutionized the economy of the American South which until then had been mainly dependent on cotton. Now the peanut is a major crop not only in the United States but also in West Africa, India and China. The economies of Senegal and Gambia depend on it to a very great extent; most other large producers have little to spare for export.

Pound for pound, peanuts are more nutritious than meat and dairy products. Western cookery uses peanuts mostly as raw or roasted 'nut nibbles', or in baked goods, confectionery, peanut butter and groundnut oil. However, Far Eastern and West African cookery has several excellent dishes based upon peanuts which appeal to the Western palate.

Nutritive values

Peanuts contain about 30 per cent proteins, 40 to 50 per cent oil, and are rich in vitamins B and E. Raw with skin: 564 calories; roasted with skin: 582 calories; roasted and salted: 585 calories; boiled: 376 calories (per 100 g/3½ oz).

Peanut Soup

6–8 servings
Use real peanuts rather than peanut butter – it makes a difference in the flavour.

500 g (1 lb) shelled roasted
   peanuts
1½ l (2½ pts) chicken or beef
   stock
1 onion, grated
½ tsp dried pepper flakes or to
   taste, or 1 tsp curry or to taste

1 tbsp cornflour
4½ dl (¾ pt) single cream and
   milk, mixed
salt
freshly ground pepper
2 tbsps finely chopped fresh mint
   or parsley

Grind the peanuts, a few at a time, in an electric blender. Do not overgrind or the peanuts will be a paste rather than a meal. Heat the stock in a large saucepan. Stir in the onion, the ground peanuts and the pepper flakes. Bring to the boil and lower the heat. Simmer without a cover for about 30 minutes, stirring frequently. Put the soup into the blender and purée. Return the puréed soup to the saucepan and to low heat. In a bowl, stir the cornflour into the cream mixture. Stir the mixture gradually into the soup. Cook, stirring constantly, until the soup is thickened. Season with salt and a little pepper. Cook for about 3 minutes longer. Sprinkle with the parsley and serve very hot.

Pepper, Sweet Pepper, Bell Pepper, Green Pepper, Paprika, Pimiento

(Capsicum annuum)

The pepper under discussion is the sweet-fleshed, mild and annual garden pepper, as opposed to the hot and pungent perennial peppers known as chilli or chile. There is a considerable range of sizes, shapes and colours. Some peppers are long, tapered and pointed, others short and wide, others again heart-shaped. However, most of the popular mild peppers are about 10 to 15 cm (4 to 6 inches) long, half as much across, three- to four-lobed and tapering only slightly towards the blossom end. Sweet peppers are green when mature, then turn red as they go on ripening. Both green and red peppers are found in our shops, but the general preference is for green peppers, where Balkan or Mediterranean people would go for the sweeter red ones, as well as for the large yellow variety found only occasionally in our shops. Sweet peppers are used as cooked or salad vegetables, pickled in brine or chopped as a flavouring ingredient.

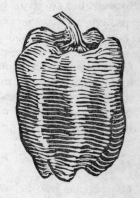

Like all capsicums, the sweet pepper is the fruit of a tropical American shrub; which part of the New World it originated in is a matter of opinion among botanists. It was long cultivated by the natives in tropical and southern America, as we learn from early Spanish records. The discovery of America brought with it a great increase of commercial trade between the various parts of the world, and capsicums seem to have been part of this dissemination into the tropical parts of Africa and Asia where they flourish with ease.

247

Vegetable Cookery

How to buy

Buy firm, well-shaped, thick-fleshed peppers with glossy sheen on their brightly-coloured skin. Avoid shrivelled, bruised, flabby peppers, and those with cuts or punctures through the walls, and peppers with soft, watery spots on the walls.

Tinned peppers, or those pickled in jars, are ready-to-use but their use is more limited: having lost their crispness, they are seldom at their best in salads.

How to keep

Refrigerate, unwashed, in the vegetable drawer. Raw, in refrigerator drawer: 1 week. Cooked and covered, or tinned (opened but covered), on refrigerator shelf: 1 to 2 days.

Nutritive values

Green sweet peppers are a valuable source of vitamins A and C and a poor source of minerals. Mature red peppers are a good source of vitamin A and a fair source of vitamin C. Raw green peppers: 22 calories; cooked green peppers: 18 calories; raw, mature red peppers: 31 calories (per 100 g/3½ oz).

How to use

Cut peppers into halves. Trim off pith, seeds and membranes. Rinse under running cold water. Then cut into slices or strips, or chop or mince them. For shells for stuffed peppers, slice off the top, remove pith and seeds, then rinse. Or cut peppers in half crosswise or lengthwise and remove pith and seeds. If peppers are to be stuffed and baked, have ready a large saucepan of boiling water. Prepare pepper shells as above and drop into boiling water. Boil for a minute, remove with a slotted spoon, taking care not to pierce the shell, and turn upside down on a plate to drain.

In Italy, and in French provincial cooking, where peppers play an important part as a vegetable, they are prepared somewhat differently: they are peeled before being put in a salad or cooked further. This is often an enormous improvement because the outer skin is bitter, whereas the flesh is sweet. Peppers may be peeled in two ways: (1) Stick a skewer lengthwise through the pepper and hold it directly over the high heat of a gas burner or electric stove. Roast the peppers, turning them frequently, until the whole outer skin is black and blistered. This will take about 5 minutes. Do not forget to blister the crevices. Under running cold water (so as not to burn your fingers with the very hot peppers) peel and slip off the blistered skin. Cut peppers open and wash off seeds and membrane. Dry on kitchen paper and then cut according to recipe direction. This is not at all as complicated as it sounds, and the smell of the roasting peppers is lovely. (2) Place peppers on a baking sheet. Bake in a hot oven (Gas 6, 400° F, 210° C), turning frequently, until blistered on all sides. Proceed as above. I find this method long and tedious.

Though peppers should have mild seeds, occasionally a hot one sneaks in. This is why it is advisable to rinse off all the seeds.

Sweet Pepper Antipasto or Salad

4 servings
It is essential that the peppers for this dish be peeled.

4 large sweet peppers, peeled	12 capers
6 tbsps olive oil	parsley sprigs
freshly ground pepper	1 tomato cut into 8 thin wedges
8 anchovies	

Seed the peppers and remove the membranes. Cut each into 4 pieces. If the peppers were somewhat torn turing the peeling, trim them to make even pieces. Turn the pepper pieces into a flat serving dish. Sprinkle with the oil and the pepper. Marinate at room temperature for about 1 hour; then chill. Peppers prepared in this way can be used without further ado as a salad. For an hors d'œuvre, however, lay 4 pepper pieces neatly on an individual salad plate. Top with the anchovies, arranged crosswise. Put 3 capers where the anchovies cross. Decorate with a few parsely sprigs and 2 tomato wedges. Repeat to make four servings. A salty white cheese (Caerphilly, *fetta*) can be used instead of the anchovies.

Piquant Stuffed Peppers

4 servings

1½ dl (¼ pt) olive oil
75 g (scant 3 oz) fresh, white
  breadcrumbs, toasted
3 tbsps currants or seedless
  raisins, plumped in water and
  drained
12 black olives, stoned and
  chopped
60 g (2 oz) *prosciutto* or ham, or
  6 anchovy fillets, cut up small
2 tbsps finely chopped parsley

2 tbsps chopped fresh basil or 2
  tsps dried basil
2 tbsps capers, drained
salt
freshly ground pepper
dash of Tabasco sauce
4 large red or green peppers,
  prepared for stuffing
1 large tomato, cut into 4 thick
  slices
chicken or beef stock, or water

Heat half the olive oil in a frying pan. Add all the other ingredients except the peppers, the tomato and the stock. Cook over high heat, stirring constantly, for about 2 to 3 minutes or until all the ingredients are well blended. If the mixture seems too dry for stuffing, stir in 1 to 2 more tablespoons of the oil. Stuff the peppers with the mixture. Place them, standing up and close together, in a small, deep baking dish. The dish must be small enough to hold up the peppers; if they fall down during baking, the stuffing will ooze out. Sprinkle the remaining oil over the peppers and top each with a tomato slice. Pour about 2 cm (not quite 1 inch) stock around the peppers in the bottom of the baking dish. Bake in a preheated moderate oven (Gas 4, 350° F, 180° C) for about 30 to 40 minutes. Serve warm or cold, but not chilled.

Peperoni al Forno

4–6 servings

4 very large green, red or yellow
  peppers, peeled and seeded
2 large ripe tomatoes, peeled
10 black olives, stoned and
  coarsely chopped
1 large onion, thinly sliced
2 garlic cloves, chopped
4 anchovies, chopped (optional)

salt
freshly ground pepper
large bunch of parsley sprigs
6 tbsps fresh basil leaves or 2
  tbsps dried basil
3–6 tbsps olive oil
30–60 g (1–2 oz) fine dry
  breadcrumbs

Cut the peppers into wide strips. Cut the tomatoes into wedges the size of the pepper strips. Put the pepper strips, the tomatoes, the olives, the onion, the garlic cloves and the anchovies into a baking dish. Season lightly with salt (more if you don't use anchovies) and with pepper. Chop together the parsley and the basil and sprinkle the mixture over the vegetables. Then sprinkle them with the olive oil and the breadcrumbs. Cook in a preheated moderate oven (Gas 4, 350° F, 180° C) for about 30 minutes. Serve either warm or cold (not chilled), as an appetizer or with plain grilled or roast meats.

Pepper and Potato Frittata

4 servings
Obviously you can also make this frittata without potatoes.

3 tbsps olive oil
2 large green or red peppers, unpeeled or peeled, seeded and cut into strips
1 medium onion, sliced very thinly
2 medium potatoes, cooked, peeled and thinly sliced
2 tbsps water
8 large eggs, slightly beaten
salt
freshly ground pepper

Heat the olive oil in a large frying pan. Add the peppers. Cook over medium heat, stirring constantly, for 3 to 4 minutes or until the peppers are soft (unpeeled peppers will take nearly twice as long to soften). Add the onion and the potatoes and mix with a fork. Cook for 5 more minutes or until the onion is soft. Beat the water into the eggs and season with salt and pepper. Pour the egg mixture over the vegetables and lower the heat. Cook over low heat until the bottom of the frittata is set. Shake the frying pan to prevent sticking. With the fork, pull the egg mixture that is still liquid over to the side of the pan, lifting the edges of the frittata to allow the egg to set. When the bottom of the frittata is firm and golden brown put a plate the size of the frying pan over the omelette and slip it out, cooked side up. Slip it back into the frying pan, cooked side up, to let the bottom firm and cook to golden brown; this takes about 2 to 3 minutes. Return to the plate and serve hot or lukewarm.

Pepper Sauce for Pasta

3–6 servings
This sauce is best for small pasta, such as any of the fancy shell pastas. It should be very well seasoned, and on the hot side.

4 large peppers, preferably red, green and yellow, peeled and seeded
4 tbsps olive oil
1 large onion, very thinly sliced
1 kg (2 lb) tomatoes, peeled and chopped
6–8 tbsps fresh basil, chopped, or 2–3 tbsps dried basil
½ hot red pepper, seeded and chopped, or to taste
salt
freshly ground pepper
1–2 tbsps drained capers
500–750 g (1–1½ lb) pasta
freshly grated Parmesan cheese

Cut the peppers into strips. Heat the olive oil in a deep frying pan. Add the onion and cook until it is soft and golden. Add the peppers. Cook over high heat, stirring constantly, for about 5 minutes. Add the tomatoes, the basil, the hot pepper, and season with salt and pepper. Reduce the heat to medium and cover the frying pan. Cook, stirring frequently, for about 10 minutes. Stir the capers into the cooked sauce. Cook the pasta while the sauce is cooking, drain it and put it into a heated deep serving dish. Pour the sauce over the pasta and toss. Serve with plenty of freshly grated Parmesan cheese.

Pigeon Pea

(Cajanus cajan)

Pigeon peas are the edible seeds of a tropical legume probably originating in Africa, which reached Asia in prehistoric times. They are usually dark grey or yellow, the size of small garden peas, growing tightly crowded in hairy, pea-like pods. The shrub (a short-lived perennial) is now extensively grown in all tropical and subtropical countries. In India, where they are known as 'red gram', they are the most important food after chick peas, used to make the basic dish of *dhal*. In Malaya they are known as *kachang* (although there is some confusion with peanuts there) and from this word they became known in England as cajan by the end of the seventeenth century.

Pigeon peas are also a popular West Indian staple, providing useful proteins in the diet of the poor people. Frequently split into halves, dried pigeon peas are treated and cooked like dried beans. They are the classic ingredients of 'peas and rice'. A large percentage of the crop is exported in tins.

Nutritive values

Fresh, raw, immature seeds: 117 calories; dried, mature seeds: 342 calories (per 100 g/3½ oz).

Potato

(Solanum tuberosum)

The potato is a perennial herb belonging to the huge Salanaceae or nightshade family, which includes tomatoes and aubergines. The plant has fibrous roots with many underground rhizomes or stems, which swell at the tip and become the edible tuber we know as potato, the world's most important single vegetable. The potato plant is handsome, with pretty white-to-purplish  flowers and decorative foliage. It is a cool weather crop, but it does not stand much frost. Potatoes are not propagated by true seeds, but by planting pieces of tubers bearing two or three eyes. With its high carbohydrate content, besides being used as food, potatoes also serve as a source of starch, dextrin and alcohol, and as fodder.

Considering the importance of the potato, it seems odd that it is a fairly recent addition to our tables. Its origin is obscure, but botanists think the potato originated in the Andes of Bolivia and Peru, or possibly in southern Chile. Different varieties were cultivated centuries before the Spanish Conquest as a leading food crop in the Andean highlands since potatoes can grow at higher altitudes than corn. The highlanders of Peru had even discovered how to preserve potatoes by freezing and drying them.

Conquering Spaniards from the expedition led by Gonzalo Jimenez de Quesada made one of their first contacts with the potato in 1537, in a high village of northern Peru, after its inhabitants had left their huts in terror. The Spaniards found corn, beans and 'truffles' of good flavour – plants with scanty flowers of a dull purple colour and floury roots, the description of which fits the potato. Later the same expedition conquered Bogotá where corn and potatoes were the main food of the people.

It is probable that Spanish sailors took the potato with them to Spain and Portugal around the middle of the sixteenth century, calling them *batata* from the Indian name *pappas*. From then on, potatoes were known in Europe. They were probably introduced into England from Spain, and grown in the British Isles in the latter part of the sixteenth century. Gerard's *Herbal* mentions them in 1596, and the seventeenth century distinguished between 'Spanish' potatoes (*Ipomoea batatas*, sweet potato), 'Canadian' potatoes (Jerusalem artichokes) and Virginia or Irish potatoes, by which were meant the purple-flowered or the white-flowered varieties of the common 'real' potato.

The Irish were the first to make great use of the potato as a crop. From the early seventeenth century on, their economy became increasingly dependent on it until the great potato blight of 1845–6 brought the dreadful famine in which about $2\frac{1}{2}$ million people died, from starvation and from the epidemics that followed.

Germany, too, became the potato land it still is quite early. The Elector Frederick William had potatoes planted first in his own gardens in 1651, and insisted, frequently with forceful persuasion, that the peasants cultivate the free potatoes he distributed to them along with a royal circular on how to plough, manure and plant the crop. The food shortages during the Seven Years War were an important factor in increasing potato production in Germany, aided by the prodding of Frederick the Great who recognized the tuber's importance for mass feeding.

France was slow in adopting the potato; not until the late eighteenth century was it considered edible there, having been decried as poisonous by doctors. In England acceptance had been equally slow, although for different reasons (the Puritans distrusting a crop which was not mentioned in the Bible, for instance). By the late eighteenth century, however, the potato had become an important food crop for the working classes.

The potato's present-day importance is best described by some figures. World production in 1970 reached the huge total of 568,300 million lb. The average yearly production from 1966–70 was: North America, 37,100 million lb; Europe, other than the U.S.S.R., 298,600 million lb; U.S.S.R., 196,400 million lb; South America, 9,400 million lb and Japan, 7,900 million lb. The Netherlands had the highest yield per acre during that period of 30,300 lb and Switzerland was next with 29,300.

Potatoes are either long or round, with brown skins (which the producers call white) or red ones. A great deal of scientific experimentation goes on among growers and agricultural research stations to produce strains that are pest- and disease-resistant (the Colorado beetle and scab being prominent among the potato's ills). Varieties are constantly changing for new improved models; and at the same time our knowledge and appreciation of the differences between available varieties dwindles from generation to generation. This is a pity, for already our potato varieties are very limited compared to those available in Holland, France or the Scandinavian countries. The different textures and tastes of the potatoes served there come as a startling revelation of the possibilities of the tuber to most mash and chips eaters. Another astonishing potato experience is the sight of a Peruvian or Colombian market with its varieties of potatoes of all shapes and with extraordinary yellow, pink, red, blue or blackish flesh, all unknown here since we only accept the white-fleshed potato.

The cooking quality of the potato depends on its starch content. Starchy potatoes become loose and mealy when boiled or baked; they are excellent for mashing and for chips. Potatoes low in starch are dry when baked; boiled, they lend themselves to pan-fried and scalloped dishes and salads where they keep their shape rather than becoming a soggy mess. Old potatoes are higher in starch than new ones, which are potatoes dug before they reach maturity and shipped immediately after being dug, whereas old potatoes are dug mature and stored.

How to buy

Buy potatoes that are well shaped whatever their size, firm, clean and relatively smooth. Avoid bruised, blemished or shrivelled potatoes, cut or skinned or frost-bitten potatoes, potatoes with signs of decay and potatoes that have sprouted (the sprouts are toxic). Also, avoid cracked potatoes which are hard and wasteful to peal and those with a green colour: the green areas contain solanin, a glycol alkaloid, which, eaten in quantity, is toxic. However, it does not affect the rest of the potato and the green parts can simply be scraped or cut away.

How to keep

Store in a cool, dry, well-ventilated area away from hot pipes or from places where potatoes can freeze. Keep in dark since light may cause potatoes to green. Do not refrigerate since low temperatures convert potato starch to sugar. Raw, general use potatoes, in cool, dry, dark area: 2 to 3 months. Raw, new potatoes, in a cool, dry, dark area: 2 weeks. Potatoes stored at room temperature should be used within a week. Cooked, covered, on refrigerator shelf: 3 days.

How to use

Scrub and wash potatoes. Whenever possible, cook with the skin since a good deal of nutrition is found on and near the skin. If the potato is to be peeled, keep the parings thin. When cooked, peeled potatoes are whiter than those cooked in their 'jackets'. If the peeled potatoes are not cooked immediately after peeling, keep them in cold water to cover to prevent darkening.

To boil: Boil new, scrubbed potatoes or older potatoes, peeled and cut into quarters. Cook prepared potatoes in boiling salted water to cover until just tender; cooking time depends on the size of the potatoes or the pieces. Drain. Return potatoes to saucepan and shake over low heat until dry. Season with salt and pepper and serve with butter. New potatoes are delicious served with a mixture of two thirds olive oil and one third lemon juice plus some grated lemon rind and freshly ground pepper.

To bake: Scrub and wash the skin and dry with kitchen paper. To keep skins soft, rub with a little fat. Pierce the skin to allow steam to escape while the potato bakes. Bake in a preheated hot oven (Gas 8, 450° F, 230° C) for about 40 minutes or until tender, that is, soft when pressed. Potatoes can be baked at any temperature; naturally, at lower temperatures the baking time will be longer. Baked along with a roast at moderate heat (Gas 4, 350° F, 180° C) they will take about 1½ hours or longer (depending on size).

To pot roast along with meat: Cut peeled large potatoes into halves lengthwise or use whole new potatoes, peeled or scraped. Wash and dry with kitchen paper. About 1 to 1½ hours before the roast is done, roll the potatoes in the pan in the dripping from the roast. Place cut side down along the roast. Turn the potatoes several times to ensure even roasting. Baste frequently with the pan dripping to keep the potatoes soft and moist.

Mashed potatoes: Peel potatoes, cut them into even-sized pieces, wash and drain. Cook, covered, in boiling salted water to cover until tender. Drain. Mash with a fork or potato masher, or put through a food mill. Do not use the blender or potatoes will acquire a plastic consistency. Return to saucepan. For each pound of potatoes, add at least 2 tablespoons *hot* milk, cream or potato water. Over low heat, beat the potatoes until they are fluffy. Serve immediately.

Potato Soup with Cucumbers

4–6 servings

2 large cucumbers
1 kg (2 lb) potatoes, peeled and cut into small cubes
1 l (1¾ pts) chicken stock or water
salt

freshly ground pepper
3 dl (½ pt) milk
3 dl (½ pt) double cream
1 tbsp grated onion
2 tbsps finely chopped dill, or more to taste

Peel the cucumbers and trim off ends. Cut them first into four, lengthwise. Scoop out the seeds with a spoon. Cut the cucumbers into small cubes and reserve. Put the potatoes and the chicken stock into a large, heavy saucepan. Bring to the boil. Reduce heat to low and season with salt and pepper. Cook until the potatoes are soft and easy to mash. Strain the potatoes with their liquid through a sieve or a food mill into a large bowl. Return the potatoes and their cooking liquid to the saucepan. Bring to boiling point and reduce heat to low. Stir in the milk, the cream and the grated onion. Add the cucumber. Simmer without a cover for about 5 minutes or until the cucumbers are tender but not mushy. Check the seasoning and stir in the dill.

Hungarian Paprika Potatoes

4–6 servings
Serve with pork or sausages.

60 g (2 oz) butter
1 medium onion, thinly sliced
1 kg (2 lb) potatoes, peeled and
  cut into bite-sized pieces
1½ dl (¼ pt) water, or beef or
  chicken stock
salt

2 tbsps sweet or hot paprika
freshly ground pepper
2 bay leaves
1 tbsp cider vinegar, or to taste
4 tbsps sour cream
2 tbsps finely chopped parsley

Heat the butter in a heavy casserole. Cook the onion until soft. Add the potatoes, the water, a little salt, the paprika and, if wanted, a little pepper and the bay leaves. Simmer, covered, over moderate heat for about 10 minutes or until the potatoes are tender but firm. Shake the pan frequently to prevent sticking, and, if necessary, add a little more water, 1 tablespoon at a time. Stir in the vinegar to taste. Cook for 1 to 2 more minutes. Remove the bay leaves. Stir in the sour cream and heat through, but do not boil. Sprinkle with the parsley and serve very hot.

Sugar-Browned Potatoes

4 servings
A favourite Danish way of cooking potatoes.

12 small new potatoes
30 g (1 oz) butter

2–3 tbsps sugar
1 tsp salt

Cook the potatoes in boiling salted water until just tender. Drain and peel. Heat the butter in a frying pan. Stir in the sugar and the salt. Cook over low heat, stirring constantly, until the sugar is melted and has turned golden-brown. Do not scorch. Add the potatoes. Cook over lowest possible heat until the potatoes are browned on all sides. Stir with a fork or shake the pan frequently to avoid sticking.

Heaven and Earth

4–6 servings

A German speciality from the Rhineland, known in Holland as 'hot lightning' for its treacherous heat-retaining properties. Excellent with all pork dishes and with duck.

4 large potatoes, peeled and cut into pieces
3 tart apples, peeled, cored and cut into quarters or eighths
salt

sugar to taste
⅛ tsp ground nutmeg
60 g (2 oz) butter, at room temperature

Cook the potatoes in water to cover for about 10 minutes or until they are about three-quarters soft. Drain off about half of the water. Add the apples, mix and cook until the apples are tender. Mash the mixture as in mashed potatoes. Season with salt and sugar to taste. Beat in the nutmeg. Beat in the butter and beat until light.

Braised Potatoes

4–5 servings

1 kg (2 lb) potatoes, peeled and washed
30 g (1 oz) butter
2 tbsps olive oil
1 garlic clove, chopped fine

4 tbsps finely chopped parsley
2–3 bay leaves, finely crumbled
1½ dl (¼ pt) chicken stock
salt
freshly ground pepper

Cut the potatoes into small cubes. Wash, drain and dry thoroughly on kitchen paper. Heat the butter and the oil in a heavy saucepan. Add the potatoes. Cook over medium heat, stirring constantly, for about 3 minutes. Add the garlic, the parsley, the bay leaves and the stock. Taste and season with salt and pepper. Cover tightly and simmer over low heat for 5 to 8 minutes or until the potatoes are tender and moist, but not soupy. Stir frequently.

Note: Different kinds of potatoes absorb liquid differently. If you need more stock, add it 2 tablespoons at a time.

German Potato Salad

4 servings

1 kg (2 lb) potatoes (preferably
  waxy new potatoes)
3 tbsps bacon fat, melted
2 tbsps cider vinegar
2½ dl (8 fl oz) stock
1 medium onion, chopped fine or
  grated

salt
freshly ground pepper
4 tbsps parsley or 3 tbsps dill,
  finely chopped
2–3 red radishes, sliced (optional)

Cook the potatoes in boiling, heavily salted water until tender (the salted water keeps them firm). Drain. Cool the potatoes only until it is just possible to handle them. Peel and cut into slices. Place in a shallow bowl and sprinkle with the bacon fat and the vinegar. Add the beef stock and the onion. Season with salt and pepper. Toss gently with two forks, coating every potato slice with the dressing. Cover and let stand at room temperature for 2 hours. Do not chill. At serving time, sprinkle with the parsley and decorate with the radish slices.

Thick Potato Skordalia

about 2½ cups
A Greek potato and garlic sauce, to be served with fried fish or cooked vegetables. It can be as garlicky as wanted and it should be solid rather than liquid.

500 g (1 lb) potatoes (baking
  potatoes are best)
boiling salted water
4–6 garlic cloves, peeled
1 tsp salt

2 dl (6 fl oz) olive oil
2 tbsps fresh lemon juice or more
  to taste
freshly ground pepper

Peel the potatoes and cut them into quarters. Wash and drain. Cook in plenty of boiling salted water until barely tender. They must not overcook or they will be watery. Drain and return to the saucepan. Over moderate heat, shake the saucepan with the potatoes to dry them out completely. Mash them to a smooth purée; keep them warm. While the potatoes are cooking, mash the garlic cloves with the salt in a heavy bowl. Add the potatoes and beat until potatoes and garlic are blended. Beating constantly, add two thirds of the olive oil in a thin, steady stream. Gradually beat in the lemon juice. If the mixture is too thick, beat in a little more olive oil, 1 tablespoon at a time. Taste and season with salt and plenty of pepper. Serve lukewarm.

Thin Potato Skordalia

In addition to the ingredients listed above, beat 1 to 2 dl (4 to 6 fl oz) chicken or fish stock into the mixture, to the desired degree of thinness.

Potherb

From the middle of the sixteenth century potherb was the general term for any herb grown in the kitchen garden. Nowadays, it is a rather old-fashioned expression for any edible greens whose fleshy leaves and stems are boiled and eaten, or used to flavour other foods. Pies made with these green vegetables turn up in one form or another in the cooking of most countries, especially southern ones. Basically, they are the food of poor country people, containing what is at hand in the way of greens, rice, eggs, milk, cheese or nuts. Sometimes, they are encased in pastry shells, other times just baked; I prefer this latter version. The cook can combine any greens that are available, provided they are leafy.

The combination of greens given below comes from Lombardy, but I added the dandelion leaves. A word of caution: there is a certain amount of waste in leafy greens, such as wilted leaves, tough stems, etc. To come out with the required amount of trimmed greens, get up to 500 g (1 lb) more, depending on their condition.

Potherb Pie

6 servings

1 kg (2 lb) chard, trimmed
1 kg (2 lb) spinach, trimmed
500 g (1 lb) dandelion leaves, trimmed
60 g (2 oz) butter
60 g (2 oz) bacon fat
2 garlic cloves, crushed
60 g (2 oz) pine nuts
3 eggs, lightly beaten
2½ dl (8 fl oz) single cream or milk

110 g (4 oz) grated Parmesan cheese
½ tsp ground nutmeg
salt
freshly ground pepper
60 g (2 oz) currants or seedless raisins, plumped in warm water and drained
butter
fine dry breadcrumbs

Wash the greens in at least three changes of cold water, or until not a trace of sand or dirt remains in the water. Drain but do not shake dry. Put the greens into a large pan with the water that clings to them. Cover the pan and cook over high heat for about 8 to 10 minutes or until tender. Do not overcook the greens because they will lose their flavour. Drain in a sieve over a bowl, saving the cooking liquid for soups, stews or sauces. Do not throw it away because it is full of vitamins. First with the back of a wooden spoon and then with the hands, squeeze as much water as possible out of the greens. Put them on a chopping board and chop medium fine. Drain the chopped greens again, squeezing with the hands. Put the greens into a large bowl. In a large, deep frying pan, heat half the butter with the bacon fat. Cook the garlic and the pine nuts over medium heat, stirring constantly, until the nuts are golden. Add the chopped greens. Cook, stirring all the time, for about 7 to 10 minutes, or until the greens are thoroughly coated with the fat. Return the cooked greens to the bowl. Beat together the eggs, the cream, two thirds of the grated Parmesan and the nutmeg. Taste and season with salt and pepper. Stir in the currants. Pour this mixture over the greens and mix well. Butter a 25-cm (10-inch) shallow baking dish or pie dish and coat it with the breadcrumbs. Turn the vegetable mixture into it and smooth out the top. Sprinkle with the remaining Parmesan and dot with the remaining butter. Bake in a preheated moderate oven (Gas 4, 350° F, 180° C) for 10 minutes. Turn the oven to low (Gas 2½, 325° F, 165° C) and bake for 20 to 30 more minutes or until set and browned. Cut into wedges and serve warm or cold, but not chilled.

Potherb Soup Chez Moi

4–6 servings
Use any greens, single or in combination, such as lettuce, dandelions, kale, beet tops, etc.

4 large potatoes, peeled and
  washed, diced small
1¾ l (3 pts) boiling water
1 kg (2 lb) potherbs, cut into
  very fine strips

4 tbsps olive oil
½ tsp hot pepper flakes, or to
  taste (optional)
salt
freshly ground pepper

Cook the potatoes in the boiling water until barely tender. Add the potherbs. Bring to the boil and stir in the olive oil, the hot pepper flakes and salt and pepper. Lower heat to medium and cook for 3 minutes, stirring frequently. The vegetables should be still crisp. Serve very hot.

Note: For a more substantial soup, add at the same time as the potherbs about 250 g ($\frac{1}{2}$ lb) sweet or hot Italian or Polish sausage, thoroughly cooked and thinly sliced.

Pumpkin

(*Cucurbita pepo*)

The pumpkin, cousin to melons, cucumbers, marrows and squash, grows on a low, trailing vine. Technically, it is a berry which we do not use as a fruit, but as a vegetable. The plant's flowers are large, handsome, creamy-white to deep-yellow blossoms and are edible as well. Pumpkins are oblong to round in shape, with a smooth or ribbed orange skin. The flesh is soft, moist, somewhat coarse and fibrous, and sweet in flavour; the colour is largely bright orange though some varieties may be a pale to warm buff. Pumpkins are large fruit, measuring an average 25 to 45 cm (10 to 18 inches) in diameter and weighing 5 to 12 kg (10 to 25 lb). The name appears to come from the Greek *pepon* (large melon) via the Latin *pepo* and its French nasalization *pompon* to the original English form 'pompion', the latter's ending being converted into a 'kin' probably in the American colonies where, like all squashes, pumpkins most likely originated.

Archaeological discoveries in Mexico have found pumpkin fragments dating back to 2000 B.C. Very likely a small, apple-shaped pumpkin was introduced into Europe in the sixteenth century. However, through the centuries, other squashes, such as our oblong vegetable marrow and the courgettes or zucchini of France and Italy, have proved infinitely more popular in Europe than the round, orange pumpkin, grown in England only in very limited quantities but increasingly imported from the Mediterranean. Pumpkin-and-apple pie, however, was a traditional English favourite from the days of Parkinson's *Earthly Paradise* (1629) to the early nineteenth century.

How to buy

Buy clean, well-matured pumpkins with a firm rind and a rich colour, free from scarring and disease and unharmed by frosts; or buy wedges newly cut from such pumpkins. Avoid broken or cracked pumpkins, with any sign of soft rot or wet breakdown.

How to keep

Store in a dry, well-ventilated place, or refrigerate. Whole, raw, on kitchen shelf: about 1 month. Whole, raw, in refrigerator: 1 to 3 months. Cut, raw, in refrigerator: 1 or 2 weeks. Fresh, cooked, on refrigerator shelf: 3 to 4 days.

Nutritive values

A good source of vitamin A and a fair source of minerals. Raw: 26 calories; tinned: 33 calories (per 100 g/3½ oz).

How to use

To boil: Cut the pumpkin into halves and scrape off pulp and seeds. Cut into small pieces and peel. Cook in boiling salted water to cover for about 10 minutes or until tender. Drain and mash or push through a sieve. Season with salt and pepper and butter for use as a vegetable, or use in pies or other desserts.

To bake: Cut pumpkin into halves and scrape off pulp and seeds. Cut into quarters and eighths. Place, cut side down, in a baking pan, add a little water and bake in a preheated moderate oven (Gas 4, 350° F, 180° C) for 35 to 45 minutes or until tender. Turn right side up, season the cavity with salt and pepper, a little scraped onion, brown sugar or molasses and a pat of butter. Bake 5 to 10 minutes longer. Alternatively, cut into pieces and place, cut side up, in a baking pan. Sprinkle with salt and pepper and brush generously with melted butter or margarine. Bake in a preheated moderate oven (as above) for 35 minutes or until tender. Brush repeatedly with melted butter. Serve as a vegetable.

Pumpkin and Tomato Casserole

4 servings

The sauce of this dish can be used for other cooked vegetables such as chick peas, green beans or dried beans. Don't overcook the vegetables and cook the sauce only briefly, for a fuller flavour.

3 tbsps olive oil	salt
2 garlic cloves, sliced	freshly ground pepper
2–3 large tomatoes, peeled and chopped	dash Tabasco sauce
	750 g (1½ lb) peeled pumpkin cut into small cubes
3 tbsps chopped fresh basil or 2 tbsps dried basil	boiling salted water

Heat the olive oil and add the garlic. Cook over medium heat for 2 to 3 minutes or until the garlic is golden (not brown). Add the tomatoes, the basil, the salt and pepper and the Tabasco sauce. Cook, stirring constantly, for about 5 minutes. Lower heat and simmer for 5 more minutes. While the sauce is cooking, cook the pumpkin in boiling salted water to cover for 3 to 5 minutes or until barely tender. Drain and add to the tomato sauce. Cook over high heat, stirring constantly, for 2 to 3 minutes or until the vegetables are blended. Serve hot.

Note: If the pumpkin (or other vegetable) is already cooked and cold, adjust the time it heats in the tomato sauce to 5 minutes over medium heat.

Pumpkin Daube

6 servings

In Martinique and Guadaloupe, this West Indian pumpkin dish is called a colombo de giraumon. In the United States, it would be made with calabaza or hubbard squash.

30 g (1 oz) butter	⅛ tsp ground cloves
6 rashers bacon, chopped fine	1 garlic clove, crushed
1 medium onion, chopped fine	salt
1 green pepper, chopped fine	freshly ground pepper
2 large tomatoes, peeled and chopped	1 tsp curry powder
500 g (1 lb) pumpkin, peeled, seeded and cut into cubes	3 tbsps water

Combine the butter and the bacon in a heavy saucepan. Cook, stirring constantly, for about 4 minutes. Add the onion and the pepper and cook for about 3 to 4 minutes or until the onion is soft. Add the tomatoes and cook for 5 minutes longer. Add the pumpkin and mix well. Cook, covered, over low heat, stirring frequently, until the pumpkin is very tender and begins to fall apart. Stir in the cloves, the garlic and the salt and pepper. Simmer, covered, for 3 more minutes. Stir the curry powder into the water and add to the pumpkin. Mix well and simmer for 5 more minutes, or until the vegetable is almost a purée.

Radish

(Raphanus sativus)

A radish is the crisp root of a hardy annual, grown in many varieties throughout the temperate world, mainly as a salad vegetable. Radishes vary in shape, size and colour. They are round, oblong or long, cylindrical or tapered, in colours ranging from a creamy white through pink, red, white-and-red and purple to black, weighing from a fraction of an ounce to several pounds,

with a flavour that goes from mild to peppery. The radishes we favour are for the greater part the size of cherries, whereas those favoured by the orientals, especially the Japanese, range from finger size to more than 60 cm (2 feet) in length and from the size of a marble to that of a basketball. China and Middle Asia are believed to be the original homes of the radish. The ancients knew and liked large radishes too. Pliny, in the first century A.D., wrote of long white radishes the size of a boy infant, to me a chilling thought. Radishes were common food in Egypt long before the pyramids were built, and the Greeks seem to have known three varieties. Gerard went one better in his 1596 *Herbal*, describing four varieties in common use since Saxon days. Radishes were probably introduced here by the Romans but there is no record of real cultivation before the ninth century.

In commercial practice these days we seem to be back to the ancients' level again, for all we find commonly in our shops are the 'Scarlet Globe' types, round radishes with red skins, the round or oblong radishes which are half-red half-white, usually known as 'Sparklers', and occasionally long white radishes called 'Icicles'. The long or round 'Black Spanish' radishes, with their pungent, crisp, snow-white flesh, are found but seldom in the markets. Home gardeners, however, grow this and another winter radish, the long pink 'China Rose', with success. On the whole, radishes are easy to grow and quick as well, the so-called spring types taking only a little over 3 weeks.

Our use of the radish is far more limited than that of the orientals, since we eat it mainly raw, not as the lovely cooked vegetable it can be. In China and Japan, where the radish crop is nearly one third of the tonnage of vegetables grown, most of the radishes are pickled in brine as we pickle cucumbers. The French chill their radishes and, as part of an hors d'œuvre, eat them with sweet butter and salt. The Germans slice them thinly, dress them with oil and vinegar and consume them as a relish or a salad.

How to buy

Buy fresh, smooth, well-formed, crisp, firm radishes with fresh tops, though the condition of the tops is not always an indication of quality. Medium-size radishes are preferable. Buy bunches of radishes rather than topped radishes in plastic bags. Avoid radishes with black spots and pits, cracked radishes, spongy, flabby, wilted radishes or very large radishes which are apt to have pithy centres. Also avoid radishes with yellow or decayed tops.

How to keep

Refrigerate in vegetable drawer. Cut off any yellowing tops and rootlets. Raw, whole, on refrigerator shelf or in vegetable drawer: 1 week.

Nutritive values

If eaten in sufficient quantities, radishes would be a fair source of minerals. Raw, common radishes: 17 calories; oriental radishes: 19 calories (per 100 g/3½ oz).

How to use

Remove all leaves and rootlets and wash thoroughly. To crisp, refrigerate radishes in a bowl of iced water.

Hot Buttered Radishes

4 servings
Serve them as a vegetable, or add to a stew at serving time.

60 g (2 oz) butter
4 tbsps finely chopped spring
   onions
2 bunches thinly sliced radishes

4 tbsps water
salt
freshly ground pepper

Heat the butter in a saucepan. Add the spring onions and cook, stirring constantly, for about 2 to 3 minutes. Add the radishes and the water. Simmer, covered, for 3 to 4 minutes, shaking the pan frequently to prevent sticking. Season with salt and pepper *after* the radishes are cooked (in cooking, the salt drains the colour).

Rice

(Oryza sativa)

Rice is the edible seed of an annual cereal grass upon which about one half of the world's population depends almost entirely. The cultivated plant grows about a metre (4 feet) in height, with long and flattened leaves. Its inflorescence, or flowering, consists of spikelets which bear flowers that produce the fruit or grain.

Rice originated in Asia; it was a staple food as early as 2800 B.C. in China, and almost as early in India. Such was its importance that for over 4,500 years, as long as imperial China existed, every 5th of February, the Emperor of China and his princes, ministers, governors and mandarins went to selected rice fields and started cultivation by getting behind the plough. The Emperor would till three rows, the princes six, the ministers nine, the governors twelve and the mandarins fifteen. The people would take some of  this nobly ploughed earth and scatter it over their own fields as a good omen. Rice was holy and wasting it an unforgivable sin in Japan. Rice was food, rice was currency and rice was the symbol of fertility pelted on newly-weds originally in China to wish them good luck and many children, a habit practised in the wasteful West to this day. Fermented and distilled rice is also the basis for the national alcoholic drinks of China (*samshu*) and Japan (*sake*).

Rice to this day dominates the agriculture of the Asian countries, and it is increasingly grown in Africa and South America by small farmers. In Europe, where rice was first introduced by the Saracens, Italy has become the leading rice producer, with southern France and Hungary increasing their production steadily.

Rice is most often grown in standing water, the hollow stem, like a built-in snorkel, permitting oxygen to reach the roots. In milling, the outer husk is first removed, exposing the grain covered by a brownish outer layer which forms the bran. This is the highly nutritious 'natural brown rice' which, thanks to the health food movement, has so greatly increased in popularity during the last few years. Rice is then further milled in an operation called 'pearling' which removes the bran; this makes a valuable feed for stock. Pearling leaves a white rice, which is frequently polished further to give it a pretty white sheen. In former years, white rice was also given a coating of glucose or of talc, which accounts for the instruction found in old recipe books: 'Wash rice until water runs clear.' Now this is no longer necessary.

In England rice was known but not much used until the later seventeenth century when it began to be imported in quantity, probably because of prohibitively high wheat prices at home. In 1689 rice replaced water-gruel in the diet at Christ's Hospital in London, but the first recommendations were still rather hesitant and indicated no great familiarity with the substance.

There are two main kinds of white rice:

Long-grain rice: The grain is about four to five times longer than it is wide. The grains tend to separate in cooking, resulting in a fluffy but still firm rice. Long-grain rice lends itself to pilafs, salads and dishes where rice is only one of the ingredients. Basmati rice is the outstanding example, with Patna rice a less expensive second.

Medium- and short-grain rice: The grains are short, plump and roundish. In cooking, the grains become moist and tend to stick together. These varieties are used in any dishes where rice has to cling together, for example in puddings, moulded dishes or risottos.

Since the Asian countries have little rice left for export after supplying home consumption other countries have taken up commercial production. The United States is the largest exporter. Their consumer research has dreamed up all kinds of pre-cooked rice which are widely marketed and expensive; among them is a proprietary long-grain rice which has been parboiled, steamed and dried, which will emerge invariably 'tender but firm and fluffy' from any way you cook it, and which has no taste whatsoever.

Wild rice, *Zizania aquatica*, is not a rice at all, but the seed of an aquatic grass of north-eastern America, which serves as food for water fowl and which only the Indians are now allowed to harvest for their own use and for sale (see page 331).

How to keep

Stored in a covered container, rice will keep almost indefinitely.

Nutritive values

Brown rice is extremely rich in nutrients, containing about 8 per cent protein, little fat, few vitamins but a good amount of thiamine (vitamin B_1), niacin, riboflavin, iron and calcium. Polished rice is largely deprived of these nutrients. Brown rice, cooked: 119 calories; white rice, cooked: 109 calories (per 100 g/$3\frac{1}{2}$ oz).

How to use

There are different ways of cooking rice, and different kinds of rice absorb liquid differently and cook for different lengths of time. No two cooks will quite agree on the best way, but the following is a useful and a fool-proof way of cooking rice for most general purposes:

2 tea-cups long-grain rice	salt
2 tea-cups water	2–3 oz butter or margarine

To wash the rice, pour boiling water over it in a bowl and stir well for a few seconds. Pour into a sieve or a small-holed colander (a metal one is best) and rinse under cold running water until the water runs clear. Drain well.

Bring 2 cups water to the boil in a pan with a little salt to taste. Throw in the drained rice, bring to the boil again and boil vigorously for 2 minutes. Cover the pan with a tight-fitting lid and simmer very gently, undisturbed, for about 20 minutes, until the water has been absorbed and the rice is cooked. It should be tender and separate, with little holes all over the surface. Turn off the heat, and allow the rice to rest for about 10 minutes.

Melt the butter or margarine in a saucepan and put it evenly all over the rice. Let it rest again, covered, for 3 minutes longer, until the melted fat has been absorbed by the rice.

One teaspoon lemon juice or vinegar will keep rice white when cooking in hard water.

Green Rice

4–6 servings

500 g (1 lb) cooked rice
3 eggs, beaten
2 bunches parsley, chopped fine
1 medium onion, grated
1 garlic clove, crushed
60 g (2 oz) melted butter

60 g (2 oz) grated Gruyère or
   Parmesan cheese
1½ dl (¼ pt) stock
salt
freshly ground pepper

Combine all the ingredients and mix well. Turn into a buttered 2-litre or 2-quart baking dish. Bake in a preheated moderate oven (Gas 4, 350° F, 180° C) for 30 minutes or until the top is golden brown.

Sushi

4–6 servings
This is a traditional Japanese way of using rice which is almost unknown in the West but which can easily be adapted to our tastes and preferences.

500 g (1 lb) rice
6 dl (1 pt) water
4 tbsps rice-wine vinegar, cider
   vinegar or white vinegar

1 tsp salt
60 g (2 oz) sugar
topping ingredients

Bring water to the boil. Add the rice and stir. Cover pan; bring to the boil again, then reduce heat to very low. Cook for 20 minutes. Take off heat and let it stand for 5 minutes. Turn rice into a bowl. Combine the vinegar, the salt and the sugar. Pour over the rice, stir lightly with a fork until well mixed, then leave to cool.

Roll the rice into balls and flatten these into small (3 cm, 1 inch) patties. Top with thinly sliced, chopped or mashed (as appropriate) raw or cooked fish, shellfish, mushrooms, or salad vegetables and serve as appetizers or hors d'œuvre, accompanied by individual pots of a light soy sauce for dipping.

Rice and Artichoke Casserole

4–6 servings

60 g (2 oz) butter
2 tbsps olive oil
2 large or 4 small artichokes, sliced
1 large tomato, peeled, seeded and chopped
1 garlic clove, chopped fine
2 tsps dried basil

5 dl (up to 1 pt, approximately) hot chicken stock
250 g (½ lb) long-grain rice
1 tsp salt
freshly ground pepper
3 tbsps chopped parsley
freshly ground Parmesan cheese

Heat about half of the butter with the olive oil in a heavy saucepan. Add the artichokes. Cook, stirring constantly, for 3 minutes. Add the tomato, the garlic, the basil and 6 tablespoons of the stock. Simmer, covered, over low heat until the artichokes are half tender. Heat the remaining butter in a 2-litre or 2-quart casserole. Add the rice. Cook over medium heat, stirring constantly, until the rice is yellow and opaque. Add the remaining stock, the salt and the pepper. Simmer, covered, over lowest possible heat until the rice is three-quarters cooked (10 to 15 minutes). Check for moisture and, if necessary, add a little more hot stock or water, a few tablespoons at a time. The dish should not be soupy. Add the artichokes to the rice and mix well. Simmer, covered, until both rice and artichokes are tender. Again check for moisture. Sprinkle with parsley and serve with plenty of freshly grated Parmesan cheese.

Country Risotto

6 servings

250 g ($\frac{1}{2}$ lb) dry white beans
9 dl ($1\frac{1}{2}$ pts) well-flavoured chicken or beef stock
2 medium potatoes, cut into small cubes
2 large carrots, sliced
2 medium artichokes, thinly sliced
2 large courgettes, sliced
2 leeks, white and green parts, sliced, or 1 bunch spring onions, white and green parts, sliced

1 turnip, cut into small cubes
250 g ($\frac{1}{2}$ lb) uncooked round-grain rice
salt
freshly ground pepper
1 kg (2 lb) fresh peas, shelled, or a 250-g ($\frac{1}{2}$-lb) package frozen peas, thawed
100 g ($3\frac{1}{2}$ oz) butter
$\frac{3}{4}$ tsp dried sage or 1 tbsp fresh sage, chopped

Pour boiling water over the beans and let them stand for 1 hour. Then put them in a deep pan, add more water to cover and cook until the beans are three-quarters done. Add all but $2\frac{1}{2}$ dl (8 fl oz) stock and bring to the boil. Add the vegetables except rice and peas. Cook over high heat for about 4 minutes. Add the rice and half of the remaining stock. Season with salt and pepper. Cook, covered, over medium heat, stirring frequently, until the rice is almost tender. Add the peas. Cook, covered, until the peas and rice are tender. If the risotto is too liquid, cook without cover to allow evaporation. If too thick, add a little more stock. Melt the butter and stir the sage into it. Stir the sage butter into the risotto.

Salsify, Oyster Plant

(*Tragopogon porrifolius*)

Scorzonera

(*Scorzonera hispanica*)

Salsify is the fleshy edible root of a herb belonging to the daisy family which, raw or cooked, tastes remarkably though not quite like an oyster. The tapering root can be as long as 25 cm (10 inches) and 5 cm (2 inches) across. It is a greyish-white in colour, with a milky-white, firm, juicy flesh. A close relation is the scorzonera, black on the outside, with a white flesh similar to that of the salsify, with which it is interchangeable in cooking and in flavour. The name scorzonera has been elaborately explained as deriving from the Spanish-Catalan word for viper since it was used as an antidote for its bites. However, the word is Italian, since the variety is very popular in Italy, and simply means 'black skin' (*scorza*, skin or rind, and *nera*, black). In German, it is called *Schwarzwurzel*, black root.

Salsify and scorzonera are far better known on the Continent than here, though occasionally one finds them (mostly the salsify) in shops during the winter. It is considered a great delicacy, and rightly so. The plant is a native of the Mediterranean, where originally it was collected from the wild. Since it runs wild in gardens and seeds, smaller wild specimens are also found near by. Salsify was known in France and Germany in the thirteenth century but it was not cultivated until the sixteenth century.

Because of its large yellow flowers, salsify served also as a garden ornament. It was sometimes known as goatsbeard, because of its thin, tufted, narrow leaves. As a food plant, salsify never gained wide acceptance, although it has had rather formidable advocates: Gerard in his *Herbal* (1596) acknowledged that its flavour surpassed that of carrot or parsnip, and two centuries later Eliza Acton observed, 'We are surprised that a vegetable so excellent as this should be so little cared for in England.' Gerard's contemporary, Parkinson, favoured scorzonera, which he candied.

How to keep

Refrigerate in the vegetable drawer for 3 to 4 days.

Nutritive values

Caloric content depends on condition of the root. The freshly-harvested, raw root: 100 calories; stored root: 82 calories (per 100 g/3½ oz).

How to use

Salsify, like artichokes and celeriac, discolours when cut. Before preparing it, have ready a bowl with acidulated cold water in which to keep the pieces until cooking time. Trim and scrape the roots, and cut them into 5-cm (2-inch) lengths, or into sticks. Wash and drain. Add, depending on the quantity cooked, 1 to 3 teaspoons lemon juice or vinegar to 3 cm (1 inch) boiling salted water. Cook, covered, for about 5 to 10 minutes, depending on the size of the pieces, or until just tender. Do not overcook. Drain, season and serve with butter and lemon juice. Or mash and treat like potatoes. Or cook in stock and serve as they are. Or sauté with a touch of dry white wine. Or serve with a light béchamel or hollandaise sauce which does not overwhelm the delicate vegetable. Or (one of the best ways) marinate the cooked, drained vegetable in a light vinaigrette dressing and chill.

Salsify in Cream

4–6 servings

1 kg (2 lb) salsify, trimmed,
scraped and cut into 5-cm
(2-inch) pieces
boiling salted water
60 g (2 oz) butter
1 tbsp grated onion

2½ dl (8 fl oz) double cream, hot
salt
freshly ground pepper
¼ tsp ground nutmeg
3 tbsps chopped parsley

Cook the salsify in 2 to 3 cm (1 inch) boiling water until three-quarters tender. Drain. Heat the butter in a casserole that can go to the table. Add the onion and cook, stirring constantly, for 1 minute. Add the salsify and toss in the butter. Add the cream and season with the salt and pepper and the nutmeg. Simmer, covered, over low heat for about 5 to 10 minutes or until the salsify is tender. Sprinkle with the parsley before serving.

Salsify Hors d'OEuvre

4–6 servings
This can also be made with cooked, peeled and sliced Jerusalem artichokes.

1½ dl (¼ pt) olive oil
fresh lemon juice to taste
2 tsps grated onion
salt

freshly ground pepper
½ tsp prepared mustard (optional)
1 kg (2 lb) cooked salsify, sliced

Combine all the ingredients except the salsify in a bowl. Mix thoroughly. Add the salsify and toss gently. Cover and refrigerate for 1 hour or more.

Fried Salsify

4 servings
Courgettes may be fried in the same manner.

1 kg (2 lb) salsify, trimmed,
scraped and cut into 5-cm
(2-inch) pieces
boiling salted water

flour
olive oil for frying
salt

Vegetable Cookery

Cook the salsify in boiling water until barely tender. Drain and dry with kitchen paper. Put the flour into a paper bag, add the salsify and shake to coat. Shake off excess flour. Heat about 5 cm (2 inches) of olive oil in a deep frying pan to smoking point. Fry a few salsify pieces at a time until they are golden. Drain on kitchen paper and keep hot in a low oven. When all the pieces are fried, pile them on a hot serving dish, sprinkle with salt and serve hot.

Samphire

(*Crithmum maritimum*)

True samphire is a succulent perennial which grows on seaside rocks and cliffs in many parts of Britain. It is gathered or, on the Continent, grown commercially, for its leaves, which are crisp and aromatic. They make an excellent salad green, or may be pickled, or cooked as a potherb. The young stems are edible as well and can be similarly prepared. The narrow spiky leaves on their thin stems are so arranged as to make the whole plant look like miniature, sparse Christmas trees.

Marsh samphire or glasswort (*Salicornia europaea*) is said to be ready for picking on the longest day and washed by every tide. You have to wade the mud to get to it, but, when you get it home, boil or steam it until just tender and serve with melted butter.

Seaweeds

Seaweeds include several thousand very different plants, of which a number are edible and mainly used in oriental cooking. Japan, Korea, the Pacific islands and Hawaii all use various kinds of seaweeds as vegetables, as pickles and as flavourings for sauces and soups. Many of these are available in a dried form from health-food shops. Usually the dried fronds are chopped and added to soups and stews, or they are nibbled as a relish.

On our own coast, perhaps the best known edible seaweed is Irish moss or carragheen (*Chrondrus crispus*), a reddish or purplish plant found in Ireland but also in Dorset and Yorkshire. When cooked, it becomes gelatinous, thickening and stiffening foods like blancmange. Before the introduction of commercial gelatine, Irish moss served in its stead and was a household staple. Irish moss (Iberian moss to chemists) was also used to clarify home-made and commercial wines before newer products were developed.

Laver (*Porphyra umbilicalis*) is common all round Britain, but is gathered and is popular especially in South Wales where a purée made by slowly simmering the translucent purple fronds is sold as laverbread. Mixed with oatmeal and fried in bacon fat it is a favourite breakfast food. In Japan, laver is cultivated and used in various ways of which the crisp cocktail crackers are the one way we are familiar with.

Shallot

(*Allium ascalonicum*)

A mildly aromatic bulb, cousin of the onion. The shallot grows in clusters, like garlic, with any number from two to six growing from a common base. The single bulbs are elongated and small, measuring usually less than 5 cm (2 inches) in length and half as much across. They are greenish at the base and purplish on the upper portion, covered by a thick outer reddish-to-grey skin. The edible parts are the green tops, which are harvested in early summer and sometimes sold as scallions, and the dried bulbs, which are used like onions or garlic.

Shallots are natives of the eastern Mediterranean countries, taking their botanical name from the city of Ascalon. Pliny mentions Ascalonicum onions as being good for sauce. Saladin's army was defeated at Ascalon in 1192, and crusaders are thought to have brought onions back to France among their spoils, as they did other foods such as sugar. In the ninth century the shallot was one of the eighteen herbs that grew in the kitchen gardens of the great Monastery of St Gall in Switzerland, then one of the great centres of civilization. Charlemagne, who was also a great expert on edible plants, grew shallots in his gardens near Aix-la-Chapelle.

In French cookery, shallots are an essential ingredient. Their flavour is complex, neither onion nor garlic, yet with traces of both. This mild, yet definite, flavour is ideally suited to sophisticated sauces and butters such as bercy and beurre blanc, all the more so since shallots emulsify more easily than onions.

How to buy

Buy dry, firm, well-filled and rounded shallots. Avoid shrunken, shrivelled bulbs.

How to keep

Store in a cool, dry, well-ventilated place for 1 to 2 months.

Nutritive values

Raw: 72 calories per 100 g (3½ oz).

How to use

Use like onion or garlic. The tiny green shoots sent up by some shallots may be utilized along with the rest of the bulb, or snipped into salads.

Beurre Blanc

This creamy shallot butter comes from Nantes, on the Loire, where it is traditionally served with pike and other poached fish. It has an excellent taste, but is somewhat tricky to make; quite often the first attempt is not successful. The trick is to cream the butter with the vinegar and shallot mixture at an extremely low heat to prevent the butter from separating, and to serve it barely warm. The consistency of beurre blanc should be that of a light hollandaise.

3 tbsps white vinegar
3 tbsps dry white wine
1½ tbsps finely chopped shallots
300 g (12 oz) butter, cut into
  small pieces

salt
freshly ground pepper

Combine the vinegar, the wine and the shallots in a small saucepan. Cook over medium heat until all the ingredients have boiled down to about 1½ tablespoons. Remove from the heat and immediately beat in about 30 g (1 oz) of the butter until it begins to look creamy. Return the saucepan to the lowest heat possible, preferably over an asbestos mat. Beat in another 30 g (1 oz) of the butter until it becomes creamy and has become almost assimilated into the sauce. Repeat until all the butter has been used up. Remove from the heat and beat in salt and pepper. Rinse a serving bowl with warm water and dry; it should be barely warm. Spoon the sauce into it and serve.

Bercy Butter

This shallot and white wine butter is served on steaks and grilled meat.

3 tbsps dry white wine
1½ tbsps finely chopped shallots
1 dl (4 fl oz) beef stock
110 g (4 oz) butter, at room temperature

1 tbsp finely chopped parsley
salt
freshly ground white pepper

Combine the wine, the shallots and the stock in a small saucepan. Cook over medium heat until all the ingredients have boiled down to about 1½ tablespoons. Cool. Mash the butter with a wooden spoon and beat it until it is light and creamy. Or beat with an electric blender. Beat the butter, a little at a time, into the wine mixture, beating well after each addition. When all the butter has been beaten in, beat in the parsley and salt and pepper to taste.

Sorrel, Dock

(genus *Rumex*)

Sorrel is a hardy perennial herb belonging to the knotweed family; its sour, pungent, arrow-shaped green leaves are used as a salad green, as a potherb and as a flavouring. The size of the edible leaves is around 7 to 17 cm (3 to 7 inches) in length. The plant is utilized in its wild and cultivated states. All the different sorrel varieties have an acid sap with varying amounts of citric, malic and oxalic acid which account for their sourness. Eaten in large quantities these might be toxic, but they are completely harmless in the limited quantities in which sorrel is eaten at the table or nibbled at in the open as a thirst-quencher.

The best-known sorrel varieties are: spinach dock, *Rumex patientia*, with 30-cm (1-foot) long mild leaves used in the spring as a salad green or potherb; sour dock or garden sorrel, *Rumex acetosa*; and curled dock, *Rumex crispus*. Sheep sorrel, *Rumex acetosella*, is the variety that has refreshed many a thirsty hiker.

Bacon called sorrel 'a cold and acid herb' and the most acid of the sorrels is sour dock or the garden sorrel, *Rumex acetosa*. Diverse varieties are widely cultivated in Europe, especially in France, where sorrel is used to make one of the best French soups. It may also be steamed, puréed or sautéed.

How to buy

Buy (or pick) sorrel as you would any green, choosing young, crisp, bright-green leaves. Avoid limp, wilted leaves or leaves with woody stems. The smaller and fresher, the more desirable.

How to keep

To store, refrigerate in vegetable drawer for 2 to 3 days. Use as soon as possible.

Nutritive values

Sorrel is extremely high in vitamin A, with small amounts of vitamin C and minerals. Raw: 28 calories; cooked and drained: 19 calories (per 100 g/3½ oz).

How to use

Treat like any other salad or potherb.

Sorrel Soup

4 servings

500 g (1 lb) sorrel	1½ dl (¼ pt) double cream
6 spring onions, chopped fine	salt
1½ l (2½ pts) chicken stock	freshly ground pepper
2 egg yolks	

Trim the sorrel, removing any wilted leaves and coarse stems. Wash in several changes of water. Shred the vegetable. Combine the sorrel, the spring onions and the stock. Bring to the boil and lower the heat. Simmer, covered, for 10 minutes. Purée the soup in a blender or leave as it is. If puréed, return to the saucepan. In a bowl, beat together the egg yolks and the double cream. Gradually stir a few tablespoons of the hot soup into the egg mixture, mixing well. Then stir the egg and soup mixture back into the soup. Heat through but do not boil or the soup will curdle. Remove from the heat, taste and season with salt and pepper. Serve hot or chilled.

Chiffonade of Sorrel

4 servings
This is delicious. Serve as a vegetable.

1 kg (2 lb) sorrel	freshly ground pepper
80 g (3 oz) butter	4 tbsps double cream (optional)
salt	

Trim the sorrel, removing any wilted leaves and tough stems. Wash in several changes of water and shake as dry as possible. Cut the sorrel into fine strips. Heat most of the butter in a casserole that can go to the table. Add the sorrel and cook, covered, over low heat for 5 minutes. Uncover and cook for 5 more minutes, stirring frequently, to let the pan juices evaporate. Season with salt and pepper and stir in the remaining butter and the cream. Heat through but do not boil. Serve very hot.

Soy Bean, Soya

(Glycine max)

The edible seeds found in the pods of an erect, bushy, annual herb belonging to the pea family. The plant grows to a height of 45 to 185 cm ($1\frac{1}{2}$ to 6 feet), with rough, brownish hairs on its stems, leaves and pods. The colour of the pods ranges from tan to nearly black and the seeds, depending on the variety, may be green, yellow, brown, black or a combination of these colours. The seeds are small, numbering from 2,500 to 3,500 seeds per pound in the commercial varieties.

The soy bean is economically the world's most important bean, equally suited for human consumption and for industrial purposes. The proteins furnished by the soy bean are the richest and most valuable of vegetable proteins: about 1 kg (2 lb) of soy flour contains as much protein as $2\frac{1}{2}$ kg (5 lb) of meat. The bean is also high in other nutrients, such as vitamins and minerals, whereas it is low in carbohydrate.

Given the richness of its food values, soy beans are comparatively inexpensive to produce, and they are playing an increasingly important role in the world's foods. In the United States, the world's largest producer of soy beans in the 1970s, soy beans are principally made into oil and meal. The oil serves for the making of margarine and for other food uses, while the meal goes into animal feed and is used for human consumption as well. The bean's industrial uses, over a hundred of them, range from fire-fighting foam to adhesives, paints and plastics. In recent years soy protein has gained notoriety in a number of meat-substitute projects, now that there is the technical possibility of literally weaving the stuff to imitate animal tissues.

Soy is believed to be native to south-western Asia, where it was grown prior to 200 B.C. in China. It is the most important food legume in China, Korea, Japan and Malaysia, furnishing essential protein in the protein-poor diets of these countries in the form of sauce, bean curd (*tofu*), bean threads, as sweets and even as boiled soy bean milk.

Soy beans were first grown as a botanical curiosity in France and in England towards the end of the eighteenth century. The first American mention dates from 1804. Not until after 1890 were soy beans taken seriously as a crop anywhere outside their native countries.

Nutritive values

Fresh soy beans, cooked and drained: 118 calories; dried soy beans, cooked and drained: 130 calories; sprouted soy beans, raw: 46 calories; sprouted soy beans, cooked and drained: 38 calories; soy sauce: 68 calories (per 100 g/3½ oz).

Chili Soy Beans

4–6 servings

3 tbsps olive or salad oil
2 medium onions, chopped
2 garlic cloves, finely chopped
1 tbsp chili powder, or to taste
500 g (1 lb) cooked, drained soy beans

500 g (1 lb) peeled, chopped tomatoes
1 tsp dried oregano
dash of Tabasco sauce (optional)
salt
freshly ground pepper

Heat the olive oil in a heavy saucepan. Add the onions and the garlic. Cook, stirring constantly, until the onion is soft and golden. Stir in the chili powder and cook for 2 more minutes. Add all the remaining ingredients. Simmer, covered, over low heat, stirring frequently, for 15 minutes. Check the moisture and, if necessary to prevent scorching, add a little water or stock, 2 tablespoons at a time.

Soy Bean Salad

4 servings
Cooked soy beans may be used like any other cooked beans.

4 tbsps olive oil
2 tbsps fresh lemon juice
2 tbsps grated onion
1 garlic clove, crushed
1 medium tomato, peeled and
  chopped

3 tbsps chopped parsley
salt
freshly ground pepper
250 g ($\frac{1}{2}$ lb) cooked soy beans,
  drained

Combine all the ingredients except the soy beans in a salad bowl
and mix well. Add the soy beans and toss with two forks. Chill
before serving.

Spinach

(Spinacia oleracea)

Spinach is a low-growing leafy annual cultivated for its broad, crinkly, tender leaves which grow in a heavy rosette and which serve as a salad green or as a vegetable. The leaf stems are also edible, but they grow tough when mature. The leaves are dark green and they may be puckered or smooth. They are oval in shape, broader at their base, the lower leaves being wider while the higher ones are narrower. Spinach may also be classified according to seed type as it can be either prickly- or smooth-seeded. The latter varieties are easier to plant accurately.

Spinach is a cool-weather plant, originating probably in Persia, where it was cultivated at the time of the Graeco-Roman civilization. The earliest mention is in a Chinese record which calls it 'the herb of Persia', and states that it was introduced into China around A.D. 647. The Moors introduced it into Spain around 1100, but it is unclear whether it spread into Europe from Spain or from the Middle East. However, by the fourteenth century spinach was grown in monastery gardens in many European countries and, by the first half of the sixteenth century, in France and in England. Parkinson, in the early seventeenth century, certainly believed it to be of Spanish origin.

Spinach has had a colourful history. As a bodybuilder, it was forced down the throats of countless unwilling children who did not like it, and who did not like it any better even when Pop-eye the Sailorman started getting his phenomenal strength from it about 1929. Its reputation was based not so much on its prodigious amounts of vitamin A and, to a lesser extent, vitamin C, but on its iron content, said to build good red blood. However, during the sixties, spinach took a fall because it was feared that the oxalic acid it contains might interfere with the body's ability to absorb calcium. Few people ever consume enough spinach for that to happen but, nevertheless, spinach is no longer as popular as it once was. Between 1957 and 1973 the consumption of fresh spinach fell 50 per cent, that of tinned spinach also declined, and only the consumption of frozen spinach remained steady. The decline in fresh spinach consumption seems to be continuing, and possibly another reason for this decline is that frozen spinach is one of the more successful frozen vegetables. Moreover, it is also already chopped, and what more can a lazy cook ask for?

How to buy

Buy fresh, crisp, flat or crinkled, dark-green leaves. Avoid straggly, long-stemmed plants or plants with seedstalks and with wilted, decayed or yellowing leaves.

How to keep

Refrigerate fresh spinach in the vegetable drawer and use as soon as possible. Fresh, in refrigerator vegetable drawer: 2 to 3 days. Cooked and covered, on refrigerator shelf: 3 days.

Nutritive values

An excellent source of vitamin A, a good source of vitamin C and a fair source of minerals. Raw: 26 calories; cooked and drained: 23 calories (per 100 g/3½ oz).

How to use

Trim off roots and cut off tough stems. Cut large leaves into pieces to save on chopping time. Wash in sink full of lukewarm water, swishing the spinach around. The lukewarm water will send the sand to the bottom of the sink. Remove spinach from sink, clean sink of sand, fill with cold water and wash spinach again. Repeat cold water wash until there is no sand left in the water. Drain the spinach. Cook, covered, for 3 to 5 minutes in the water that clings to the leaves. Do not overcook. Drain in a sieve and squeeze dry by pressing the spinach with a spoon against the sides of the sieve, or squeeze dry with hands. Season with salt and pepper and serve with butter and lemon juice. For salads, use only the smallest, tenderest leaves. Wash as above and dry with kitchen paper.

Spinach and Rice Soup

4 servings

1½ l (2½ pts) chicken or beef
  stock
80 g (3 oz) uncooked rice
1 kg (2 lb) spinach, washed,
  drained and shredded

salt
freshly ground pepper
⅛ tsp ground nutmeg
freshly ground Parmesan cheese

Heat the stock in a soup pot. Add the rice. Simmer, covered, for about 10 minutes or until the rice is almost tender. Add the spinach and season with the salt and pepper and the nutmeg. Cook 3 more minutes or until the spinach is tender but still crisp. Serve hot with plenty of Parmesan cheese.

Baked Spinach Omelette

4 servings

1½ kg (3 lb) spinach, washed,
  drained and coarsely shredded
60 g (2 oz) butter
salt
freshly ground pepper
dash of Tabasco sauce

6 eggs
40 g (1½ oz) freshly grated
  Parmesan cheese
mushroom or tomato sauce
  (optional)

Cook the spinach in the water that clings to it for 3 minutes. Drain the spinach and squeeze it dry in a sieve, using a wooden spoon or hands. Return the spinach to the saucepan. Add the butter. Cook over high heat, stirring constantly, until the spinach is well coated with the butter. Remove from heat and season lightly with salt (the cheese will be salty), pepper and the Tabasco sauce. Beat together the eggs and the Parmesan cheese. Butter a 20-cm (8-inch), medium deep baking dish. Place it for a few moments over direct low heat to heat it up. Pour in half of the egg mixture. Cook like an omelette, for 2 minutes or until set. Remove from the heat. Spread the spinach evenly on top of the eggs. Top the spinach evenly with the remaining eggs. Bake in a preheated moderate oven (Gas 4, 350° F, 180° C) for about 15 minutes or until set and golden. Unmould on a plate and serve hot with a mushroom or tomato sauce. Or serve lukewarm, with sliced tomatoes.

Spinach with Yoghurt

4 servings

1½ kg (3 lb) spinach, trimmed,
  coarsely chopped and washed
1 medium onion, chopped fine
1 garlic clove, chopped fine
2 tbsps olive oil
salt

freshly ground pepper
30 g (1 oz) pine nuts
3 dl (½ pt) plain yoghurt, or
  more depending on taste
2 tbsps finely chopped fresh mint
  or 2 tsps dried mint

Combine the spinach, the onion and the garlic in a saucepan. Cook, covered, over medium heat, without additional water, for 5 minutes, tossing the pan frequently to prevent sticking. Drain off any moisture. Add the olive oil. Cook, stirring constantly, for 3 more minutes. Season with salt and pepper. Mix in the pine nuts. Remove from heat and stir in the yoghurt. Turn into a serving dish and sprinkle with the mint.

Spinach Salad Bowl

6 servings

1½ dl (¼ pt) olive oil
juice of 1 lemon
2 tbsps wine vinegar
1 garlic clove, crushed
salt
freshly ground pepper

500 g (1 lb) fresh young spinach
2 tbsps grated Parmesan cheese
2 hard-boiled eggs, chopped
6 bacon slices, fried crisp and
  crumbled
croûtons

Combine the olive oil, the lemon juice, the vinegar, the garlic clove and salt and pepper to taste. Mix well. Clean the spinach by pulling the leaves off the stems and washing them thoroughly in several waters. Tear the drained spinach leaves into bite-sized pieces with your fingers. Dry with kitchen towel. Place them in a salad bowl. Add the dressing and the Parmesan cheese and toss. Add the eggs, the crumbled bacon and a handful of croûtons and toss once more.

Spinach Soufflé

4 servings

60 g (2 oz) butter
30 g (1 oz) flour
2½ dl (8 fl oz) single cream or
  milk
salt
freshly ground pepper

⅛ tsp ground nutmeg
110 g (4 oz) grated Gruyère or
  Emmenthal cheese
500 g (1 lb) spinach, washed,
  cooked and squeezed dry
4 eggs, separated

Heat the butter in a saucepan large enough to take all the ingredients except the eggs. Stir in the flour and cook, stirring constantly, for about 2 minutes. Stir in the cream, and cook, stirring all the time, until thickened and smooth. Season with the salt and pepper and the nutmeg. Turn heat to very low and stir in the cheese and the spinach. Cook until the cheese has melted. Remove from the heat and cool. Beat the egg yolks until thick and beat them into the spinach. Beat the egg whites until they are stiff but not dry. Carefully fold the egg whites into the spinach mixture. Turn into a buttered 1½- to 2-litre (or quart) baking dish. Bake in a preheated slow oven (Gas 3, 335° F, 170° C) for about 30 to 40 minutes or until set. Serve immediately.

Spring Onion

(*Allium cepa*)

Spring onions are onions that are pulled when the tops are still green. They have a definite bulb formation with the same concentric arrangement of dry onion. The varieties pulled before the bulb has formed are scallions. Spring onions look like cylinders with tightly furled leaves, from 20 to 30 cm (8 to 12 inches) in length and about 1 cm ($\frac{1}{4}$ to $\frac{1}{2}$ inch) across, white at the root base

and green at the top, like miniature leeks. Their history is the same as that of dry onions, and they are equally popular throughout the world; in China more use is made of spring onions than of dry ones.

Spring onions are mostly eaten raw, by themselves as appetizers, in salads, in sandwiches or snipped as a fresh green into cooked dishes. Cooked, they are a delicious, delicate vegetable.

How to buy

Buy young, tender, clean spring onions with well-trimmed bulbs, firm, with fresh, bright-green tops. Avoid soft, withered, wilted spring onions with broken, bruised, diseased or damaged leaves.

How to keep

Refrigerate in vegetable drawer for 2 days and use as soon as possible.

Nutritive values

Raw, bulb and top: 36 calories per 100 g ($3\frac{1}{2}$ oz).

300

How to use

Trim, wash and use sliced or chopped in salads. Or cook whole, or cut into two pieces, in boiling salted water to cover for 3 to 4 minutes; drain, season and serve with butter and lemon juice.

Squashes

(Cucurbitae)

Squashes are members of the gourd family (Cucurbitaceae) of which there are some 700 different species, many of which are cultivated to be eaten as a cooked vegetable. The squash plant is a trailing or climbing vine, or a bush with large leaves and generally large, yellow flowers. The edible part is a pepo, a berry-like structure, filled with seeds. The squash flowers are also edible.

Squashes are native to the Americas (probably Peru and Chile) where many varieties were cultivated long before the European conquests. They were, along with corn and beans, a staple Indian food. Few Europeans seriously cultivate any at all with the exception of the courgette and its larger forerunner, the rather insipid vegetable marrow, a summer squash like the custard marrow which has been grown in England for at least 400 years without ever achieving popularity as a food plant. In the United States an astonishing variety of both summer and winter squashes is readily available everywhere, but we so far make do with the pumpkin, the only squash other than the marrow which is both grown here and imported in some quantity.

The word 'squash' itself comes from the Massachusetts Indian word *askutasquash* meaning 'eaten raw and uncooked'.

Further notes and recipes will be found under Courgette, Marrow and Pumpkin.

Swede

(Brassica napus var. *napobrassica)*

A root vegetable of the cabbage family which resembles and is often confused with the turnip. The swede is distinguished by an ochre-coloured swollen 'neck' bearing a number of ridges, which are the leaf-base scars, and it has smooth, bluish leaves. A turnip has little or no neck and thin, hairy, medium-green leaves. Swedes are also larger than turnips. There are purple, white and yellow varieties but the commercially available ones are yellow.

The origin of the swede is not quite clear. It is believed to be a hybrid of cabbage and turnip, possibly of the seventeenth century, for it is not recorded earlier, and probably came from Bohemia. Certainly it was known on the Continent before it was known in England where it is said to have arrived from Holland about 1755. The 'turnip-rooted cabbage' did not become popular here, except as an animal feed, until fairly recently.

Swedes are a hardy, long-lasting, easy-to-store, cold-weather crop. They flourish in cool central and northern Europe, where they have long been the diet of the poor as well as animal fodder. As a staple crop of northern Europe, they have fed people through more wars and famines than one likes to think. As recently as the Second World War, many would have starved to death without the swede, which was vegetable, fruit for preserves and even the material for ersatz coffee.

Swedes are not one of the more delicate or interesting vegetables

303

but they are at least a fresh one, which counts in winter. Cooked with a little imagination and care, they can be turned into surprisingly palatable dishes.

How to buy

Buy roots that are firm, solid and heavy for their size. They should be smooth, and well-shaped, whether they are round or oblong. Avoid cracked, punctured, cut or blemished roots.

How to keep

Store in cool, moist area or refrigerate in a plastic bag. Raw: about 1 month. Cooked and covered, on refrigerator shelf: 3 to 4 days.

Nutritive values

A moderate source of vitamins and minerals. Raw: 46 calories; cooked: 35 calories (per 100 g/3½ oz).

How to use

Swedes must be peeled before any cooking.

Peel, cut into slices, sticks or dice, wash and drain. Cook in boiling salted water to cover for 5 to 15 minutes, depending on the size of the pieces. Do not overcook. Season with salt and pepper and serve with butter; or mash or cream them. A half teaspoon of sugar added to the cooking water improves the flavour.

Finnish Swede Pudding

4–6 servings
This recipe, which can be halved, makes a good deal out of an ordinary vegetable. Serve with any meat.

1 kg (2 lb) swedes, peeled and
   diced
boiling salted water
salt
freshly ground pepper
⅛ tsp ground nutmeg
1 tsp sugar or 2 tsps dark syrup
   or molasses

3 tbsps fine dry breadcrumbs
3 tbsps single or double cream
2 eggs, beaten
60 g (2 oz) butter, cut into small
   pieces

Cook the swedes in boiling salted water to cover until soft. Drain and reserve 1½ dl (¼ pint) of the cooking liquid. Mash as when making mashed potatoes. Beat in half the reserved cooking liquid, the salt, the pepper, the nutmeg and the sugar. If too dry, add a little more of the cooking liquid, 1 tablespoon at a time. Combine the breadcrumbs and the cream and stir in the eggs. Beat this mixture into the swedes and beat until light. Place the mixture in a generously buttered 2-litre (or quart) baking dish. Smooth the surface and dot with the butter. Bake in a preheated moderate oven (Gas 4, 350° F, 180° C) for about 30 to 45 minutes or until a skewer, stuck into the pudding, comes out clean and the pudding is gently browned on top.

Mashed Swedes

4 servings

1 kg (2 lb) swedes, peeled and
   cut into cubes
boiling salted water
60–80 g (2–3 oz) butter, at room
   temperature

3 tbsps chicken or beef stock
salt
freshly ground pepper
⅛ tsp ground mace
3 tbsps dry sherry

Cook the swedes in boiling salted water to cover for 10 minutes or until very tender. Drain and put through a sieve. Return to the saucepan. Over low heat, stir in the butter, beginning with 60 g

(2 oz). Stir in the stock and season with the salt and pepper and the mace. Beat as you would mashed potatoes; if too dry, beat in the remaining butter. Beat in the sherry. Cook, beating constantly, for 2 to 3 more minutes. Serve very hot.

Sweet Potato

(*Ipomoea batatas*)

The sweet potato is the edible tuberous root of a vine belonging to
the morning glory family. Among the many varieties there are
oblong or roundish, forked or beet-shaped sweet potatoes, with
skins of many colours, from nearly white to magenta and purple,
though in our shops the red-skinned ones predominate. The flesh
is usually white, though there are yellow varieties, and it may be
moist or dry. Most sweet potatoes taste sweet though some of the
tubers are as dry as any Irish potato. The average size is 15 to 25
cm (6 to 10 inches) long, and 5 to 8 cm (2 to 3 inches) across.
Sweet potatoes must not be confused with yams, which belong to
another botanical genus (*Dioscorea*). However, for cooking
purposes sweet potatoes and yams are interchangeable.

The sweet potato is a truly American vegetable, grown by the
Incas of Peru and the Mayas of Central America long before the
conquest. Columbus mentions it in his records, and de Soto
found sweet potatoes growing in Indian gardens in 1540 in what is
now Louisiana. The tuber reached São Tomé off the African
coast before 1574 and a Portuguese navigator described it as one
of the most essential articles of the people's food. Since the sweet
potato needs a hot, moist climate, it flourished in the Philippines
and the East Indies to which it is believed it was introduced
by early Spanish explorers. Portuguese travellers brought it
to India, China and Malaya. It is now a staple in all of these
countries.

The sweet potato was introduced into Spain from the West
Indies in 1526. It has never become popular in Europe, not even
in the Mediterranean countries. It reached England by the third
quarter of the sixteenth century. Gerard calls it the Spanish
potato in his 1596 *Herbal*. Most people find its taste too pronounced to accept it as a basic foodstuff like ordinary potatoes (to
which it is not closely related) but at least sweet potatoes have

become more readily available with the spread of West Indian and African communities.

How to buy

Buy firm, well-shaped, clean sweet potatoes with evenly coloured skins that are free from blemishes. Choose thick, chunky, medium-sized potatoes tapering towards the ends. Avoid potatoes with any signs of bruises or decay since they rapidly go bad.

How to keep

Store in a cool, dry, well-ventilated area. Do not refrigerate since chilling damages sweet potatoes. Store for short time only. Raw: 2 to 3 weeks. Cooked and covered, on refrigerator shelf: 4 to 5 days.

Nutritive values

An excellent source of vitamin A and vitamin C. Boiled in skin: 114 calories; baked in skin: 141 calories (per 100 g/3½ oz).

How to use

Scrub and cut off any woody or bruised parts. Sweet potatoes are usually boiled or baked before peeling and then finished. They cook and bake quicker than ordinary potatoes and also reheat better. For cooking methods, see Potatoes section, page 257.

Fried Sweet Potatoes

4–5 servings

3 medium sweet potatoes (approx. 750 g or 1½ lb)
boiling salted water
flour

60 g (2 oz) butter or 4 tbsps vegetable oil
salt

Wash the sweet potatoes and cook in boiling salted water to cover for 15 to 20 minutes or until tender but still firm. Drain and cool.

Peel them and cut them into slices. Dip the slices in flour and shake off excess flour. Heat the butter in a deep frying pan. Cook the sweet potato slices, a few at a time, until they are golden brown. Sprinkle with salt and serve hot.

Chicken and Sweet Potato Soup

6 servings

2 l (2 qts) chicken stock
2 carrots, diced
2 sticks celery, diced
1 medium onion, chopped
2 large sweet potatoes (approx.
   750 g or 1½ lb), peeled and
   diced

250–350 g (½–¾ lb) chicken,
   cooked and chopped
1 tsp ground thyme
½ tsp ground sage
¼ tsp dried hot pepper flakes
salt
freshly ground pepper

Combine the stock, the carrots, the celery and the onion in a soup pot. Bring to the boil and lower the heat. Simmer, covered, for 10 minutes. Add the sweet potatoes and all the other ingredients. Simmer, covered, for 15 more minutes.

Festive Sweets

6 servings

4 large sweet potatoes (approx.
   1½ kg or 3 lb)
60 g (2 oz) butter, melted
80 g (3 oz) brown sugar
1 tsp salt
⅛ tsp pepper

½ tsp ground mace
1½ dl (¼ pt) cream
4 tbsps sherry
2 tsps grated orange rind
150 g (5 oz) dried apricots,
   cooked and chopped

Cook, drain and peel the sweet potatoes. Mash until very smooth. Add all the other ingredients, except the apricots. Lightly fold in the apricots. Turn into a buttered shallow 1½-litre (or-quart) baking dish. Bake in a preheated moderate oven (Gas 4, 350°F, 180° C) for 15 to 20 minutes.

Sweet Potato Orange Casserole

6 servings
This dish may be made with yams.

6 medium sweet potatoes (approx.
   1½ kg or 3 lb)
boiling salted water
80 g (3 oz) light brown sugar
juice of 2 fresh oranges

juice of 1 fresh lemon
grated rind of ½ orange
grated rind of ½ lemon
¼ tsp salt
60 g (2 oz) butter, cut into pieces

Wash the sweet potatoes and cook in boiling salted water to cover
for about 15 to 20 minutes or until tender but still firm. Drain and
cool. Peel the sweet potatoes and cut them into thinnish slices.
Place them in a buttered shallow baking dish in one or two layers.
Sprinkle with the sugar. Combine the orange and lemon juice, the
grated rinds and the salt and mix well. Sprinkle the mixture over
the potatoes. Dot with the butter. Bake in a preheated slow oven
(Gas 3, 335° F, 170° C) for 25 minutes or until golden.

Tomato

(Lycopersicon esculentum)

The fruit of a vine that, along with potato, tobacco, pepper and aubergine, belongs to the nightshade family. Botanically speaking, the tomato is a berry, being pulpy and containing seeds that are not stones. Tomatoes are eaten as a vegetable rather than as a fruit, prized for their flavour, their colour and their high vitamin content. Tomatoes can be almost totally round or oval, pear, plum or chili shaped; from 2 cm (barely 1 inch) to more than 10 cm (4 and more inches) in size, weighing up to 1 kg (2 lb); red or yellow or colourless. The flesh may be white, orange, pink or red. The flavour of a tomato depends largely on the ratio of sugar to acid. If there is not enough sugar, the tomato will be sour and flavourless.  Tomatoes are more or less watery. Those which are watery rather than fleshy will have a poorer flavour. Tomatoes are grown for specific purposes such as for the table, for juice and for canning. The solidly-fleshed Italian plum tomato, used mainly for sauces and for canning, very often has more flavour for salad use than the usual table varieties.

Tomatoes are said to be natives of the Peruvian and Bolivian Andes, where tomatoes the size of large currants and cherries are still to be found. The Indians cultivated and improved them so long before the white man came that the large forms of the tomato have never been found wild and no markedly different types either in form or colour have appeared since tomatoes were first found in the New World. The northward migration of the fruit is also wrapped in antiquity. The Aztecs and Toltecs and

311

other Mexican tribes not only ate tomatoes but also named them since the word is derived from their *tomatl*. In 1554 tomatoes were eaten in Italy, where they were called *pomo d'oro* (today's *pomodoro*), 'golden apple', from which we may deduce that they belonged to a golden variety. The French of the time, in a hopeful manner, called the tomato the 'love apple'. By the end of the sixteenth century tomatoes were grown in England, Germany and Belgium – largely as an ornament, since they seemed to be too odd a food.

Commercially speaking, the tomato became popular only after 1880. Since then, few if any vegetables have had as much attention from scientists, from breeders of new varieties, from producers of standard varieties, from manufacturers of planters, sprinkler and cooling systems, cultivators, mechanical harvesters, graders, packing-house cooling systems and packing materials, from home gardeners, and finally, from cooks. No other vegetable, I think, has suffered as much from what is now known as 'agribusiness'. As any commercial grower will tell you, with the exception of hot-house tomatoes, it is not practical to harvest red-ripe tomatoes since the fruit is too tender to pack and ship. So-called vine-ripe tomatoes are not that at all, but harvested at the barely-pink stage. But most tomatoes that are shipped long distances are harvested at what euphemistically is called the 'mature-green' stage, when they have a shiny, thick skin that cannot be torn and an inner jelly-like substance. They are then ripened, or shall I say reddened, in storage. These are the horrid, pallid, woolly tomatoes we all pay far too much for. In most parts of the country, it is possible only during the summer months to savour the glorious flavour and colour of a naturally ripened tomato when tomatoes are grown locally and allowed really to ripen on the vine. Even the little red or yellow cherry tomatoes, once nuggets of true tomato flavour, have become insipid during recent years.

How to buy

Buy, preferably, ripe but not over-ripe tomatoes only; home-ripened tomatoes are never as flavourful. Buy firm, well-formed tomatoes that are heavy for their size. Avoid blemished or cracked tomatoes, or tomatoes with a torn skin or with watery, dark or sunken spots.

How to keep

Keep in a cool, dry place, at a temperature around 50° F, 10° C. Refrigerate for a short time only and only when fully ripe; chilling injures tomatoes. Ripen green and under-ripe tomatoes at room temperature; then chill. Fresh, ripe, on refrigerator shelf: 2 to 3 days. Tinned, open and covered, or cooked and covered: 4 to 5 days.

Nutritive values

A good source of vitamins A and C and of minerals. Fresh, raw: 22 calories; boiled: 26 calories (per 100 g/3½ oz).

How to use

To peel tomatoes, spear on a fork and dip into boiling water for about 1 to 2 minutes. Then dip into cold water. Slip off skin. Or hold tomato over direct heat until the skin splits; then slip off.

To seed and juice peeled or unpeeled tomatoes, cut into halves crosswise. Squeeze each half gently over a bowl to extract the seeds and the juice.

To slice tomatoes, cut them into vertical rather than horizontal slices. This is the French way and tomato slices stay firmer.

To stew tomatoes, cut into pieces and cook, covered, without water over low heat for 8 to 10 minutes. Stir frequently. Since the water content of tomatoes varies, check for scorching; if necessary, add a little water. For more flavour, add a little chopped onion or celery or a bay leaf. Season with salt and pepper. If tomatoes are sour, add a pinch of sugar. To grill, remove the stem from firm tomatoes. Cut into halves and cut criss-cross the surface of each half. Place on baking sheet. Season with salt and pepper and dot with butter. Grill under moderate heat for 5 to 10 minutes or until topping is browned. Or bake in a preheated hot oven (Gas 7, 425° F, 220° C) for 10 minutes.

Fresh Tomato Soup

4 servings
Once you've made fresh tomato soup you won't like tinned tomato soup.

60 g (2 oz) butter
1 tbsp groundnut or vegetable oil
1 medium onion, chopped fine
3 tbsps flour
6 large ripe tomatoes, peeled,
   seeded and chopped
1 l (1¾ pts) boiling water

1 large bay leaf
3 parsley sprigs
2 sprigs fresh thyme or 1 tsp dried
   thyme
salt
freshly ground pepper
croûtons

Heat half the butter and the oil in a large, heavy saucepan. Cook the onion, stirring constantly, until it is soft and golden. Stir in the flour and cook, stirring all the time, until golden; do not brown. Add the tomatoes and the water. Tie the bay leaf, the parsley sprigs and thyme in a triple layer of cheesecloth to make a *bouquet garni*. Add to the tomatoes. Season with salt and pepper. Simmer, covered, over low heat for 30 minutes. Remove the *bouquet garni* and stir in the remaining butter. Serve in a heated tureen with croûtons.

Fried Tomatoes

4–6 servings

8 large ripe tomatoes, washed
salt
freshly ground pepper
4 tbsps olive oil
2 tbsps finely chopped basil or
  2 tsps dried basil

2 tbsps finely chopped parsley
1 tbsp finely chopped mint or 1
  tsp dried mint

Cut the tomatoes lengthwise into halves. Lay them, cut side up, side by side in a large frying pan or use two frying pans; the tomatoes must be in *one* layer. Sprinkle each half with salt and pepper, a little olive oil, a little basil, a little parsley and a little mint. Cook over low heat for about 5 to 7 minutes, shaking the pan to prevent sticking. Cover the frying pan and cook for 3 to 5 more minutes; the cooking time depends on the firmness of the tomatoes.

Roman Stuffed Tomatoes

4–6 servings

It is impossible to give totally accurate amounts for the rice used since the size of the tomatoes varies. If the tomatoes are very large, about 2 tablespoons of uncooked rice are needed for each tomato. If any rice stuffing is left over, cook it alongside the tomatoes. The saffron in the rice makes for a pretty colour effect.

8 large ripe but firm tomatoes
4–5 tbsps olive oil
4 tbsps finely chopped parsley
2 garlic cloves, chopped fine
250 g ($\frac{1}{2}$ lb) long-grain rice

1 tsp saffron (optional)
$4\frac{1}{2}$ dl ($\frac{3}{4}$ pt) hot chicken stock
salt
pepper
$\frac{1}{8}$ tsp ground cinnamon

Cut a slice from the top of each tomato, under the stem, and scoop out the pulp with a teaspoon. Be careful not to break the shells. Strain the pulp through a sieve and reserve. Place the tomatoes side by side in a shallow baking dish. Sprinkle each tomato with a few drops of olive oil. Heat the remaining oil in a saucepan. Cook the parsley and the garlic for 2 minutes. Add the rice and cook, stirring constantly, for 3 more minutes. Stir the saffron into the stock. Add the hot stock to the rice and cover the saucepan. Cook over low heat, stirring frequently, for about 10 minutes or until the rice is three-quarters done. Remove from the heat and season the rice with the salt and pepper and the cinnamon. Fill the tomato shells with the rice mixture. Pour the strained tomato pulp over the tomatoes to the depth of about 1 cm ($\frac{1}{2}$ inch); if there is not enough strained pulp add a little water. Bake in a preheated moderate oven (Gas 4, 350° F, 180° C) for about 30 minutes or until the rice is tender and the liquid has been absorbed. Check for scorching; if necessary, add a little more hot water. Baste occasionally with the pan juices. Serve hot or lukewarm or cool but not chilled.

Pizzaiola Sauce

4 servings
Serve with steaks or on thin pasta. The tomatoes in this sauce are cooked just long enough to soften and keep their fresh taste.

3 tbsps olive oil
750 g–1 kg (1½–2 lb) ripe
   tomatoes, peeled, seeded and
   chopped
2 garlic cloves, chopped fine

salt
freshly ground pepper
1 tsp dried oregano
3 tbsps chopped parsley

Heat the olive oil in a heavy saucepan. Add all the other ingredients. Cook over high heat, stirring all the time, for about 5 to 7 minutes or until the tomatoes are just soft and hot.

Salsa Fria

This sauce is found on all Mexican tables; it can be as hot as desired. Serve it on beans and on any dishes that can stand a little livening up.

2 large ripe tomatoes, peeled and
   chopped
1 medium onion, chopped fine
1 jalapeno or other hot pepper,
   or more to taste, fresh or
   tinned and drained, seeded and
   chopped fine

2 tbsps olive or vegetable oil
juice of 1 lemon
½ tsp dried oregano
salt
freshly ground pepper

Combine all the ingredients and mix well. Refrigerate, covered, until serving time.

Truffle

(Tuber melanosporum, Tuber aestivum)

A truffle is a fungus which, unlike other fungi, grows underground in woods. It is an irregularly shaped, roundish lump, with a light- or dark-brown or greyish, warty skin and solid flesh. It measures about 7 to 10 cm (3 to 4 inches) in width. The truffle's odour and flavour are indescribable but most distinctive, delicious to most people but repulsive to some. Their nutritive values are of no importance. There are several varieties, of which the two finest and most prized are the black-fleshed truffle of the Périgord and other regions of France, and the truffle of Piedmont in northern Italy, which has off-white to very light-brown flesh and a vaguely garlicky taste. Lesser truffles are also found in England, in some parts of the Continent and in North Africa.

Truffles have been prized as the height of sophisticated eating since the days of the Romans, when Apicius, in the first century A.D., gave recipes on how to cook and sauce them. Truffles never lost this reputation and they are priced accordingly and often astronomically. Raw or cooked, the *haute cuisine* of France relies on them in numerous ways, such as in pâtés (that small black square in the middle of a *foie gras* pâté), braised whole in wine or cream, baked or sautéed, in a salad or minced in stuffings. The Italians, who say their white truffles are tastier than the French black ones, shave their raw truffles with a special cutter on pasta or egg dishes; all truffles show a great affinity for eggs.

The magic of truffles is also connected to the way they grow and are harvested. Truffles like a light, porous, limestone soil in oak, beech or birch forests under the trees that nourish them. When ripe, only their odour betrays them. Since the human sense of smell is not sensitive enough to detect them, truffle pigs and truffle hounds scent out the ripe truffles and dig them out of the ground which is cracked from the swelling of the ripe fungus. Dogs

317

are better for the purpose because they do not want to eat the precious nuggets. In England's southern counties, Spanish poodles were used for truffle hunting until the 1920s. Truffles usually grow wild and unpredictably, but they keep on growing in the same spots. They are also cultivated, after a fashion, by planting tiny oak trees in places where truffles are known to exist. Joseph Talm of France's Vaucluse region is credited with inventing, or perhaps, rather, discovering, this method. He planted acorns in a flinty soil, and that did the trick for him. The method has worked for others, but is not foolproof.

Both black and white truffles are tinned and imported into this country. Personally, I consider tinned truffles without perfume and with little flavour, a show of riches that could be better employed. But others do not agree with me. Fresh truffles have an overpowering scent which penetrates anything close to them. But the fresh truffle season is very short, in late autumn, and to be good fresh truffles should be used within a week of the harvest.

A French dish with the words *à la périgord* or *périgourdine* in its title means that it contains some truffle, being made in the fashion of Périgord where the finest truffles come from. An Italian dish with the word *trifolato* (truffled) in its title does not mean at all that it contains any truffles. It simply means that one or more of the ingredients is sliced very fine, like truffles.

How to keep

Store cleaned or partially used raw truffles or truffle scraps in a tightly lidded glass container in the refrigerator and use as soon as possible. If you are using tinned truffles and have some left over, transfer them to a tightly lidded glass container and cover them with sherry, port, Madeira or brandy. Close the jar well and keep refrigerated for up to a week.

How to use

Slice them thinly, or dice, chop or cut them into thin strips, adding them to a dish towards the end of the cooking period to avoid overcooking and loss of flavour. Or use raw, thinly sliced, in salads. Since tinned truffles are already cooked, add them to a dish which is ready and will heat them through. Use the tinning liquids for flavouring soups, stews and sauces.

Whole, raw black truffles may be cooked in many ways but I suggest this simple method. Place cleaned black truffles in a heavy cast-iron casserole. Add enough of a good, full-bodied, dry white wine, such as a Chablis or other Burgundy, to come about three quarters of the way up the truffles. Add for each truffle about 1 or 2 cm ($\frac{1}{2}$ to $\frac{3}{4}$ inch) lean bacon cut into thin strips. Bring quickly to the boil, reduce heat to low, cover tightly and simmer for about 15 to 20 minutes, depending on size. Season with a little salt and pepper. Serve hot as a separate course with a spoonful or two of the cooking liquid, or as a vegetable. Some recipes call for champagne in this dish but I think it is better with a really good white wine.

White truffles, always to be used raw, are delicious when sliced thinly, or grated, over a dish of pasta or rice dressed with butter and grated Parmesan cheese, or into an egg dish or salad.

Scrambled Eggs with Truffles

3 servings

6 large eggs	butter
salt	4 tbsps double cream
freshly ground pepper	hot buttered toast
1 medium black or white truffle, fresh or tinned, or to taste	

Break the eggs into a bowl and beat them. Season lightly with salt and pepper. Chop the truffle and stir it into the eggs. If tinned truffles are used, also add the liquid in the tin to the eggs. Cover and refrigerate for 1 to 2 hours. Melt a generous amount of butter in a small, heavy frying pan. Stir the cream quickly into the eggs. Add the eggs to the butter and scramble lightly in the usual manner over low heat. Do not dry out the eggs. Serve immediately, with hot buttered toast.

Sautéed Black Truffles

3–4 servings
I had this once in France, made with fresh truffles and goose fat and served with a little plain boiled rice. It was an unforgettable experience.

500 g (1 lb) black truffles, ready
    for cooking, fresh or tinned
30 g (1 oz) butter
1 tbsp bacon fat

salt
freshly ground pepper
2½ dl (8 fl oz) dry Madeira

Slice or chop the truffles. Heat the butter and the bacon fat in a small, heavy casserole. Add the truffles. Season with a little salt and pepper. Cook over medium heat, stirring very gently with a fork, for about 3 to 4 minutes. With a slotted spoon, transfer the truffles to a heated serving dish and keep warm. Stir the Madeira into the pan juices, scraping up all the little brown bits at the bottom. Turn the heat up to high and cook for 2 to 3 minutes or until the sauce is reduced by about one quarter. Pour over the truffles and serve immediately.

Turnip

(Brassica rapa)

The turnip is a root vegetable belonging to the cabbage family; its leaves can also be eaten, as a potherb. Some coarse turnip varieties are grown as forage plants. The roots measure an average of 5 to 8 cm (2 to 3 inches) across, are round or conical in shape and, depending on the varieties, have white, green or purplish crowns. The hairy leaves are green, thin and radish-like. The flesh is crispy and either white or yellow, but most commercial varieties have white flesh. The flavour of the turnip resembles that of all the vegetables whose names end in 'nip', but it is milder. Even when yellow fleshed, turnips must not be mistaken for swedes.

Like most members of the cabbage family, turnips are of European and north Asian ancestry. The Romans cultivated long, flat or elongated turnips. As a cold-weather crop, turnips became popular among the Flemings in the fifteenth century. At the time of Henry VIII, turnips were baked or roasted in the ashes of fires and the young leaves served as a salad and as cooked greens. Gerard thought the turnips grown on the sandy ground of Hackney (now in London) were by far the best.

Turnips and their green tops are extensively used in Chinese, Japanese and other oriental cooking; they remain, as well, one of the more popular vegetables in middle and northern Europe and in the British Isles.

Vegetable Cookery

How to buy

Buy small to medium turnips which are firm with a smooth, unblemished skin. The tops should be fresh and green. Avoid large, fibrous turnips with too many leaf scars around their tops, and those with wilted, yellowing, blemished tops.

How to keep

Turnips like very cool surroundings. Remove tops and store in a well-ventilated, cool, dry place. Or refrigerate in a plastic bag. Wash greens and shake dry. Wrap in plastic and refrigerate. Fresh raw roots, on refrigerator shelf: 3 weeks. Cooked and covered roots, on refrigerator shelf: 2 to 3 days. Fresh green tops, on refrigerator shelf: 2 to 4 days.

Nutritive values

The roots are a moderate source of vitamins and minerals. The greens are an excellent source of vitamins A and C and a good source of minerals. Raw root: 30 calories; cooked and drained root: 23 calories; raw greens: 28 calories; cooked and drained greens: 20 calories (per 100 g/3½ oz).

How to use

When turnip roots are used imaginatively, they can be an excellent and interesting vegetable. As with many vegetables, their size when cut up affects their taste. They are at their mildest when cut into thin strips in the French manner, or when diced or thinly sliced. Small turnips must be peeled before cooking, though large turnips may be baked in their skins. To cook, place peeled and sliced, diced or match-stick turnip roots in boiling salted water just to cover for 5 or more minutes or until tender. Do not overcook. Season with salt and pepper and serve with butter. Or cook further according to recipe.

Turnips, Luzerne Style

4 servings
Serve with boiled beef or with sausages.

12 small or 6 medium white turnips, trimmed and peeled	1 large onion, chopped fine
boiling salted water	salt
3 rashers bacon, cut up	freshly ground pepper
	2 tbsps finely chopped parsley

Cut the turnips into strips. Wash and drain. Cook them in a little boiling salted water until barely tender. Drain. In a frying pan, cook the bacon until it is limp. Add the onion and cook, stirring constantly, until soft and golden. Add the turnips. Season with salt and pepper. Cook over low heat, stirring occasionally, for about 10 minutes or until the turnips are golden brown. Serve sprinkled with chopped parsley.

Curried Turnips

4–6 servings

This may also be made with parsnips. Serve with ham.

60 g (2 oz) butter	1 kg (2 lb) turnips, peeled and cut into cubes
1 medium onion, chopped fine	
1 tbsp curry powder, or to taste	salt
1½–3 dl (¼–½ pt) hot chicken stock or water	freshly ground pepper
	1 dl (4 fl oz) yoghurt

Heat the butter in a heavy saucepan. Cook the onion in it until soft. Stir in the curry powder. Cook, stirring constantly, for 2 to 3 minutes. Stir in the smaller amount of stock. Add the turnips. Cook, covered, over very low heat for about 10 to 15 minutes or until the turnips are tender. Check the moisture; if necessary to prevent scorching, add more stock, 2 tablespoons at a time. The cooked turnips should be dry. Season with salt and pepper. Remove from the heat and stir in the yoghurt. Serve immediately.

Watercress

(Nasturtium officinale)

Watercress is a perennial, succulent, leafy plant of the mustard family; it is gathered or grown for its peppery green leaves which serve as salad greens and flavouring. The plant grows best in running water and is found wild by or in springs and clear streams in many parts of the country (beware of those that grow near sheep meadows, they often harbour a parasite). Commercially, it is grown in shallow pools of flowing clean water with an adequate lime content.

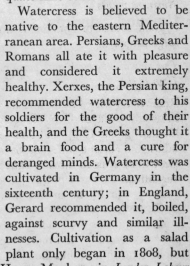

Watercress is believed to be native to the eastern Mediterranean area. Persians, Greeks and Romans all ate it with pleasure and considered it extremely healthy. Xerxes, the Persian king, recommended watercress to his soldiers for the good of their health, and the Greeks thought it a brain food and a cure for deranged minds. Watercress was cultivated in Germany in the sixteenth century; in England, Gerard recommended it, boiled, against scurvy and similar illnesses. Cultivation as a salad plant only began in 1808, but quickly became widespread. Henry Mayhew, in *London Labour and the London Poor* (1861–2), describes the early-morning trade of the 'worter-crease costers' of the mid nineteenth century.

Watercress is used largely as a garnish by hotels and restaurants. It is an excellent salad green by itself or combined with other greens. The French combine watercress with potatoes for an excellent soup and the Chinese, too, have long used it in their soups. Cooked watercress has far more flavour than many greens.

How to buy

Buy fresh, bright-green watercress, with crisp leaves and stems which snap easily. Avoid watercress with yellowing or wilted leaves.

How to keep

Untie each bunch, and remove any poor leaves and stems. Place in a container with a tight-fitting lid and refrigerate. Refrigerator shelf: 3 to 5 days.

Nutritive values

A good source of vitamins A and C and of minerals if eaten in large amounts.

How to use

Remove all wilted stems and leaves. Snap off tough stems. Wash in several changes of cold or ice water and shake dry or dry with kitchen paper. Chop and add to sandwiches, soups, eggs, vegetables and cottage cheese or leave whole and add to salad greens. Or use as a salad with a light French dressing. Or cook as a vegetable.

Watercress Soup

6 servings

1½ l (2½ pts) chicken stock
6 spring onions, white and green
  parts, thinly sliced
1 large potato, peeled and diced
2 bunches watercress, trimmed,
  washed and tough stems
  removed (reserve 2 large
  sprigs)

salt
freshly ground pepper
3 dl (½ pt) cream

Put the stock into a large heavy saucepan and bring to boiling
point. Lower the heat. Add the onions, the potato and the watercress. Simmer, covered, for 10 to 15 minutes. Do not overcook or
the soup will lose its fresh flavour. Season with salt and pepper.
Purée in a blender. Return to saucepan and add the cream. Heat
through but do not boil. Garnish with the leaves of the reserved
watercress sprigs. Serve hot.

Note: For chilled watercress soup, proceed as above but do not
add the cream. Chill the soup and the cream separately and
thoroughly. At serving time, stir the cream into the soup and
garnish with the watercress leaves.

Braised Watercress

4 servings
Serve with rich meats such as duck, pork or ham.

4 bunches watercress
60 g (2 oz) butter, cut into pieces
salt

freshly ground pepper
3 tbsps chicken stock
sour cream (optional)

Trim off the heavy stems. The easiest way to do this if you have a
very regular bunch of watercress is to lay it on its side and cut off
the stems to the height of the leaves. Plunge in a bowl of cold
water and agitate to loosen dirt and sand. Remove any wilted
leaves. Change the water until there is no dirt and sand left in the
bowl. Drain. Do not shake dry. Place in a saucepan. Cook,
covered, over low heat for about 5 minutes, shaking the saucepan

frequently to prevent sticking. Stir in the butter and season with salt and pepper. Add the stock. Return to heat until the pan liquid has evaporated and the watercress is the consistency of chopped spinach. Serve hot, with a bowl of sour cream on the side.

Watercress and Mushroom Salad

4–6 servings

2 bunches watercress, trimmed, washed and tough stems removed

110 g (4 oz) mushrooms, thinly sliced

1 tbsp fresh lemon juice

4 slices crisp fried bacon, crumbled

Dressing:

4 tbsps olive oil

2 tbsps lemon juice

1 garlic clove, crushed

½ tsp salt

¼ tsp freshly ground pepper

¼ tsp dry mustard

1 egg yolk

Dry the watercress with kitchen paper. Place in a salad bowl. Top with the mushrooms. Sprinkle the lemon juice over the mushrooms. Top with the crumbled bacon. Chill while you make the dressing. Combine the olive oil, the lemon juice, the garlic, the salt and pepper, and the mustard. Mix well. Beat in the egg yolk and blend thoroughly. Chill until serving time. Then pour the dressing over the salad and toss.

Wheat

(Triticum aestivum, Triticum durum)

Wheat is the edible fruit of a cereal grass; it is the oldest of the cereal crops, and the most important, except in Asia. Its leading role is due to the fact that it can be grown in a great many diverse soils and climates of the temperate zones, that it produces a good yield, and that it is easy to store. As a human food, wheat is high in protein and other nutrients and agreeable in flavour. Further-

more, wheat proteins have the unique ability of forming gluten, the substance which when mixed with water becomes sticky and elastic, giving dough the adhesiveness it needs to be able to rise in bread-making. Cereals with no gluten (e.g. rice) or with little gluten (e.g. rye) must be mixed with wheat flour for bread-making. The wheat grain used for flour (and the seed planted to produce new plants) consists of three parts: (1) The tiny, inner core, that is, the embryo or germ, which produces the new plant; (2) the starchy endosperm, which feeds the germinating seed; and (3) the bran, or outer coating, which protects the endosperm. If the whole kernel is ground, the product is whole wheat flour. If the endosperm alone is ground, we have wheat or plain flour.

Wheat is believed to have originated in the Euphrates Valley from where it spread East and West. There are thousands of varieties due to a long history of hybridization. Wheat has been cultivated since prehistoric times and it is one of the reasons for man's original transition from nomadic to settled life. When man discovered that grains could be cultivated and did not need to be consumed immediately, his former life as a hunter and gatherer of wild foods was no longer necessary. This was the first step towards civilization, for this needs a settled life to develop properly. Life as we know it today would be inconceivable without wheat and its products. Yet only when mechanical cultivation became possible did wheat production become an enormous agricultural business.

Two main varieties of wheat are now grown for human consumption: (1) Bread wheat, *Triticum aestivum* or *vulgare*, the most widely grown and economically the most important of wheats, and (2) durum wheat, *Triticum durum*, known also as winter and spring wheat, containing an even higher proportion of gluten and used to make pasta.

If the embryo itself is extracted from the wheat it is sold as wheat germ. Cracked or bulgur wheat is the parched, crushed kernel of bread wheat, an important staple in the diet of the Near and Middle East. It has a delicious nutty flavour and an agreeable texture and can be used in lieu of rice.

Nutritive values

Plain flour: 367 calories; whole wheat flour: 333 calories; Bulgur wheat, cooked: 168 calories (per 100 g/3½ oz).

Tabbuleh

6 servings
A famous Middle Eastern salad.

250 g (½ lb) fine or medium
  cracked wheat (bulgur)
water
1 bunch spring onions, trimmed
2 or 3 bunches of parsley, heads
  only, chopped fine
2–4 tbsps chopped fresh mint
  leaves, depending on taste

1 dl (scant 4 fl oz) olive oil
juice of 2 or 3 lemons, to taste
salt
freshly ground pepper
lettuce
2 tomatoes, sliced

Soak the wheat in water to cover for 30 minutes. Drain and squeeze dry with hands. Place in a bowl. Chop together the spring onions, the parsley, the mint, chopping them very fine.

Vegetable Cookery

Add to the wheat, together with the olive oil and the lemon juice (which should dominate the taste) and salt and pepper. Mix well. Serve in a salad bowl lined with lettuce; top with slices of tomato.

Wild Rice

(Zizania aquatica)

The edible grain of a water grass native to eastern North America, in no way related to true rice, *Oryza sativa*. The plant grows in shallow water to a height of up to 4 metres (12 feet). The ripened grains are 1 or 2 cm ($\frac{1}{2}$ to $\frac{3}{4}$ inch) long, and reddish-brown to olive-brown in colour. The flavour is deliciously nut-like and more definite than that of true rice. Wild rice is used as a vegetable or as a stuffing. Unlike true rice, wild rice has never been domesticated and to this day is a true wild plant.

Wild rice has served for centuries as a food for both the Indians of the region and for wild fowl; it is gathered largely in Minnesota and Wisconsin where, by law, it can only be harvested by the Indians. Father Jacques Marquette, a Jesuit priest who did much pioneer exploration in the Middle West in the seventeenth century, even then described the Indians gathering wild rice. In September they paddle through the marshes in canoes, bend the grass over the boat and knock the grains into the canoe with a stick.

Wild rice has been known and used in Britain since the early nineteenth century, originally under the names of Canadian or Indian rice.

How to buy

Wild rice is sold in packages, usually pre-washed; consult package directions for cooking.

Nutritive values

Wild rice is high in proteins and minerals. Raw: 353 calories per 100 g ($3\frac{1}{2}$ oz).

Vegetable Cookery

How to use

Wild rice may be used as any rice, though it is more delicate and must not be overcooked. Its yield, cooked, is greater than that of true rice. It is excellent as a casserole, and as a stuffing or as an accompaniment for game birds, especially wild duck – the traditional Indian way of using it. One measure raw wild rice makes 3 to $3\frac{1}{2}$ measures cooked.

Yam

(genus *Dioscorea*)

A true yam is a thick, edible, oblong tuber which develops at the base of the stem of a confusing number of vines with twining or creeping stems and broad leaves. The genus *Dioscorea* to which it belongs numbers hundreds of species with any number of varieties, mostly from the warm weather and tropical countries. Some are grown as ornamentals, others for their tuberous roots, and others again produce potato-like tubers on their stems and are aptly called air potatoes, *Dioscorea bulbifera*. In appearance and flavour yams resemble sweet potatoes, though these belong to a botanically different species. The name is said to be a corruption of an African word pronounced 'nyam'. Early Negro slaves who had used the word for the true yam or any other similar edible tuber in Africa, applied it in America to the sweet potato, a confusion which has persisted.

The most commonly cultivated true yam is *Dioscorea alata*, and its varieties, a native of southern Asia but grown in all warm climates. The many varieties vary in size, shape, colour and weight. The best ones are small and weigh preferably less than 500 g (1 lb). In the monsoon zone of West Africa, the other large producing area, the dominant species is *Dioscorea rotundata*, the white yam. The Chinese or oriental yam, *Dioscorea esculenta*, is a well-flavoured grey or blackish tuber with an inner purple skin and a white moist flesh; it is sometimes found in the Chinese stores of our big towns.

How to buy

Buy firm yams with unwrinkled skins. Avoid soft yams with skin blemishes or sunken spots.

How to keep

Store whole, uncut yams in a cool, dry, well-ventilated place for no more than 1 week. Refrigerate cooked and covered yams for 2 to 3 days.

Nutritive values

Yams consist of little but pure starch. Raw: 101 calories per 100 g (3½ oz).

How to use

Yams can be cooked in any way potatoes and sweet potatoes are cooked. Peel, wash and slice or cube yams. Cook in boiling salted water to cover until tender. Drain and mash like sweet potatoes. Or use according to recipe.

Curried Yams

4–6 servings

1 kg (2 lb) yams	3 dl (½ pt) chicken stock
30 g (1 oz) butter	salt
1 medium onion, chopped fine	freshly ground pepper
1 tbsp curry powder, or to taste	juice of ½ lemon

Cook the yams in their skins until three-quarters tender (12 to 15 minutes). Drain, peel and slice or cut into cubes. Heat the butter in a saucepan. Add the onion and cook, stirring constantly, for 2 to 3 minutes. Stir in the curry powder and cook 2 minutes longer. Stir in the stock. Bring to boiling point and lower the heat to low. Cook, stirring occasionally, for 3 minutes. Taste and, if necessary, season with salt and pepper. Add the yams and mix well with a fork. Simmer, covered, for about 5 to 10 minutes or until the yams are tender. Remove from the heat and sprinkle with the lemon juice.

Candied Yams

4 servings

4 large yams
boiling salted water
salt
freshly ground pepper

110 g (4 oz) dark-brown sugar
4 tbsps water
60 g (2 oz) butter

Cook the yams in boiling salted water to cover until barely tender. Cool, peel and cut into halves lengthwise. Sprinkle with a little salt and pepper. In a frying pan combine the sugar, the water and the butter. Cook over low heat, stirring constantly, until the sugar has melted; do not scorch. If necessary, add 1 or 2 tablespoons more water. Lay the yam halves side by side in the frying pan. Cook over very low heat, turning over once, until the yams are candied on both sides. This will take about 10 to 12 minutes. Transfer to a heated serving dish and serve hot.

Weights, Measures and Oven Temperatures

SOLID MEASURES

British	*Metric*
16 oz = 1 lb	1000 grammes (g) = 1 kilogramme (kilo)

APPROXIMATE EQUIVALENTS

British	*Metric*
1 lb (16 oz)	450 g
½ lb (8 oz)	225 g
¼ lb (4 oz)	100 g
1 oz	25 g

Metric	*British*
1 kilo (1000 g)	2 lb 3 oz
½ kilo (500 g)	1 lb 2 oz
¼ kilo (250 g)	9 oz
100 g	4 oz

LIQUID MEASURES

British

1 quart	=	2 pints	=	40 fl oz
1 pint	=	4 gills	=	20 fl oz
½ pint	=	2 gills		
		or 1 cup	=	10 fl oz
¼ pint	=	8 tablespoons	=	5 fl oz
		1 tablespoon	=	just over ½ fl oz
		1 dessertspoon	=	⅓ fl oz
		1 teaspoon	=	⅙ fl oz

Weights, Measures and Oven Temperatures

Metric

1 litre = 10 decilitres (dl) = 100 centilitres (cl) = 1000 milli-
litres (ml)

APPROXIMATE EQUIVALENTS

British	Metric	Metric	British
1 quart	1·1 litre	1 litre	35 fl oz
1 pint	6 dl	½ litre (5 dl)	18 fl oz
½ pint	3 dl	¼ litre (2·5 dl)	9 fl oz
¼ pint (1 gill)	1·5 dl	1 dl	4 fl oz
1 tablespoon	15 ml		
1 dessertspoon	10 ml		
1 teaspoon	5 ml		

American

1 quart	=	2 pints	=	32 fl oz
1 pint	=	2 cups	=	16 fl oz
		1 cup	=	8 fl oz
		1 tablespoon	=	⅓ fl oz
		1 teaspoon	=	⅙ fl oz

APPROXIMATE EQUIVALENTS

British	American	American	British
1 quart	2½ pints	1 quart	1½ pints + 3 tbsps (32 fl oz)
1 pint	1¼ pints		
½ pint	10 fl oz (1¼ cups)	1 pint	¾ pint + 2 tbsps (16 fl oz)
¼ pint (1 gill)	5 fl oz		
1 tablespoon	1½ tablespoons	1 cup	½ pint − 2 tbsps (8 fl oz)
1 dessertspoon	1 tablespoon		
1 teaspoon	⅓ fl oz		

Vegetable Cookery

OVEN TEMPERATURES

Gas no.	F	C
¼	240	120
1	290	145
2	310	160
3	335	170
4	350	180
5	380	195
6	400	210
7	425	220
8	450	230
9	475	240

Index

Index

Index

Index

Index

Index

More About Penguins
and Pelicans

Danish Cooking *Nika Hazelton*

Nowhere in the world is good food better prepared than in Denmark, where the practical spirit of modern Scandinavian cooking blends with the exotic *haute cuisine* of France's Golden Age. Danish layer cakes, cheeses and pastries are justly famous here, and smørrebrød is now almost an English word – but few English cooks even dream of such delicious dishes as Gypsy Cheese Salad and Veiled Country Lass dessert. Here is your chance to make them, and over three hundred other intriguing recipes from country cottage to cordon bleu standard.

Indian Cookery *Dharamjit Singh*

Through Indian and Tandoori restaurants many English-speaking people have been introduced to the delights of Indian food. But whilst appreciating the taste (and occasionally cooking our own curry), we may not really understand the hows and whys of Indian dishes. For Indian cookery has a philosophy of its own. Its knowledge and skills have been handed down by word of mouth and practical example, and only now, when the tradition is threatened, have attempts been made to record it.

In this book Dharamjit Singh, describes this background tradition, and sets out the practical steps necessary to produce in your own home dishes more subtle and aromatic than you will find in most Indian restaurants.

Caribbean Cookery *Elizabeth Lambert Ortiz*

The recipes in this book came from islands all over the Caribbean including Trinidad and Tobago, Jamaica, Barbados, Antigua, Guadeloupe, Cuba, Haiti and the Virgin Islands. They have been carefully checked to ensure that all the ingredients are available in the British shop or market and have been tried and tested in the author's kitchen.

Elizabeth Lambert Ortiz has provided something for every taste from conejo tapado (Smothered Rabbit) and lambchi and boonchi (Skewered Lamb with Yard-long Beans) to guava pie and coconut ice cream. And, although (particularly in our case) the sun might be notable by its absence, she shows that it is possible to recreate the richness and the subtlety, the delicacy, and the variety of these wonderful tropical dishes.

Jane Grigson

Fish Cookery

There are over 50 species of edible fish; and Jane Grigson feels that
most of us do not eat nearly enough of them. If anything will make
us mend our ways, it is this delightful book with its varied and
comprehensive recipes, covering everything from lobster to conger eel,
from sole to clam chowder. Many of her dishes come from France,
others are from the British Isles, America, Spain, Italy – any country
where good fish is cooked with loving care and eaten with
appreciation.

Charcuterie and French Pork Cookery

Although it could be said that European civilization has been
founded on the pig, this unfortunate animal has encountered much
prejudice and degradation in the past. But ever since Charles Lamb
stated that there was no other taste comparable to that of roast pork,
the pig has never looked back. And it is hoped that this book – the
first of its kind – will further its popularity in the English kitchen.
Together with a guide to *charcuterie* and a host of French pork dishes,
it gives new and unusual information on the history and growth of
this art. Certain to delight both adventurous housewife and diffident
traveller to France, this book allows you to make a true pig of
yourself.

Good Things

Bouchées à la reine, civet of hare, Mrs Beeton's carrot jam to imitate
apricot preserve, baked beans Southern style, wine sherbet . . .
  These are just a few of the delicious and intriguing dishes in *Good
Things*: Jane Grigson is a firm believer in the pleasure food gives.
Echoing the great chef Carême — 'from behind my ovens, I feel the
ugly edifice of routine crumbling beneath my hands' – she
emphasizes the delights and solaces of a truly creative activity.

and

ENGLISH FOOD